∿ At a Glance

Essays

FIFTH EDITION

Lee Brandon
Mt. San Antonio College

WADSWORTH
CENGAGE Learning™

Australia • Brazil • Japan • Korea • Mexico • Singapore • Spain • United Kingdom • United States

WADSWORTH
CENGAGE Learning™

To Sharon

At a Glance: Essays, Fifth Edition

Lee Brandon

Senior Publisher: Lyn Uhl

Director of Developmental English and College Success: Annie Todd

Development Editor: Karen Mauk

Assistant Editor: Melanie Opacki

Editorial Assistant: Matthew Conte

Media Editor: Amy Gibbons

Senior Marketing Manager: Kirsten Stoller

Marketing Coordinator: Ryan Ahern

Marketing Communications Manager: Stacey Purviance

Content Project Manager: Aimee Chevrette Bear

Art Director: Jill Ort

Print Buyer: Susan Spencer

Rights Acquisition Specialist: Katie Huha

Production Service: Books By Design, Inc.

Cover Designer: Walter Kopek

Cover Image: Getty Images

Compositor: S4Carlisle Publishing Services

For product information and technology assistance, contact us at **Cengage Learning Customer & Sales Support, 1-800-354-9706**

For permission to use material from this text or product, submit all requests online at **www.cengage.com/permissions.** Further permissions questions can be emailed to **permissionrequest@cengage.com.**

Library of Congress Control Number: 2010933767

ISBN-13: 978-0-495-90630-8
ISBN-10: 0-495-90630-1

Wadsworth
20 Channel Center Street
Boston, MA 02210
USA

Cengage Learning is a leading provider of customized learning solutions with office locations around the globe, including Singapore, the United Kingdom, Australia, Mexico, Brazil and Japan. Locate your local office at **international.cengage.com/region**

Cengage Learning products are represented in Canada by Nelson Education, Ltd.

For your course and learning solutions, visit **www.cengage.com.** Purchase any of our products at your local college store or at our preferred online store **www.cengagebrain.com.**

Printed in the United States of America
1 2 3 4 5 6 7 14 13 12 11 10

Contents

Preface

In this, the fifth edition of *At a Glance: Essays*, the surf writer, gallantly perched on a pencil, once more celebrates the "flow of writing." Like waves at a beach, writing is cyclical, moving forward and backward and forward again. The surf writer will always be searching for the "perfect wave," meaning the best possible expression. The recursive movement of writing and rewriting is the essence of good writing. Instruction in this book—comprehensive, flexible, relevant, and stimulating—is predicated on that systematic, relentless revision.

At a Glance: Essays is the third-level book in the *At a Glance* series. Along with *At a Glance: Sentences, At a Glance: Paragraphs*, and *At a Glance: Reader*, it meets the current need for succinct, comprehensive, and up-to-date textbooks that students can afford. All four books provide basic instruction, exercises, and writing assignments at the designated level, as well as support material for instructors. *At a Glance: Sentences* and *At a Glance: Paragraphs* include a transition to the next level of writing, and *At a Glance: Paragraphs, At a Glance: Essays*, and *At a Glance: Reader* each ends with a handbook that students can refer to for help with sentence-level issues or for problems with mechanics. *At a Glance: Reader* presents brief writing instruction and thirty sources for reading-based writing. Each book in the *At a Glance* series can be used alone, with one of the other *At a Glance* books, or with another textbook. Two or more *At a Glance* books can be shrink-wrapped and delivered at a discount.

Comprehensive Coverage

Using instruction with exercises, examples, and writing applications, the fifth edition of *At a Glance: Essays*

- focuses on writing essays (Chapters 1–12) and the research paper (Chapter 13);
- features the writing process with attention to prewriting, organization, writing, revision, and editing—each phase illustrated with student examples (Chapters 1–3);

- includes brief instruction for using the Writing Process Worksheet, an optional one-page form that guides student work through the stages of exploring the topic, organizing the writing, and writing (Chapters 1–3), with a blank sheet for copying in the book following the Student Overview and on the Instructor and Student Companion Sites;
- incorporates professional and student writing in instruction on how to read critically and how to write summaries, reactions, and two-part responses (Chapter 4);
- leads students through eight patterns of essay writing, each with instruction, student and instructor examples of paragraphs (40 altogether, 14 of them new to this edition), and an abundance of writing prompts and topics covering reading-based, general (often keyed to model student and professional examples), cross-curricular, and career-related subjects, with each chapter including a pattern for organization while recognizing that a specific pattern is seldom used alone (Chapters 5–12);
- features a handbook that addresses sentence-level issues, such as subjects and verbs, fragments, comma splices, run-ons, sentence combining, verbs, pronouns, modifiers, punctuation, and capitalization (Chapter 14);
- and supports handbook instruction with an abundance of material on the Companion Sites for students (exercises, additional instruction, worksheets, documentation guides, and so on) and for instructors (syllabi, diagnostic and final quizzes, teaching suggestions, and more).

∼ Instructional Approach

Using explanation, student examples, exercises, and applications, *At a Glance: Essays* presents the writing process in Chapters 1–3 and reading-based writing in Chapter 4. Each of Chapters 5 through 12 uses the same sequence of instruction: a writing strategy for a particular pattern, a box of transitional terms, an exercise that gives students practice in organizing the pattern, student examples and professional examples with questions for students to answer and discuss, topic suggestions (reading-based, cross-curricular, career-related, and general topics) for writing such paragraphs or short essays, and a concluding summary of guidelines specific to the pattern. Chapter 13 presents the research paper in ten steps, following the MLA 2009 Update (with an APA Style option on the Instructor and

Student Companion Sites). Chapter 14 is a handbook section on sentence writing, punctuation, and other fundamentals.

◯ New and Enhanced Material

- Mode-specific boxes of transitional words in eight chapters
- 60 percent reading selections (14 new to this edition)
- Updated lists of reading-based, general, cross-curricular, and career-related topics and prompts in Chapters 5–12
- An enhanced Writing Process Worksheet designed to provide guidance for students and save time and effort for instructors
- An updated Self-Evaluation Chart to help students track their needs and goals while promoting self-reliance
- Additional instruction, writing topics, and writing prompts on reading-based writing as the summary, reaction, and two-part response as assignments to help students write with more substance and become better prepared to write across the curriculum, and avoid plagiarism
- MLA 2009 Update with examples of documented student essays
- Instruction with student examples on career-related writing in five chapters
- APA Guide for writing research papers available on the *At a Glance* Student and Instructor Companion Sites
- An abundance of printable quizzes on the Instructor Companion Site (for reading selections and sentence writing—diagnostic, final, and unit quizzes)
- A research paper unit organized around the ten steps of the writing process

◯ Special Brandon Features at a Glance

Reading-Based Writing

Reading-Based Writing as an Option: Because this book does focus on writing essays of all types, instructors whose pedagogy favors assigning mostly personal narratives will continue to find *At a Glance* hospitable and effective. However, this book now has another instructional dimension as an optional approach: **reading-based writing**. Instructors who wish to help students transition from personal experience to more analytical thought with reading-based writing have choices that include: (1) beginning with the personal narrative and phasing in reading-based writing; (2) interspersing reading-based writing with other assignments; or (3) using reading-based writing throughout the course. Students who work with reading-based writing will be able to function better in writing across the curriculum and move more smoothly into advanced courses.

Reading-Based Writing Defined: Reading-based writing requires students to read a source, write an analytical reply, and give credit to the originator for the ideas they borrow and the words they quote. Credit can be noted formally (MLA with 2009 Update in this book—or with APA form, as presented on both the Student and the Instructor Companion Sites) or informally (by using clear references with acknowledged credit and quotations with quotation marks), depending on the instructor's preference. As for structure, reading-based writing can be a summary, a reaction (paragraph or essay), or a two-part response (with separated summary and reaction). Although the reaction can include personal experience to clarify and support conclusions, the text should be at the center of the writing. The reaction can also incorporate summary to convey a broad aspect of the text. But summary is never the major concern of the reaction.

The Writing Process Worksheet

The Writing Process Worksheet provides a flexible, systematic approach to specific assignments and leaves a word trail so that instructors can help students confront problems during the exploration and planning of assignments and reconstruct what went right and wrong after the paper is written. This classroom-tested form can save students and instructors time and effort, and produce effective results. A copy of the worksheet is located in the textbook following the Student Overview, on the Student Companion Site, and on the Instructor Companion Site. It is discussed in detail in Chapters 1, 2, and 3. Instructors who require this sheet can ask their students to photocopy the generic version from the Student Companion Site or enlarge and copy it from their textbook. They can also customize the Word copy on the Instructor Companion Site to fit their pedagogy or particular assignments.

Career-Related Writing

Especially to accommodate the interests and needs of career-minded students, career-related writing instruction, topics, and exemplary student writing selections are included in Chapter 5 (workplace report), Chapter 7 (career report), Chapter 8 (workplace content),

Chapter 10 (workplace comparison), and Chapter 12 (writing a proposal). Because the same basic principles of writing apply to all topics within each of those chapters, career-related assignments can easily fit within the complete range of reading assignments, lectures, and discussions without your changing the design of your course.

⌒ Support Material for Instructors

- **Instructor's Guide for *At a Glance*.** The Instructor's Guide—available both in print at Cengage Learning, Higher Education, at 800-354-9706, and online at the Instructor's Companion Site—provides helpful hints for teaching *At a Glance* in the classroom. It includes sample syllabi; suggestions for working with basic writing students and ESL students; grading tips; Answer Keys; quizzes on sentence writing, handbook material, readings; and more.
- **Instructor Companion Site for *At a Glance*.** The instructor site provides helpful resources in addition to the Instructor's Guide, such as PowerPoint slides, at login.cengage.com.
- **Student Companion Site for *At a Glance* at www.cengagebrain .com.** The student site provides helpful resources such as sentence writing exercises, a 2009 MLA Guide and an APA Guide to documented papers, a printable Writing Process Worksheet, tips on writing resumes and letters of application, additional reading selections, and more.

⌒ Acknowledgments

I am profoundly indebted to the many instructors who have reviewed *At a Glance: Essays* for these five editions and helped it grow and remain fresh and innovative. Here are a few of those thoughtful and imaginative reviewers: Connie A. Gramza, Erie Community College; Janice Hart, Central New Mexico Community College; Charlotte Laughlin, McLennan Community College; Buzz R. Pounds, Lewis University; Cindi Clarke, Belmont Technical College; Tim Kelley, Northwest-Shoals Community College; Darin Cozzens, Surry Community College; James Crooks, Shasta College; Joanne Kara, Pennsylvania Institute of Technology; Howard Sage, Hunter College; Denton Tulloch, Miami Dade College; Karen

J. Weyant, Jamestown Community College; Deborah Burson-Smith, Southern University at New Orleans; David Lang, Golden Gate University; Kathy Masters, Arkansas State University; Steve Stremmel, American River College; and Anne-Marie Williams, Cuesta College.

I also deeply appreciate the expert, dedicated work of freelance principal editor Karen Mauk, production manager Nancy Benjamin with Books By Design, editorial specialist Ann Marie Radaskiewicz, permissions editor Maria Leon Maimone, and my colleagues at Cengage Learning: Annie Todd, Kirsten Stoller, Katie Huha, Matthew Conte, Melanie Opacki, Ryan Ahern, Stacey Purviance, Courtney Morris, and Aimee Chevrette Bear.

I am especially grateful to my family for their cheerful, inspiring support: Sharon, Kelly, Erin, Michael, Kathy, Jessica, Deborah, Shane, Lauren, Jarrett, and Matthew.

                                                          Lee Brandon

Student Overview

This book is designed to help you write better essays and research papers. Chapter 1 defines the essay and discusses what you need to know and do to write effective essays. Chapters 2 and 3 focus on the writing process itself—how to get started and how to develop, revise, and edit your working drafts. Every stage is illustrated by the work of one student, whom we follow through the entire process. Chapter 4 introduces you to writing about what you read.

Each of Chapters 5 through 12 describes a different pattern for developing an essay. For example, Chapter 5 is about writing an essay by using both description and narration techniques, and Chapter 12 is about writing an essay of argument. Each of Chapters 5 through 12 includes one essay written by a student and one or more written by a professional writer. In addition, several chapters contain a student career-related essay that demonstrates how patterns of writing can be applied to workplace situations in a practical, realistic way. In every chapter, questions and exercises help you put into practice what you have learned.

Chapter 13 explains and illustrates the ten steps to writing the research paper and describes the special considerations that kind of essay involves. Chapter 14 is a handbook, to which you can refer whenever you need assistance in grammar, usage, punctuation, and capitalization.

Following are some strategies to help you make the best use of this book and to jump-start the improvement in your writing skills.

1. **Be active and systematic in learning.** Take advantage of your instructor's expertise by being an active participant in class—one who takes notes, asks questions, and contributes to discussion. Become dedicated to systematic learning: determine your needs, decide what to do, and do it. Make learning a part of your everyday thinking and behavior.
2. **Read widely.** Samuel Johnson, a great English scholar, once said he didn't want to read anything by people who had written more than they had read. William Faulkner, a Nobel Prize winner in

literature, said, "Read, read, read. Read everything—trash, classics, good and bad, and see how writers do it." Read to learn technique, to acquire ideas, to be stimulated to write. Especially read to satisfy your curiosity and receive pleasure. If reading is a main component of your course, approach it as systematically as you do writing. Reading-based writing will offer you opportunities to polish your critical-thinking skills as you compose responses to what you read, much as you do in classes across the curriculum.

3. **Keep a journal.** Keeping a journal may not be required in your particular class; regardless of whether it is required, though, jotting down your observations in a notebook is a good idea. Here are some ideas for daily, or almost daily, journal writing:

   - Summarize, evaluate, or react to reading assignments.
   - Summarize, evaluate, or react to what you see on television and in movies, and to what you read in newspapers and magazines.
   - Describe and narrate situations or events you experience.
   - Write about career-related matters you encounter in other courses or on the job.

   Your journal entries may read like an intellectual diary, a record of what you are thinking about at certain times. Because your entries are not structured writing assignments, organization and editing are not important. Mainly, keeping a journal will help you to understand reading material better, to develop more language skills, and to think more clearly—as well as to become more confident and write more easily so that writing becomes a comfortable everyday activity. Your entries may also provide subject material for longer, more carefully crafted pieces. It is important to get into the habit of writing something each day.

4. **Evaluate your writing skills.** Use the Self-Evaluation Chart inside the front cover of this book to list areas you need to work on. You can add to your lists throughout the entire term. Drawing on your instructor's comments, make notes on matters such as the organization, development, and content of your essays; spelling, vocabulary, and diction; and so on. Use the chart for self-motivated study assignments and as a checklist in all stages of writing. As you master each problem area, you can check it off or cross it out.

   Here is a partially filled out Self-Evaluation Chart, followed by some guidelines for filling out your own.

Self-Evaluation Chart

Organization/ Development/ Content	Spelling/ Vocabulary/ Diction	Grammar/ Sentence Structure	Punctuation/ Capitalization
Avoid top-heavy introductions 44–45 Use specific examples 100 Repeat key words such as *causes* and *effects* 42	all right separate sophomore avoid "into" as "into rap" 40	Vary sentence beginnings Watch for pronoun antecedent problems, such as "a person . . . they" 262 RO-CS—*Then* isn't a conjunction 45	comma after long introductory modifier 266 colon to introduce list 269 cap beginning for words replacing names, such as, "I told Mother," but "I told my mother" 272

- *Organization/Development/Content.* Note your instructor's suggestions for all aspects of planning your essays and supporting your ideas.
- *Spelling/Vocabulary/Diction.* List words marked as incorrectly spelled on your assignments. Master the words on your list and add new words as you accumulate assignments. List suggestions made by your instructor about word choice (such as avoiding slang, clichés, and vague terms). Also include new, useful words you encounter in this class and others; add the words here, with simple definitions. Use another page if you need more space.
- *Grammar/Sentence Structure.* List any grammar points you need to remember or any sentence problems, such as fragments, comma splices, and run-ons. If you tend to begin sentences in the same way or to choose the same patterns, use your chart to remind yourself to vary your sentence beginnings and patterns.
- *Punctuation/Capitalization.* List any problems you encounter with punctuation and capitalization. Because the items in this column may be covered in Chapter 14, you can often use both rule numbers and page numbers for the references here.

5. **Take full advantage of the *At a Glance* Student Companion Site at www.cengagebrain.com and other technology.** Using a computer will enable you to write, revise, and edit more swiftly as you move, alter, check, and delete material with a few keystrokes. The Student Companion Site offers additional exercises and instruction. Many colleges have writing labs with good instruction and facilities for networking and researching complicated topics. The Internet, used wisely, can provide resource material for compositions.

6. **Use the Writing Process Worksheet.** Record details about each of your assignments, such as the due date, topic, length, and form. The worksheet will also remind you of the stages of the writing process: explore, organize, and write. A blank Writing Process Worksheet for you to enlarge and photocopy for assignments appears on page xxi, and a printable copy is on your Student Companion Site.

7. **Be positive.** All the elements you record in your Self-Evaluation Chart are probably covered in *At a Glance: Essays.* The table of contents, the index, and the Correction Chart on the inside back cover of the book will direct you to the additional instruction you decide you need. Soon, seeing what you have mastered and checked off your list will give you a sense of accomplishment.

Finally, don't compare yourself with others. Compare yourself with yourself and, as you make progress, consider yourself what you are—a student on the path toward effective writing, a student on the path toward success.

Writing Process Worksheet

Title _____

Name _____ **Due Date** _____

Use separate paper if you need more space.

Assignment   In the space below, write whatever you need to know about your assignment, including information about the topic, audience, pattern of writing, length, whether to include a rough draft or revised drafts, and whether your paper must be typed.

Stage One   **Explore**   Freewrite, brainstorm (list), cluster, or take notes as directed by your instructor.

Stage Two   **Organize**   Write a topic sentence or thesis; label the subject and focus parts.

Write an outline or a structured list. For reading-based writing, include references and short quotations with page numbers within the outline.

Stage Three   **Write**   On separate paper, write and then revise your paragraph or essay as many times as necessary for **co**herence, **l**anguage (usage, tone, and diction), **u**nity, **e**mphasis, **s**upport, and **s**entences (**CLUESS**). Read your work aloud to hear and correct any grammatical errors or awkward-sounding sentences.

Edit any problems in fundamentals, such as **c**apitalization, **o**missions, **p**unctuation, and **s**pelling (**COPS**).

1

The Essay and Its Parts

~ The Essay Defined

An **essay** is a group of paragraphs, each of which supports a controlling idea called a **thesis**. The number of paragraphs in an essay varies, but in college writing that number is likely to be between three and nine. Many college essays are about five paragraphs long, often because of the nature of the assignment and the length of time allowed, but there is no special significance in the number five.

Each paragraph in an essay is almost always one of three types:

1. The **introductory paragraph** presents the thesis, the controlling idea of the essay, much as a topic sentence presents the main idea of a paragraph.
2. The **paragraphs in the body of the essay** present evidence and reasoning—the support for the thesis of the essay.
3. The **concluding paragraph** provides an appropriate ending—often a restatement of or a reflection on the thesis.

Figure 1.1 shows the basic form of a typical essay, although the number of support paragraphs may vary.

Figure 1.1
Essay Form

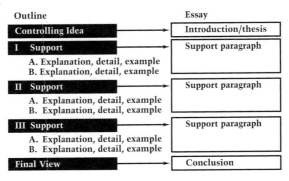

1

～ Student Writing: A Sample Essay

The following essay was written by Leah, an inmate at a women's prison in California who enrolled in a small, low-cost college program. The parts of her essay are marked to show the organization of the paragraphs. Although only the final draft appears here, Leah's essay also provides the examples for the stages and techniques of the writing process discussed in Chapters 2 and 3.

Razor Wire Sweat Lodge

Leah

Introductory paragraph   My Indian tribe is Pomo, one of twenty-one represented at this prison. I have always had tremendous interest in my ancestors and their customs, and in the cultures of all Indian tribes. The sacred sweat ceremony itself is at the center of my life. Here at prison it has taken on a special meaning. In fact, many women of other races here have also found peace within themselves as a result of participating with me and other **Thesis** Native Americans in the sweats. Each Saturday we have a routine: we make preparations, we sweat, and we conclude with a post-sweat activity.

Topic sentence

<u>Before we sweat, we must prepare ourselves and the facility</u>. For twenty-four hours before the sweat, we fast. We do not eat anything and drink only water or juices, but if someone has a health problem, we will excuse her. As for clothing, we wear simple, loose dresses such as the prison-issued muu-muus. We bring tobacco ties, sage leaves, sweet grass, and sometimes a pipe. Preparing the facility is more complicated than preparing ourselves. About thirty-five lava rocks must be heated in a fire approximately three hours before we start sweating. The wood for the fire has to be placed in a tepee

Support paragraph

shape around the pile of rocks and ignited. Once the fire is hot, we tend to the sweat lodge itself. Since we have no tarp to put on the sweat lodge frame, the state provides us with blankets. We use these to cover the lodge fully, draping it with about three layers and leaving an opening to the east.

Finally we are ready to go inside. The preparation period is very important, but everyone looks forward to its being over.

Topic sentence

From this point on through the ceremony, everything must be done according to rules. First we enter counterclockwise, and once inside we conduct all parts of the ceremony counterclockwise. There are four rounds in the sweat, each of which lasts about twenty to thirty minutes. We stress that no one

Support paragraph

should break our circle inside the sweat lodge, but it sometimes happens. Some women can't handle the steam and the heat, so we never make them stay. Those who do stay are free to participate in the singing and praying or not. The four rounds are similar. For each, six hot rocks are brought in, and six dippers of water are poured onto the rocks. The number six indicates the four directions and the sky and the ground. As someone finishes a prayer (usually in Sioux because our sponsor is a Sioux), she mentions her relatives, for this ceremony is also for others. Then another person follows. As sweet grass burns outside on the fire, we sit in the hot steam and rub sage leaves on our bodies for purification. We maintain ourselves with humility during the whole sweat.

Topic sentence

When the sweat is over, we enter the final phase. We come out and throw our tobacco ties into the fire pit, and the smoke takes our prayers to the sky. Then we hose ourselves down with plenty of cold water and

Support paragraph

open the refreshments we brought. Once we've eaten and changed our clothes, we start dismantling the sweat. The blankets have to be taken off the same way they were put up and then folded carefully. The leftover wood has to be put away, and the blankets and wood must be covered. Any garbage that's been left around is thrown into the Dumpster. Then we

```
lock the gate to our facility and bid

farewell.

    Using a sweat lodge is a custom of most

Indian tribes. Certain Indian tribes go about

it differently from others, but in here when

we are together in the lodge, we feel like
```
Concluding `one whole being. Each week we look forward to`
paragraph
```
this ceremony. It helps us cope better with

the prison system. After it's over, we feel

physically refreshed, clean, and peaceful.
```

⌒ The Thesis Defined

If you tell a friend you are about to write an essay, be prepared for the question, "What are you writing about?" If you answer, "Public schools," your friend will probably be satisfied with the answer but not very interested. The problem is that the phrase *public schools* doesn't suggest a focus or direction. It just indicates your subject, not what you are going to do with it. An effective controlling statement, called the *thesis of the essay*, has both a subject and a focus. The **subject** is what you intend to write about. The **focus** is what you intend to do with your subject.

<u>Overall, public schools</u> <u>do not assign enough homework.</u>
       subject   focus

⌒ Sources for the Thesis

The thesis of an essay can come from any of several places. You may generate it early on through prewriting techniques, you may develop it from something you have read, or you may be assigned a topic. In any case, you need to work on your thesis statement—just that one sentence—until you have developed an interesting subject and a narrowed focus. Your working thesis may be a bit different from the one you finally use in your essay, but it can easily be reworded once you begin writing and revising.

〜 Writing the Thesis

An effective thesis includes a focus that can be developed with supporting information. An ineffective thesis presents a focus that is vague, too broad, or too narrow.

VAGUE	<u>Public schools</u> <u>are great.</u> 　　subject　　　focus
BETTER	<u>Public schools</u> <u>do as well academically as private</u> 　　subject　　　　　　　focus <u>schools, according to statistics.</u> (made more specific)
TOO BROAD	<u>Public schools</u> <u>are having trouble.</u> (trouble with 　　subject　　　focus what?)
BETTER	<u>Bidwell Elementary School</u> <u>is too crowded.</u> 　　　subject　　　　　　focus (limiting the idea of trouble)
TOO NARROW	<u>American public schools</u> <u>were first established</u> 　　subject　　　　focus <u>in Philadelphia in 1779.</u> (only a fact)

▐ Exercise 1 ▌ Evaluating the Thesis

Underline and label the subject (S) and focus (F) in each of the following theses. Also judge each one as effective (E) or ineffective (I).

EXAMPLE:　　I　　　<u>Basketball</u> <u>is an interesting sport.</u>
　　　　　　　　　　　　S　　　　　　F

———　　1. Students who cheat in school may be trying to relieve certain emotional pressures.

_____ 2. Shakespeare was an Elizabethan writer.

_____ 3. The quarterback in football and the general of an
           army are alike in significant ways.

_____ 4. Animals use color chiefly for protection.

_____ 5. Portland is a city in Oregon.

_____ 6. Life in the ocean has distinct realms.

_____ 7. Rome has had a glorious and tragic history.

_____ 8. Boston is the capital of Massachusetts.

_____ 9. The word *macho* has a special meaning to the
           Hispanic community.

_____ 10. The history of plastics is exciting.

Exercise 2 Writing the Thesis

Convert each of the following subjects into an effective thesis.

1. Bumper stickers _____

2. Rudeness _____

3. The true character of my neighbor _____

4. Many homeless people _____

5. Being able to use a computer _____

6. Dieting _____

Patterns of Support for the Thesis

If the foundation of an effective essay is a strong thesis—one with a specific subject and a well-defined focus—the strength of the essay is in the support. Whether that support comes from research or personal experience, it will almost certainly be suggested by the focus imposed on the subject. After settling on a thesis, you should pose two questions:

1. What kinds of information will best support or explain my thesis?
2. How should I divide and present that supporting information?

The way you choose to divide and present your information will determine the organization of your support paragraphs.

Among the most common forms of dividing and organizing ideas are the following:

- Descriptive narration (telling a story with relevant descriptions)

  Division: parts of the story
  I. Situation
  II. Conflict
  III. Struggle
  IV. Outcome
  V. Meaning

- Analysis by division (examining the parts of a unit; for example, a pencil can be divided into an eraser, a wooden barrel, and a lead core with a point at the end)

  Division: parts of the unit
  I. First part
  II. Second part
  III. Third part

- Process analysis (how to do something or how something was done)

  Division: preparation and steps
  I. Preparation
  II. Steps
     A. Step 1
     B. Step 2
     C. Step 3
     D. Step 4

- Cause and effect

  Division: causes or effects (sometimes mixed)
  I. Cause (or effect) 1
  II. Cause (or effect) 2
  III. Cause (or effect) 3

Other patterns of developing an essay include exemplification, comparison and contrast, definition, and argument. All of these forms are presented individually in Chapters 5 through 12. Although a single form is often dominant at either the paragraph or short-essay level, a rich combination of forms is common.

∼ Special Paragraphs Within the Essay

Introductions

A good introductory paragraph does many things. It attracts the reader's interest, states or points toward the thesis, and moves the reader smoothly into the support, or body, paragraphs. Here are some introductory methods:

- A direct statement of the thesis
- Background
- Definition of term(s)
- Quotation(s)
- A shocking statement
- Question(s)
- A combination of two or more methods in this list

You should not decide that some of the methods are good and some are bad. Indeed, all are valid, and the most common one is the last, the combination. Use the approach that best fits each essay. Resist the temptation to use the same kind of introduction in every essay you write.

Each of the following statements is an introductory paragraph. The thesis is the same in all of them, yet each uses a different introductory method. Notice the great variety here.

Direct Statement of Thesis

Anyone on the road in any city near midnight on Friday and Saturday is among dangerous people. They're not the product of the witching hour; they're the product of the "happy hour." They're called drunk drivers. These threats to our lives and limbs need to be controlled by federal laws with strong provisions.

Subject
Focus

Background

In one four-year period in California (2005–2009), 17,942 people were injured and 6,632 were killed by drunk drivers. Each year, the same kinds of figures come in from all our states. The state laws vary. The federal government does virtually nothing. Drunk driving has reached the point of being a national problem of huge proportions. This slaughter of innocent citizens should be stopped by following the lead of many other nations and passing federal legislation with strong provisions.

Subject
Focus

Definition

Here's a recipe. Take two thousand pounds of plastic, rubber, and steel, pour in ten gallons of gas, and start the engine. Then take one human being of two hundred pounds of flesh, blood, and bones, pour in two glasses of beer in one hour, and put him or her behind the wheel. Mix the two together, and the result may be a drunken **Subject** driver ready to cause death and destruction. This prob- **Focus** lem of drunk driving can and should be controlled by federal legislation with strong provisions.

Quotation

The National Highway Traffic Safety Administration has stated that 50 percent of all fatal accidents involve intoxicated drivers and about "75 percent of those drivers have a Blood Alcohol Content of .10 percent or greater." That kind of information is widely known, yet **Subject** the carnage on the highways continues. This problem of **Focus** drunk driving should be addressed by a federal law with strict provisions.

Shocking Statement and Questions

Almost 60,000 Americans were killed in the Vietnam War. What other war kills more than that number every four years? Give up? It's the war with drunk drivers. The war in Vietnam ended more than three decades ago, but our DUI war goes on, and the drunks are winning. **Subject** This deadly conflict should be controlled by federal laws **Focus** with strong provisions.

Questions and a Definition

What is a drunk driver? In California it's a person with a blood alcohol content of .08 percent or more who is operating a motor vehicle. What do those drivers do? Some of them kill. Every year more than 16,000 people nationwide die. Those are easy questions. The difficult one is, What **Subject** can be done? One answer is clear: Drunk drivers should be **Focus** controlled by federal laws with strong provisions.

All these introductory methods are effective. Some others, however, are ineffective because they are vague, or too general, to communicate the thesis or because the wording is mechanical. The mechanical approach may be direct and explicit, but it usually destroys the reader's imagination and interest.

VAGUE	The purpose of this essay is to write about the need for strong national laws against drunk driving.
MECHANICAL	I will now write a paper about the need for strong national laws against drunk driving.

The length of an introduction can vary, but the typical length for an introduction to a student essay is three to five sentences. If your introduction is shorter than three, be certain that it conveys all that you want to say. If it is longer than five, be certain that it only introduces and does not try to expand on ideas. That function is reserved for the body paragraphs; a long and complicated introduction may make your essay top-heavy.

Exercise 3 Writing Introductory Paragraphs

Pick one of the following theses (altering it a bit to suit your own ideas, if you like) and write two different introductory paragraphs for it, each one featuring a different method. Underline the thesis in each paragraph, and label the subject and focus parts.

1. Families come in different shapes and sizes.
2. Career choices are greatly influenced by a person's background.
3. *Friendship* is just one word, but friends are of different kinds.
4. The spirit of sports has been corrupted by money.
5. Sexual harassment at work often goes unreported for practical reasons.

Support Paragraphs

Support paragraphs, also called **developmental paragraphs**, form the body of an essay and provide information and reasoning that justify the thesis presented in the paragraph of introduction.

The following paragraph is both a definition and an example of the developmental paragraph:

Topic sentence	The developmental paragraph contains three parts: the subject, the topic sentence, and the support. The subject
Support	is what you will write about. It is likely to be broad and

Support   must be focused or qualified for specific treatment. The topic sentence contains both the subject and the focus—what you will do with the subject. It carries the central idea to which everything else in the paragraph is subordinated. For example, the first sentence of this paragraph is a topic sentence. Even when not stated, the topic sentence as an underlying idea unifies the paragraph. The

Support   support is the evidence or reasoning by which a topic sentence is developed. It comes in several basic patterns and serves any of the four forms of expression: narration, description, exposition, and argumentation. These forms, which are usually combined in writing, will be presented with both student and professional examples in the following chapters. The developmental paragraph, therefore, is a group of sentences, each with the

Concluding   function of supporting a controlling idea called the topic

sentence   sentence.

Incompleteness of support is more common among beginning writers than is overdevelopment of support. Besides having enough support, be sure that the points are presented in the best possible sequence.

Consider the following paragraph. Is it complete? Does the writer make the main idea clear and provide adequate support for it? Are the ideas in the right order?

A cat's tail is a good barometer of its intentions. By various movements of its tail a cat will signal many of its wants. Other movements indicate its attitudes. An excited or aggressively aroused cat will whip its entire tail back and forth.

At first glance, this paragraph seems complete. It begins with a concise topic sentence telling us that a cat's tail is "a good barometer of its intentions." It adds information of a general nature in the following two sentences. Then it presents a supporting example about the aggressively aroused cat. But the paragraph is not explicit; it contains insufficient supporting material for the opening generalization. The paragraph leaves the reader with too much information to fill in. What are some other ways that cats communicate their intentions with their tails? How do they communicate specific wishes or desires? Is their communication effective? If the passage is to answer these questions that may come into the reader's mind, it must present more material to support the beginning generalization. The original paragraph that follows begins with a concise topic sentence that is then supported with details.

> A cat's tail is a good barometer of its intentions. An excited or aggressively aroused cat will whip its entire tail back and forth. When I talk to Sam, he holds up his end of the conversation by occasionally flicking the tip of his tail. Mother cats move their tails back and forth to invite their kittens to play. A kitten raises its tail perpendicularly to beg for attention; older cats may do so to beg for food. When your cat holds its tail aloft while criss-crossing in front of you, it is trying to say. "Follow me"—usually to the kitchen or, more precisely, to the refrigerator. Unfortunately, many cats have lost their tails in refrigerator doors as a consequence.

> —*Michael W. Fox*, "What Is Your Pet Trying to Tell You?"

We can strengthen our understanding of good support by analyzing the structure of our model paragraph, putting to use the information we have assimilated to this point in the discussion. The paragraph begins with the highest generalization (the main idea in the topic sentence): "A cat's tail is a good barometer of its intentions." It follows immediately with six major supporting statements and ends with a final sentence to add humor to the writing. If we place this material in outline form, we can easily see the recurrent pattern in the flow of thought from general to particular.

TOPIC SENTENCE (HIGHEST GENERALIZATION)	A cat's tail is a good barometer of its intentions.
MAJOR SUPPORT	A. An excited or aggressively aroused cat will whip its entire tail back and forth.
MAJOR SUPPORT	B. When I talk to Sam, he holds up his end of the conversation by occasionally flicking the tip of his tail.
MAJOR SUPPORT	C. Mother cats move their tails back and forth to invite their kittens to play.
MAJOR SUPPORT	D. A kitten raises its tail perpendicularly to beg for attention;
MAJOR SUPPORT	E. older cats may do so to beg for food.

MAJOR SUPPORT   F. When your cat holds its tail aloft while crisscrossing in front of you, it is trying to say, "Follow me"—usually to the kitchen or, more precisely, to the refrigerator.

CONCLUDING SENTENCE
(ADDED FOR HUMOR)   Unfortunately, many cats have lost their tails in refrigerator doors as a consequence.

Basic Frames

Two effective frames of conventional paragraph structure are shown in Figure 1.2. Frame A merely states the controlling idea as the topic sentence and develops it; Frame B adds a concluding sentence following the development. Two other forms—the paragraph with an unstated but implied topic sentence and the paragraph with the topic sentence at the end of the paragraph—are valid, but they are used less frequently in college writing.

Figure 1.2
Paragraph Frames

Frame A

Topic Sentence

Support

Support

Support

Development

Frame B

Topic Sentence

Support

Support

Support

Concluding Sentence

Development

Following is an example of Frame A:

Pity, Anger, and Achievement Performance

Topic sentence
Support

It is generally thought that pity and sympathy are "good" emotions and that anger is a "bad" emotion. However, attribution theorists have pointed out that the consequences of these emotional expressions are complex. In one investigation, Graham (1984) gave subjects (twelve-year-old children) false failure feedback during an achievement task. For some children, this was accompanied by the remark: "I feel sorry for you" as well as body postures and facial gestures that accompany sympathy (head down, hands folded, etc.). To other students, the experimenter said: "I am angry with you." Students receiving the pity feedback tended to blame the failure on themselves (low ability) and their performance declined. On the other hand, students receiving anger feedback attributed their failure to lack of effort

Support

and their performance subsequently increased. This is not to advocate that sympathy is always detrimental and anger always facilitative. Rather, the consequences of feedback depend on how that feedback is construed and what it means to the recipient of the communication. Other kinds of feedback, such as praise for success at an easy task and excessive and unsolicited helping, also tend to convey that the student is "unable" and therefore have some negative consequences.

—Seymour Feshbach and Bernard Weiner, Personality

Here is an example of Frame B:

Primitive Methods of Lie Detection

Topic sentence
Support

Throughout history there have been efforts to distinguish the guilty from the innocent and to tell the liars from the truthful. For example, a method of lie detection practiced in Asia involved giving those suspected of a crime a handful of raw rice to chew. After chewing for some time, the persons were instructed to spit out the rice. The innocent person was anticipated to do this easily, whereas the guilty party was expected to have grains of rice sticking to the roof of the mouth and tongue. This technique relied on the increased sympathetic nervous system activity in the presumably fearful and

Support

guilty person. This activity would result in the drying up of saliva that, in turn, would cause grains of rice to stick in the mouth. A similar but more frightening technique involved placing a heated knife blade briefly against the tongue, another method used for criminal detection. An innocent person would not be burned while the guilty party would immediately feel pain, again because of the relative dryness of the mouth.

Concluding sentence

Many of these methods relied (unknowingly) on the basic physiological principles that also guided the creation of the polygraph.

—Seymour Feshbach and Bernard Weiner, Personality

Exercise 4 Analyzing a Paragraph

1. Is the following paragraph developed according to Frame A (topic sentence/development) or Frame B (topic sentence/development/ concluding sentence)?

2. Identify the parts of the paragraph frame by underlining the topic sentence and the concluding sentence, if any, and by annotating the support in the left margin. Use the two example paragraphs as models.

But now I can say that I am a Japanese-American. It means I have a place here in this country, too. I have a place here on the East Coast, where our neighbor is so much a part of our family that my mother never passes her house at night without glancing at the lights to see if she is home and safe; where my parents have hauled hundreds of pounds of rocks from fields and arduously planted Christmas trees and blueberries, lilacs, asparagus, and crab apples, where my father still dreams of angling a stream to a new bed so that he can dig a pond in the field and fill it with water and fish. "The neighbors already came for their Christmas tree?" he asks in December. "Did they like it? Did they like it?"

—Kesaya E. Noda, "Growing Up Asian in America"

Exercise 5 Analyzing a Paragraph

1. Is the following paragraph developed according to Frame A (topic sentence/development) or Frame B (topic sentence/development/ concluding sentence)?

2. Identify the parts of the paragraph frame by underlining the topic sentence and the concluding sentence, if any, and by annotating the support in the left margin. Use the two example paragraphs as models.

> I can see myself today as a person historically defined by law and custom as being forever alien. Being neither "free white," nor "African," our people in California were deemed "aliens, ineligible for citizenship," no matter how long they intended to stay here. Aliens ineligible for citizenship were prohibited from owning, buying, or leasing land. They did not and could not belong here. The voice in me remembers that I am always a Japanese-American in the eyes of many. A third-generation German-American is an American. A third-generation Japanese-American is a Japanese-American. Being Japanese means being a danger to the country during the war and knowing how to use chopsticks. I wear this history on my face.
>
> —*Kesaya E. Noda*, "Growing Up Asian in America"

Conclusions

Your concluding paragraph should give the reader the feeling that you have said all you want to say about your subject. Like introductory paragraphs, concluding paragraphs are of various types. Here are some effective ways of concluding a paper:

- Conclude with a final paragraph or sentence that is a logical part of the body of the paper; that is, it functions as part of the support. In the following example, there is no formal conclusion. This form is more common in the published essay than in the student essay.

> One day he hit me. He said he was sorry and even cried, but I could not forgive him. We got a divorce. It took me a while before I could look back and see what the causes really were, but by then it was too late to make any changes.
>
> —*Maria Campos*, "A Divorce with Reasons"

- Conclude with a restatement of the thesis in slightly different words, perhaps pointing out its significance or making applications.

> Don't blame it on the referee. Don't even blame it on the fight managers. Put the blame where it belongs—on the prevailing mores that regard prize fighting as a perfectly proper enterprise

and vehicle of entertainment. No one doubts that many people enjoy prize fighting and will miss it if it should be thrown out. And that is precisely the point.

—*Norman Cousins*, "Who Killed Benny Paret?"

- Conclude with a review of the main points of the discussion— a kind of summary. This is appropriate only if the complexity of the essay makes a summary necessary.

As we have been made all too aware lately in this country, the more energy we conserve now, the more we'll have for the future. The same holds true for skiing. So take the Soft Path of energy conservation as you ski. You'll not only be able to make longer nonstop runs, but you'll have more energy to burn on the dance floor.

—*Carl Wingus*, "Conserving Energy as You Ski"

- Conclude with an anecdote related to the thesis.

Over the harsh traffic sounds of motors and horns and blaring radios came the faint whang-whang of a would-be musician with a beat-up guitar and a money-drop hat turned up at his feet. It all reminded me of when I had first experienced the conglomeration of things that now assailed my senses. This jumbled mixture of things both human and nonhuman was, in fact, the reason I had come to live here. Then it was different and exciting. Later it was the reason I was leaving.

—*Brian Maxwell*, "Leaving Los Angeles"

- Conclude with a quotation related to the thesis.

He [Johnny Cash] had, of course, long since attained a legendary stature few performers ever achieved. Terri Clark, a country songstress two generations removed, captured a sense of it in a statement released Friday. "What really made him stand out, more than the back-beats, the TV shows, the hit records, was how he stood up for the little people, the way he believed in the right things. . . . He was a beacon for both musical and personal integrity, and he set a bar most of us can only gaze at."

—*Dave Tianen*, "A Music Legend Fades to Black"

There are also many ineffective ways of concluding a paper. Do not conclude with the following:

- a summary when a summary is unnecessary
- a complaint about the assignment or an apology about the quality of the work

- an afterthought—that is, something you forgot to discuss in the body of the paper
- a tagged conclusion—that is, a sentence beginning with such phrases as *In conclusion, To conclude, I would like to conclude this discussion,* or *Last but not least*
- a conclusion that raises additional problems that should have been settled during the discussion.

The conclusion is an integral part of the essay and is often a reflection of the introduction. If you have trouble with the conclusion, reread your introduction. Then work for a roundness or completeness in the whole paper.

Exercise 6 Writing a Conclusion

For Exercise 3, you wrote two introductions. Select the better one, consider the basic information you would probably use for support (jotting down a few ideas if you like), and then write a simple conclusion of three to five sentences. This exercise demonstrates that the conclusion connects with the introduction, is a consequence of the development of the essay, and ends on a note of finality. In your regular assignments, you will not write your conclusion until after you have written the paragraphs of support.

Writer's Guidelines at a Glance: The Essay and Its Parts

1. An **essay** is a group of paragraphs, each of which supports a controlling statement called a **thesis**.
2. Each paragraph in an essay is almost always one of three types: introductory, support (developmental), or concluding.
3. An effective thesis has both a subject and a focus. The **subject** is what you intend to write about. The **focus** is what you intend to do with your subject.

   EXAMPLE   <u>Bidwell Elementary School</u> is <u>too crowded</u>.
                             subject   focus

4. An effective thesis presents a focus that can be developed with supporting information.
5. An ineffective thesis is vague, too broad, or too narrow.

6. Supporting information is presented in one of the following patterns—such as descriptive narration, analysis by division, process analysis, cause and effect, exemplification, comparison and contrast, definition, and argument—or in a combination of patterns.

7. A good **introductory paragraph** attracts the reader's interest, states or points toward the thesis, and moves the reader smoothly into the support, or body, paragraphs.

8. Introductory methods include a direct statement of the thesis, background, definition of term(s), quotation(s), a shocking statement, question(s), and a combination of two or more methods in this list.

9. **Support paragraphs**, also called **developmental paragraphs**, form the body of an essay and provide information and reasoning that justify the thesis presented in the paragraph of introduction. The developmental paragraph contains three parts: the subject, the topic sentence, and the support. It may also have a concluding sentence.

10. Your **concluding paragraph** should give the reader the feeling that you have said all you want to say about your subject.

11. Some effective methods of concluding are restating the thesis in slightly different words, perhaps pointing out its significance or applying it; reviewing the main points; presenting an anecdote related to the thesis; and using a quotation.

2

The Writing Process: Prewriting

Chapter 1 focused on organizing and writing an essay. However, it stopped short of presenting an overall plan for completing a specific writing assignment. The reason for that omission is simple: Each assignment has its own guidelines that vary according to the kind of topic, the source of ideas, the time permitted, the conditions for writing (especially in or outside class), and the purpose. Obviously, if one is to use a system, it must be flexible because a technique that is an asset for one assignment may be a burden for another. Therefore, a good writer should know numerous techniques, treating each as a tool that can be used when needed. All of these tools are in the same box, one labeled "The Writing Process."

The Writing Process Defined

The writing process consists of strategies that can help you proceed from your purpose or initial idea to a final developed essay. Those strategies can be divided into prewriting techniques and writing stages. Using prewriting techniques, you explore, experiment, gather information, formulate your thesis, and develop and organize your support. In the writing stages, you write a first draft, revise your draft as many times as necessary, and edit your writing. For the typical college writing assignment, the writing process looks like the following:

Prewriting
- Explore, experiment, and gather information
- Write the controlling idea
- Organize and develop support

Writing
- Draft, revise, and edit

22

A flexible set of steps is included in the Writing Process Worksheet on page xxi. The worksheet can be enlarged, photocopied, and submitted with your assignment, if your instructor asks you to do so.

Prewriting is discussed in this chapter, and writing is discussed in Chapter 3. The examples come from Leah's essay, "Razor Wire Sweat Lodge."

〜 Prewriting Strategies

Prewriting strategies include freewriting, brainstorming and listing, clustering, composing the thesis, and outlining.

Freewriting

Freewriting is an exercise that Peter Elbow, its originator, has called "babbling in print." In freewriting, you write without stopping, letting your ideas tumble forth. You do not concern yourself with the fundamentals of writing, such as punctuation and spelling. Freewriting is an adventure into your memory and imagination. It is discovery, invention, and exploration. If you are at a loss for words on your subject, write down a comment such as "I don't know what is coming next" or "blah, blah, blah," and continue when relevant words come. It is important to continue writing. Freewriting immediately eliminates the blank page and thereby helps you break through an emotional barrier, but that is not the only benefit. The words that you sort through in that fashion will include some you can use. You can then underline or circle those words and even add notes on the side so that the freewriting continues to grow even after its initial, spontaneous expression.

The way you proceed depends on the type of assignment:

> working with a topic of your choice
> working from a restricted list of topics
> working with a prescribed topic

Working with the topic of your choice gives you the greatest freedom of exploration. You would probably select a subject that interests you and freewrite about it, allowing your mind to wander among its many parts, perhaps mixing fact and fantasy, direct experience, and hearsay. A freewriting about music might uncover areas of special interest and knowledge, such as jazz or folk rock, that you would want to pursue further in freewriting or other prewriting strategies.

Working from a restricted list requires a more focused freewriting. With the list, you can, of course, experiment with several topics to discover what is most suitable for you. If, for example, "career choice," "career preparation," "career guidance," and "career prospects" are on the restricted list, you would probably select one and freewrite about it. If it works well for you, you would probably proceed with the next step of your prewriting. If you are not satisfied with what you uncover in freewriting, you would explore another item from the restricted list.

When working with a prescribed topic, you focus on a particular topic and try to restrict your freewriting to its boundaries. If your topic specifies a division of a subject area such as "political involvement of your generation," then you would tie those key words to your own information, critical thinking, and imaginative responses. If the topic is restricted to, let's say, your reaction to a particular reading selection such as a poem, then that poem would give you a framework for freewriting about your own experiences, creations, and opinions. An analysis of the piece would probably include underlining pertinent ideas, annotating it (writing in the margins), and even taking notes on it. Freewriting can help you get words on paper to generate topics, develop new insights, and explore ideas.

Freewriting can lead to other stages of prewriting and writing, and it can also provide content for details and insights as you develop your topic. Let's back up and see how Leah used freewriting to begin exploring her ideas for her essay. Leah was assigned to write a personal essay of 500 to 800 words. Her instructor suggested she concentrate on a recent development or prison event that changed her life, for better or worse.

Several topics interested her. There was the problem of overcrowding: she lived in an institution built for 900 inmates, and the population was now 2,200. She also considered education. After spending some time in routine prison work and aimless activities, she had discovered school and found it highly satisfying. And then there were the accomplishments of her Native American friends at the prison. After years of arguing their case, they had finally obtained permission from the institution to build a sweat lodge for religious purposes, and it was now in operation. That was a subject she knew well, and it was one for which she held the most enthusiasm.

Leah started freewriting, which enabled her to probe her memory and see which aspects of the subject she was most interested in. She wrote without stopping, as she liberated and associated the many thoughts she had on the subject of *sweat lodge*. Following is some of Leah's freewriting.

Now <u>we have a sweat lodge</u> where we can go

for our ceremonies. It makes me feel good. I

look forward to it. I <u>have used it once a</u>

<u>week for most</u> of the <u>last year</u>. When I am

nervous and when things are tense on the

prison grounds, I think about the sweat lodge

and just thinking about it gives me some

peace. Then <u>when I go there and sweat</u> for a

period of time I seem to feel that I am

leaving the prison grounds and I am <u>at peace</u>

Ceremony   with the universe. It is <u>a ceremony</u> that is
important

<u>important</u> to me and also to the prison. We

even have women who are not Indians who are

interested and we teach them about Indian

ways and we all learn from what we do. What

else is there to say. I could go on and on.

That is what I have to say. I love the sweat

lodge which we call the sweats. I think it is

the most important thing in my life now. I

used to be bitter toward the prison for

denying me my rights, but now I am even

At peace   at peace with them—most of the time.

I remember when we were trying to get

approval and . . . [partial]

After her freewriting session, Leah examined what she had written for possible ideas to develop for a writing assignment. As she recognized those ideas, she underlined key words and phrases and made a few notes in the margins. By reading only the underlined words, you can understand what is important to Leah; she did not need to underline whole sentences.

In addition to putting words on that dreaded blank sheet of paper, Leah discovered that she had quite a lot to say about the sweat lodge and that she had selected a favorable topic to develop. The entire process took no more than five minutes. Had she found only a few ideas or no promising ideas at all, she might have freewritten on another topic. In going back over her work she saw some errors, especially in wording and sentence structure, but she did not correct them because the purpose of freewriting is discovery, not revising or correcting grammar, punctuation, and spelling. She was confident that she could continue with the process of writing a paper.

Exercise 1 Freewriting

Freewrite for a few minutes on one of the following topics. After you finish freewriting, take two minutes or so to mark the key words and phrases. Then make a few notations if you find some promising ideas that could be developed.

An event that was important to you in your youth
A concert, a movie, or a television program
Types of smartphones
Drug abuse—causes, effects, a friend with a problem
Gang membership—causes, effects, an experience
Ways of disciplining children
A family reunion, wedding, funeral, or graduation
A great or terrible party

A bad or good day at school
Why a college education is important
How music (rock, rap, country) affects or reveals the attitudes
of its fans
Your most memorable job
A date from hell or heaven

Brainstorming and Listing

Brainstorming is a strategy for coming up with fresh, new ideas in a hurry. What key words and phrases pop into your mind when you think about your topic? One effective way to get started brainstorming is to ask the big six questions about your subject area: *Who? What? Where? When? Why?* and *How?* Then let your mind run free as you jot down answers in single entries or lists. Using the big six questions also helps you begin to organize ideas for your writing. Some of the big six questions may not fit, and some may be more important than others, depending on the purpose of your writing. For example, if you were writing about the causes of an accident, the *Why?* question could be more important than the others. If you were concerned with how to succeed in college, the *How?* question would predominate. If you were writing in response to a reading selection, you would confine your thinking to questions related to the content of the reading selection.

Whatever the focus of the six questions, the result is likely to be numerous ideas that will provide information for continued exploration and development of your topic. Thus your pool of information for writing widens and deepens.

An alternative to the big six questions approach is simply to make a list of words and phrases related to your subject area or specific topic.

Leah continued with the subject of the sweat lodge, and her topic tightened to focus on particular areas. Although she could have listed the annotations and the words she underlined in her freewriting, she instead used the big six questions for her framework.

Who?   American Indian inmates and others
What?   sweat lodge, how it was started, the politics, the ceremonies
Where?   California Institution for Women—off the yard
When?   1989, before, after, long time in planning and building

Why?   spiritual, physical, self-esteem, educational
How?   preparation, steps

Leah's listing might have taken this form:

Sweat Lodge	Ceremony	Result
Problems in	Preparation	Relaxed
building it	Blankets	Spiritually clean
Reasons	Rocks	Peaceful
Fairness	Fire	
Who helped	Water	
Time to build	Tobacco and	
	sweet grass	
	Sweating	
	Passing pipe	
	Tearing down	

Exercise 2 Brainstorming or Listing

Brainstorm or make a list for the topic that interested you in Exercise 1.

Clustering

Clustering (also called *mapping*) is yet another prewriting technique. Start by double-bubbling your topic; that is, write it down in the middle of the page and draw a double circle around it, like the hub of a wheel. Then respond to the question, "What comes to mind?" Single-bubble other ideas on spokes radiating from the hub. Any bubble can lead to another bubble or to numerous bubbles in the same way. This strategy is sometimes used instead of or before making an outline to organize and develop ideas.

The more specific the topic inside the double bubble, the fewer the number of spokes that will radiate from it. For example, a topic such as "high school dropouts" would have more spokes than "reasons for dropping out of high school."

Leah's cluster on her topic of the prison sweat lodge is shown on page 29.

Notice that after completing her basic cluster, Leah went back and drew a broken boundary around subclusters that offered encouraging areas for focus. Some subclusters, usually with further clustering to provide details, can be as good as an outline in offering structure and content for the development of an essay.

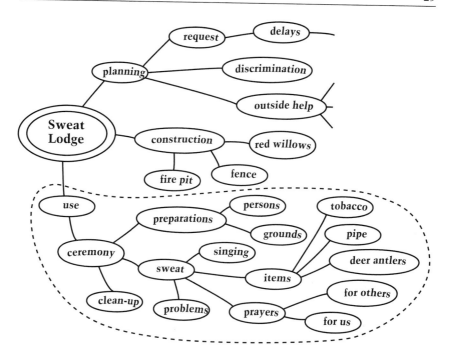

Exercise 3 Clustering

Make a cluster on the topic you chose in Exercise 1. After you finish, draw broken boundaries around subclusters that have potential for further development.

Composing the Thesis

After freewriting, brainstorming, and clustering, Leah was ready to focus. She was ready to concentrate on one aspect of her larger topic that could reasonably be developed into an essay of 500 to 800 words. She also wanted to establish a direction for the essay that would target her audience, who knew little about her topic. She would have to explain her topic in detail as a controlling idea, or thesis, so that uninformed readers could easily understand. Moreover, she would avoid any Native American words that her audience might not know. Although the sweat lodge was developed in an atmosphere of controversy in which she and others often had to be persuasive, she anticipated that readers of her essay would be open-minded and interested. She would simply inform them about her experience with the sweat lodge, giving a personal perspective. She would also have to avoid using prison slang because this essay was for an assignment in a college writing class.

Leah made three attempts to write a sentence with both a subject (what she would write about) and a focus (what she would do with her subject). She wanted the focus to be just right, not vague or too broad or too narrow.

> I want to explain how we use the sweats and why.
>
> Using the prison sweat lodge involves specific practices that contribute to my well-being.

Subject I want to discuss the <u>prison sweat lodge</u>,
Focus <u>what we do in the preparation period</u>, <u>what we do when we're inside for the ceremony</u>, and <u>what we do afterward</u>.

Her third attempt satisfied her, and the statement became her thesis. Later she would reword it.

Exercise 4 Writing a Thesis

After consulting your freewriting, brainstorming or listing, and clustering, write a thesis. Label the subject and focus parts.

Outlining

Outlining is the tool that most people think of in connection with organizing. Outlining does basically the same thing that listing and clustering do. Outlining divides the controlling idea into sections of support material, divides those sections further, and establishes sequence.

An outline is a kind of framework, and it can be used in two ways: It can indicate the plan for a paragraph or an essay you intend to write. It can also show the organization of a passage you are reading. The outline of a reading passage and the outline as a plan for writing are identical in form. If you intend to write a summary of a reading selection, then a single outline might be used for both purposes.

The two main outline forms are the **sentence outline** (each entry is a complete sentence) and the **topic outline** (each entry is a key word or phrase). The topic outline is more common in writing paragraphs and essays.

In the following topic outline, notice first how the parts are arranged on the page: the indentations, the number and letter sequences, the punctuation, and the placement of words. Then read the outline and see how the ideas relate to one another.

Main idea (usually the topic sentence for a paragraph or the thesis for an essay)

I. Major support
   A. Minor support
      1. Explanation, detail, example
      2. Explanation, detail, example
   B. Minor support
      1. Explanation, detail, example
      2. Explanation, detail, example
II. Major support
   A. Minor support
      1. Explanation, detail, example
      2. Explanation, detail, example
   B. Minor support
      1. Explanation, detail, example
      2. Explanation, detail, example

Leah's next task was to organize her material. For this strategy, she went back to her bubble cluster, which she had divided into "planning," "construction," and "use." She had already decided she wanted to work with the "use" aspect and explain it from her perspective. Therefore, she focused on only one part of the cluster—the part indicated by the broken boundary line.

She might have started to write a first draft at this point, but instead she decided she wanted to recall and organize more detail, so she began an outline. She used her own memory and private reference sources for information. If she had been working on a reading-related topic, she would have gone back to the reading. If she had been working on a topic subject to research, she would have consulted library sources.

Leah's outline shows the relationship of ideas, suggests ways to divide the essay according to her thesis, and indicates support. The divisions are Preparation, Ceremony, and Ceremony Completion and Site Restoration. Those items are Leah's Roman-numeral headings.

I. Preparation
   A. Fasting
      1. Duration
      2. Only water or juices
   B. Heat rocks
      1. Thirty to fifty
      2. Build fire
   C. Set up lodge
      1. Permission from sponsor
      2. Cover framework
II. Ceremony
   A. Movement
      1. Going and coming
      2. Passing sacred objects
   B. Establishing attitude
   C. Sweating
   D. Praying and singing
   E. Purification rites
      1. Tobacco ties
      2. Sage
      3. Sweet grass
III. Ceremony completion and site restoration
   A. Personal
      1. Water down
      2. Eat and drink
      3. Change
   B. Site
      1. Remove and store blankets
      2. Move rocks

Exercise 5   Completing Outlines

Fill in the missing parts of the following outlines. It may be helpful to ask, in each case, whether you are dealing with time, examples, causes, effects, parts, or steps. The answers will vary, depending on your individual experiences and views.

1. <u>Borrowing</u>   <u>is the mother of trouble.</u>
      subject   focus

I. Received five credit cards in mail

II. Saw numerous commercials on television

   A. One about _____

   B. Another about _____

III. Made purchases

IV. Two months later _____

2. <u>A successful job interview</u>   <u>depends on several factors</u>.
         subject   focus

   I. Presenting good appearance

      A. _____

      B. _____

   II. Behaving properly

   III. Being qualified

      A. Education

      B. _____

   IV. Knowing something about the employer

3. <u>Joe's drug addiction</u>   <u>had significant effects on his life</u>.
        subject   focus

   I. Developed mental-health problems

      A. _____

      B. _____

   II. Developed _____

   III. Lost his job

▋Exercise 6▐ Writing an Outline

Make a topic outline for your essay. Your Roman-numeral headings will probably correspond to some of the major divisions of your cluster.

Writer's Guidelines at a Glance: Prewriting

1. The writing process consists of strategies that can help you produce a polished essay.
   Prewriting includes exploring, experimenting, gathering information, writing the controlling idea, and organizing and developing support. **Writing** includes drafting, revising, and editing.
2. Prewriting includes one or more of the following strategies.

   - **Freewriting:** writing without stopping so that you can explore, experiment, and invent
   - **Brainstorming or listing:** responding to *Who? What? Where? When? Why?* and *How?* questions or making lists on likely divisions of your subject
   - **Clustering:** showing related ideas by double-bubbling a subject and then connecting single bubbles of related ideas on spokes radiating out and branching from the hub
   - **Composing the thesis:** writing a sentence that has two parts— the subject (what you are writing about) and the focus (what you will do with the subject)
   - **Outlining:** dividing the controlling idea into sections of support material, dividing those sections further, and establishing a workable sequence

3

The Writing Process: Writing, Revising, and Editing

Writing Your First Draft

Once you have developed your thesis and your outline (or list or cluster), you are ready to begin writing your essay. The initial writing is called the **first**, or **rough**, **draft**. Your thesis statement is likely to be at or near the beginning of your essay and will be followed by your support as ordered by your outline.

Paying close attention to your outline for basic organization, you should proceed without worrying about the refinements of writing. This is not the time to concern yourself with perfect spelling, grammar, or punctuation. After you have finished that first draft, take a close look at it. If your thesis is sound and your outline has served you well, you now have a basic discussion. You have made a statement and supported it.

Don't be embarrassed by the roughness of your work. You should be embarrassed only if you leave it that way. You are seeing the reason why a first draft is called "rough." Famous authors have said publicly that they wouldn't show their rough drafts even to their closest, most forgiving friends.

The Recursive Factor

The process of writing can be called **recursive**, which means "going back and forth." In this respect, writing is like reading. If you do not understand what you have read, you back up and read it again. After you have read an entire passage, you may need to read it again selectively. The same can be said of writing. If, for example, after having developed an outline and started writing your first draft, you discover

35

that your subject is too broad, you will have to back up, narrow your thesis, and then adjust your outline. You may even want to return to an early cluster of ideas to see how you can use a smaller grouping of them. Revision is usually the most recursive of all parts of the writing process. You will go over your material again and again until you are satisfied that you have expressed yourself as well as you possibly can.

Your Audience

When you speak to a person, you routinely adjust what you say and how you say it. You should do the same for your audience when you write. To the extent that you can, consider the needs, interests, knowledge, biases, and abilities of your intended readers and appropriately adjust your subject, explanations, style, and word choice to achieve your objective, whether it be to inform or to persuade.

◠ Revising Your Writing

The term *first draft* suggests quite accurately that there will be other drafts, or versions, of your writing. Only in the most dire situations, such as an in-class examination when you have time for only one draft, should you be satisfied with a single effort.

What you do beyond the first draft is called revising and editing. Revising concerns itself with organization, content, and language effectiveness. Editing involves a final correcting of mistakes in spelling, punctuation, and capitalization. In practice, revising and editing are not always separate activities, although writers usually wait until the next-to-the-last draft to edit some minor details and attend to other small points that can be easily overlooked.

Successful revision almost always involves intense, systematic rewriting. You should learn to look for certain aspects of skillful writing as you enrich and repair your first draft. To help you recall these aspects so that you can keep them in mind and examine your material comprehensively, this textbook offers a memory device—an acronym in which each letter suggests an important feature of good writing and revision. This device enables you to memorize the features of good writing quickly. Soon you will be able to recall and refer to them automatically. These features need not be attended to individually when you revise your writing, although they may be. And they need not be attended to in the order presented here. Consider using the acronym CLUESS (pronounced "clues"), which provides a comprehensive guide to revision:

Coherence
Language
Unity
Emphasis
Support
Sentences

Coherence

Coherence is an orderly relationship of ideas, each leading smoothly and logically to the next. You must weave your ideas together so skillfully that the reader can easily see how one idea connects to another and to the central thought. This central thought, of course, is expressed in the topic sentence for a paragraph and in the thesis for an essay. You can achieve coherence efficiently by using an overall pattern, transitional words and expressions, repetition of key words and ideas, pronouns, and a consistent point of view.

Overall Pattern

Several chapters in this book discuss strategies for an overall plan, or pattern, of organization. Three basic patterns prevail: time (chronology), space, and emphasis (stress on ideas). Sometimes you will combine patterns. The coherence of each pattern can be strengthened by using transitional words such as these:

Time: *first, then, soon, later, following, after, at that point*
Space: *up, down, right, left, beyond, behind, above, below, before*
Emphasis: *first, second, third, most, more*

Transitional Terms

Use transitional terms, conjunctive adverbs, to help your reader move easily from one idea to another. Each of the following sentences has one or more of these terms.

First I realized I had to get a job to stay in school.
At the same time, however, my track coach wanted the team to spend more hours working out.
We were, *after all,* the defending champions.
Finally I dropped one of my courses.

Other transitional terms include *moreover, in fact, nevertheless, then, thus, now, soon, therefore, consequently,* and *accordingly.*

Repetition of Key Words and Ideas

Repeat key words and phrases to keep the main subject in the reader's mind and to maintain the continuity necessary for a smooth flow of logical thought.

Pronouns

Pronouns, such as *this, that, those, he, her, them,* and *it,* provide natural connecting links in your writing. Why? Every pronoun refers to an earlier noun (called the **antecedent** of the pronoun) and thus carries the reader back to that earlier thought. Here are some examples:

> I tried to buy *tickets* for the concert, but *they* were all sold.
>
> Assertive *people* tend to make decisions quickly. However, *they* may not make the wisest decisions.

Language

In the revision process, the word *language* takes on a special meaning; it refers to usage, tone, and diction.

Usage

Usage is the kind or general style of language we use. All or almost all of us operate on the principle of appropriateness. If I used *ain't* as part of my explanations in this textbook, you would be surprised and probably disappointed. You would think about my word choice rather than about what I have to say. Why would you be surprised? Because *ain't* is not appropriate for my audience in this situation. If you write an essay containing slang, you will probably be understood, but if the slang is not appropriate, you will draw unfavorable attention to your words. That does not mean that slang does not have its place—it does. It can be imaginative and colorful. Often, though, it is only a weak substitute for more precise vocabulary.

Usage is an important part of writing and revising. Judge what is appropriate for your audience and your purpose. What kind of language is expected? What kind of language is best suited for accomplishing your purpose?

Tone

Have you ever heard someone say, "Don't talk to me in that tone of voice" or "I accepted what she was saying, but I didn't like the tone she used when she told me"? **Tone** in these contexts means that the sound of the speaker's voice and maybe the language choices conveyed disrespect to the listener. The tone could have represented any number of feelings about the subject matter and the audience. Tone can have as many variations as you can have feelings: it can, for example, be sarcastic, humorous, serious, cautionary, objective, groveling, angry, bitter, sentimental, enthusiastic, somber, outraged, or loving.

Let's say you are getting a haircut. Looking in those omnipresent mirrors bordered with pictures of people with different styles of haircuts, you see that the stylist is cutting off too much hair. You could use different tones in giving him or her some timely how-to instructions.

> *Objective, serious:* "If you don't mind, what I meant to say was that I would like a haircut proportioned just like that one there in the picture of Tom Cruise from *Rain Man.*"
>
> *Humorous:* "I hesitate to make suggestions to someone who is standing at my back and holding a sharp instrument near my throat, but I'm letting my hair grow out a bit, and I don't want you to take off a lot in the back and on the sides."
>
> *Angry and sarcastic:* "Look man, when I sat down, I said I wanted my hair cut in the design of Tom Cruise in *Rain Man.* The way you're hacking at it, you must've thought I said *Top Gun.*"
>
> *Conciliatory:* "I really like the way you cut my hair, and I can see that you are proportioning it with great care, but I would like my hair to be a bit longer than the style that I think you're working on. Do you remember how I used to get my hair cut about a year ago, a little longer on the sides and more bushy on top?"
>
> *Friendly:* "You came up with a great style that everyone liked. Could you give me one similar to that?"
>
> *Overbearing:* "Damn it, buddy. Will you watch what you're doing! I asked for a haircut, not a shave. If God had wanted me to have bare skin above my shoulders, he would've put the hair on my feet."

In speech, feelings and attitudes are represented by inflection, loudness, word choice, and language patterns. In writing, tone is conveyed mainly by word choice and order; it is closely related to style—the variations in the way you write, depending on your purpose. Your purpose is simply to present a particular idea in a particular context. The context implies the audience; it is important to use the tone appropriate for your audience.

Usually your tone will be consistent throughout your presentation, although for the informal essay often assigned in college, you may choose to begin in a lighthearted, amusing tone before switching to a more serious, objective mode.

Diction

Diction is word choice. If you use good diction, you are finding the best words for a particular purpose in addressing a certain audience. There is some overlap, therefore, between usage and diction.

The following list shows the difference between general and specific words.

General	Specific	More Specific
food	pastry	Twinkie
mess	grease	oil slicks on table
drink	soda	mug of root beer
odor	smell from grill	smell of frying onions

Another aspect of diction is freshness and originality of expression. To achieve those distinctions, you should avoid clichés, which are trite, familiar phrases. Consider this sentence:

> When the prince married Cinderella, her sisters went green with envy because she was now on easy street, leaving them out in the cold.

Those words were written by a person who doesn't care about communicating in a clear and interesting manner. It would be far better to say,

> When the prince married Cinderella, her sisters were envious because they had few prospects.

Here are some clichés to avoid:

young at heart	quick as a flash
rotten to the core	slow but sure
uphill battle	other side of the coin
more than meets the eye	breathless silence
bitter end	acid test
as luck would have it	better late than never
last but not least	six of one, half dozen of the other

These clichés are ready-made expressions. A cliché master manipulates language as if it were a prefabricated building going up, not bothering to use any imagination and leaving little opportunity for his or her audience to use theirs. Good diction reflects the writer as an individual and is fresh, original, and clear.

Unity

A controlling idea, stated or implied, unifies every piece of good writing. It is the point around which the supporting material revolves. For a paragraph, the elements are the topic sentence and the supporting sentences. For an essay, the elements are the thesis and the supporting paragraphs. All the supporting material should be related to the topic sentence or the thesis.

Unity can be strengthened and made more apparent if you use a strong concluding statement at the end of the unit and if you repeat key words and phrases from time to time. A good check on unity is to ask yourself if everything in your paragraph or essay is subordinate to and derived from the controlling idea.

Don't confuse unity and coherence. Whereas coherence involves the clear movement of thought from sentence to sentence or paragraph to paragraph, unity means staying on the topic. A unified and coherent outline would become incoherent if the parts were scrambled, but the outline technically would still be unified. These qualities of writing go together. You should stay on the topic and make clear connections.

Emphasis

Emphasis, a feature of most good writing, helps the reader focus on the main ideas. It can be achieved in several ways but mainly through placement of key ideas and through repetition.

Placement of Ideas

The most emphatic part of any passage, whether a sentence or a book, is the last part, because we usually remember most easily what we read last. The second most emphatic part of a passage is the beginning, because our mind is relatively uncluttered when we read it. For these reasons, among others, the topic sentence or the thesis usually comes at the beginning of a piece, and it is often restated or reflected on at the end in an echoing statement.

Repetition of Key Words and Ideas

Repetition is one of the simplest devices in your writer's toolbox. The words repeated may be single words, phrases, slightly altered sentences, or synonyms. Repetition keeps the dominant subject in the reader's mind and maintains the continuity necessary for a smooth flow of logical thought.

You can use this valuable technique easily. If, as is done in the following example, you are discussing the effects of the school dropout problem, then the word *effect(s)*, along with synonyms such as *result(s)* or *consequence(s)*, and *school dropout(s)*, are likely to be repeated several times. Moreover, phrases giving insight into the issue may be repeated, perhaps with slight variation.

```
The causes of the school dropout problem

have received much attention recently, but the

effects are just as important. One obvious

result is that of unemployment or low-paying

employment. The student who drops out of school

is likely to be dropping into poverty, perhaps

even into a lifelong condition. Another effect

is juvenile crime. The young person who has no

prospects for a good job and no hope all too

frequently turns to illegal activities. A third

result concerns the psychological well-being of

the dropout. Although withdrawing from school

seems to offer a quick, viable solution to

perceived problems, it almost immediately has
```

```
consequences for the dropout's self-esteem. Of

course, these effects may also be tied to

causes, such as drugs, poverty, crime, or

psychological problems, but devastating

repercussions are there at the far end of the

causes-and-effects continuum, and youngsters

who are contemplating dropping out should

consider them with care.
```

A word of warning: The effective use of word and phrase repetition should not be confused with an irritating misuse of word repetition. We all at times get "hung up" on certain words, and the result is a negative response from our audience. Consider this awkward use of repetition:

> She looked at him and frowned. He returned the look and then looked away at a stranger looking for his lost keys.

That's too many *look*'s. Consider this version:

> She looked at him [or, *perhaps even better,* She frowned at him]. He glared back and then glanced away at a stranger searching for his lost keys.

The second version preserves the idea of people "looking" by using synonyms. It does not grate on the reader's mind as the first does.

Support

How much support does a piece of writing need? A good support paragraph fulfills its function by fully developing the topic sentence. An essay is complete when it fulfills its function of developing a thesis. Obviously, you will have to judge what is complete. With some subjects, you will need little supporting and explanatory material. With others, you will need much more. The points of support, in the form of examples, details, quotations, and explanations, should be placed in the best possible order. (See "Patterns of

Support for the Thesis," p. 8, and "Support Paragraphs," p. 12, in Chapter 1 for more information.)

Sentences

In the revision process, the word *sentences* pertains to the variety of sentence patterns and the correctness of sentence structure. A passage that offers a variety of simple and complicated sentences satisfies the reader, just as a combination of simple and complicated foods go together in a good meal. The writer can introduce variety by including both short and long sentences, by using different sentence patterns, and by beginning sentences in different ways.

Length

In revising, examine your writing to make sure that sentences vary in length. A series of short sentences is likely to make the flow seem choppy and the thoughts disconnected. But single short sentences interspersed with longer sentences often work very well. Because short sentences are uncluttered with supporting points and qualifications, they often are direct and forceful. Consider using short sentences to emphasize points and to introduce ideas. Use longer sentences to provide details or show how ideas are related.

Variety of Sentence Patterns

Good writing includes a variety of sentence patterns. Although there is no limit to the number of sentences you can write, the conventional English sentence appears in only four basic patterns:

SIMPLE	She did the work well.
COMPOUND	She did the work well, and she was well paid.
COMPLEX	Because she did the work well, she was well paid.
COMPOUND-COMPLEX	Because she did the work well, she was well paid, and she was satisfied.

Each sentence pattern listed above has its own purposes and strengths. The simple sentence conveys a single idea. The compound sentence shows, by its structure, that two somewhat equal ideas are connected. The complex sentence shows that one idea is less important than another; that is, it is dependent on, or subordinate to, the idea in the main clause. The compound-complex sentence has the scope of both the compound sentence and the complex sentence.

Variety of Sentence Beginnings

Another way to provide sentence variety is to use different kinds of beginnings. A new beginning may or may not be accompanied by a changed sentence pattern. Among the most common beginnings, other than those starting with the subject of the main clause, are those that start with a prepositional phrase, a dependent clause, or a transitional connective (conjunctive adverb), such as *therefore, however,* or *in fact.*

- Prepositional phrase (in italics)

    In your fantasy, you are the star.

    Like casino owners, game show hosts want you to be cheery.

- Dependent clause (in italics)

    When the nighttime Wheel of Fortune *debuted,* the slot was occupied by magazine shows.

    As Pat Sajak noted, viewers often solve the puzzle before the contestants do.

    —Lewis Grossberger, "A Big Wheel"

- Transitional connective (in italics)

    Now you know.

    Therefore, you feel happy, excited, and a bit superior.

Problems with Sentences

A complete sentence must generally include an independent clause, which is a group of words that contains a subject and a verb and can stand alone. Some groups of words may sound interesting, but they are not correct sentences. Three common problem groupings are fragments, comma splices, and run-ons (see pp. 249–250 in Chapter 14, "Handbook").

- **Fragment:** A word grouping that is structurally incomplete is only a fragment of a sentence.

    Because he left. (This phrase is a dependent clause, not a complete sentence.)

    Went to the library. (This phrase has no subject.)

    She being the only person there. (This phrase has no verb.)

    Waiting there for help. (This phrase has neither subject nor verb.)

    In the backseat under a book. (This phrase has two prepositional phrases but no subject or verb.)

- **Comma splice:** The comma splice consists of two independent clauses with only a comma between them.

    The weather was bad, we canceled the picnic. (A comma by itself cannot join two independent clauses.)

- **Run-on:** The run-on differs from the comma splice in only one way: it has no comma between the independent clauses.

    The weather was bad we canceled the picnic.

Fragments, comma splices, and run-ons can easily be fixed. You cannot fix them, however, until you can confidently identify them in your writing. Watch for them during the revision and editing stages of your writing.

If you frequently have problems with sentence structure and awkwardness of phrasing, be especially suspicious of long sentences. Test each sentence of fifteen or more words for flaws. Try writing shorter, more direct sentences until you gain more confidence and competency. Then work with more sophisticated patterns.

⁓ Adding Editing to Revision

Editing, the final stage of the writing process, involves a careful examination of your work. Look for problems with capitalization, omissions, punctuation, and spelling (COPS).

Before you submit your writing to your instructor, do what almost all professional writers do before sending their material along: read it aloud, to yourself or to a willing accomplice. Reading material aloud will help you catch any awkwardness of expression, omission and misplacement of words, and other problems that are easily overlooked by an author.

As you can see, writing is a process and is not a matter of just sitting down and "banging out" a statement. The parts of the process from prewriting to revising to editing are connected, and your movement is ultimately forward, but this process allows you to go back and forth in the recursive manner discussed earlier. If your outline is not working, perhaps the flaw is in your thesis. You may need to go back and fix it. If one section of your essay is skimpy, perhaps you will have to go back and reconsider the pertinent material in your outline or cluster. There you might find more details, or you might alter your thesis so that you can move into more fertile areas of thought.

Let's return to Leah, whose work was shown in Chapters 1 and 2. After completing her first draft, Leah began revising, guided mainly by CLUESS:

Coherence	making one idea lead smoothly into the next
Language	ensuring proper usage, tone, and diction
Unity	using the thesis to unify the essay parts and using the topic sentences to unify ideas within the developmental paragraphs
Emphasis	repeating words and phrases and placing of key parts at the beginning or end of units
Support	presenting evidence and reasoning in relation to the thesis and topic sentences
Sentences	using a variety of beginnings and patterns; avoiding fragments, comma splices, and run-ons

The following partial draft is an early version that shows her revision process. The draft also includes some editing (for capitalization, omissions, punctuation, and spelling, or COPS). Her final draft is on pages 2–6 in Chapter 1.

Razor Wire Sweat Lodge

My tribe is

I am a Pomo Indian, one tribe of many twenty-one represented

here on the prison grounds. I have always had

tremendous interest in my Ancestry ancestors and their in

customs, and the cultures of all Indian

tribes. The sacred sweat ceremonies, I've

Rewrite

found to be one of the most interesting. Many cultural practices

women of all other races here in the facility have

also taken interest an and found peace other benefits within

themselves from participating in the sweats.

I want to discuss the prison sweat lodge,

what we do in the preparation period, what we

do when we're inside for the ceremony, and

what we do afterwards.

Rewrite for stronger topic sentence

The first step to sweating *in our prison facility* is the

preparation period. Before anyone can sweat

there are many requirements ~~in~~ *concerning* what we wear/,

~~how we are instructed (depending on how many~~

~~times we've gone),~~ and how we act. *For* Twenty-

four hours before the sweat, we fast. ~~We can~~

Coherence

~~only drink~~ *Participants should drink only* water or juices, but if someone

has health problems, we will excuse her. The

lava rocks have to *heat* in the fire approximately

three hours before we start sweating. The

fire has to be built just right in a little

house shape. ~~Putting~~ *We put* all the rocks in the

middle with the wood standing like a teepee

Organize Be more concise

around them; then the paper *is* stuffed between

and around the wood. Once there's a good fire

going, we ~~start~~ tend to the sweat lodge

itself. Since we have no tarp to put on the

sweat lodge, the state has provided us with

plenty of blankets. The blankets have to cover

the s^weat lodge fully. We put at least three

layers of blankets on the sweat lodge. We make

sure we leave about eight inches of blanket

around the bottom of the sweat lodge. ~~Around~~ ^By

Coherence [this time some women have started making their

tobacco ties. These ties are used for ^sending ~~putting~~

~~your~~ prayer on. We've ~~got to~~ ^must make sure the

sponsor is somewhere by the sweat lodge at all

times. ~~Also about~~ ^As for the rock^s, we use thirty to

fifty of them ^; it depends on their size and how

many women are sweating that day. Then the

women are told to change into only muumuu^s; the

state provides them also. Then we're read^y to go

inside. The preparation period is very

important ^, but ~~and~~ everyone looks forward to it

being over.

    Once everyone is inside the sweat lodge,

there are certain things ^we ~~you~~ must do. ~~The way~~

~~we enter is~~ first we enter counter‿clockwise ^,

and ^once^ inside we ~~maintain everything we do~~ ^conduct all parts of the ceremony^

counter‿clockwise. There are four rounds in

the sweat ^, each of^ which lasts about twenty to thirty

minutes ~~each~~. We stress that no one ^should^ break our

circle inside the sweat lodge, but it ~~is~~ ^sometimes happens.^

Coherence — ~~possible.~~ Some women can't handle the heat

inside; we never make them stay. The praying

Rephrase — and singing is in the Sioux language since

our outside sponsor is Sioux. Not everyone

has to sing or pray. It's up to ~~them~~ ^the individual.^ As

someone finishes a prayer ~~they say for all~~ ^she mentions all her relatives^

~~their relations,~~ then the next person prays.

Agreement — Before ^we^ ~~anyone even~~ enters the sweat ^we^ ~~they~~

have to make sure they have peace and

good feelings with all other members. The

tobacco ties hang over our heads in the

sweat or around our necks. (Also) we take in

sage with us and smudge ourselves with it ^for purification^.

After each round, new hot rocks are brought

Verb tense — in. As these rocks are place^d^ in the fire

sweet grass is put on them. ~~All~~ ^What^ we do inside

Be more
concise

the sweat lodge is not only for ourselves,

but ~~for~~ our prayers ^through^ for others. We maintain

ourselves with humility during the whole

sweat.

When the sweat is over^,^ we enter the final

phase. We come out and throw our tobacco ties

in ^to^ the fire pit. The^n^ ~~first thing~~ we ~~do is~~ hose

ourselves down with plenty of cold water. The

refreshments are opened and someone goes after

food. Once we've eaten and changed our clothes^,^

we start taking down the sweat. The blankets

have to be taken off the same way they were

put on and folded up ^carefully^ ~~good~~. The left-over wood

has to be put away and ~~on both~~ the blankets

and the wood ^must be covered^ ~~we put their covers~~. Any garbage

that's been left around is thrown in ^to^ the

dumpster. Then we lock the gate and bid our

farewells until the next weekend. After it's

Move
to end

all over ~~you really~~ ^we^ feel ^physically^ ~~a sense of~~

refreshn^ed^ess, and cleanl~~iness~~ and peaceful~~ness~~.

Rewrite

Using the
~~The~~ sweat lodge is a custom of most~~ly all~~

Indian tribes. Certain Indian tribes go about

from
it differently ~~than~~ others‸but once they're

all inside everyone feels of one whole being.

All three of the steps I've gone through are

Each week we
helpful for a successful sweat ceremony. ~~Many~~

~~of us members~~ look forward to these

ceremonies ~~every week~~. They help us cope

better with the prison system.

Exercise 1 Revising and Editing a First Draft

Treat the following passage by Tara Newsome as your own rough draft and revise and edit it. First consider coherence, language, unity, emphasis, support, and sentences (CLUESS). Then edit, correcting fundamentals such as capitalization, omissions, punctuation, and spelling (COPS).

Quitting School

Quitting school was not a big deal for me until I

realize all the effects of quitting would bring to my

life. At that time I didn't care. I plan to marry a few

months later after my high school graduation. I was happy

at the time.

Quitting school was a big mistake because when I went

out to look for a job I couldn't qualify for any of the

good positions because of my lack of education. Instead

I took a job as in a fast-foods place where I had no future. Then I went to work in a big company just doing simple office work. When it came time for promotions I couldn't pass the tests they gave. That was not all. As a result of quitting school later. I couldn't even help my children with their homework or buy the special things for them.

I started my family when I was not even eighteen years. The first year of my marriage was fine, then things started to fall apart. My husband had quit school too, and he didn't make much money, and as I mentioned, I didn't make much either. We argued a lot mainly over money. We couldn't get a big enough house for our family so that we could have the privacy we needed. I quit work to raise my kids and that when I really got in deep. My car was getting old and money was not enough to make big payments I had to buy another old car, which broke down all the time. I started freaking out. The fighting got worse and we had a divorce.

I was lucky that my parents decided to help me, and now I am dedicated to getting a good education. I will work hard to learn so me and my children can have a better life.

Writer's Guidelines at a Glance: Writing, Revising, and Editing

1. **Writing**
   Write your first draft, paying close attention to your outline or list or cluster. Do not concern yourself with perfect spelling, grammar, or punctuation.

2. Revising (CLUESS)

Coherence

- Are the ideas clearly related, each one to the others and to the central idea?
- Is there a clear pattern of organization (time, space, or emphasis)?
- Is the pattern supported by words that suggest the basis of that organization (time: *now, then, later*; space: *above, below, up, down*; emphasis: *first, second, last*)?
- Is coherence enhanced by the use of transitional terms, pronouns, repetition, and a consistent point of view?

Language

- Is the general style of language usage appropriate (properly standard and formal or informal) for the purpose of the piece and the intended audience?
- Is the tone (language use showing attitude toward material and audience) appropriate?
- Is the word choice (diction) effective? Do the words convey precise meaning? Are they fresh and original?

Unity

- Are the thesis and every topic sentence clear and well stated? Do they indicate both subject and focus?
- Are all points of support clearly related to and subordinate to the topic sentence of each paragraph and to the thesis of the essay?

Emphasis

- Are ideas properly placed (especially near the beginning and end) for emphasis?
- Are important words and phrases repeated for emphasis?

Support

- Is there adequate material—such as examples, details, quotations, and explanations—to support each topic sentence and the thesis?
- Are the points of support placed in the best possible order?

Sentences

- Are the sentences varied in length and beginnings?
- Are the sentences varied in pattern (simple, compound, complex, and compound-complex)?
- Are all problems with sentence structure (fragments, comma splices, run-ons) corrected?

3. **Editing**

- Are all problems in such areas as capitalization, omissions, punctuation, and spelling (COPS) corrected?

4

Reading for Thinking, Discussion, and Writing

～ Reading-Based Writing

The Writing Component

Reading-based writing was invented to help you fill those daunting blank pages with thoughtful statements centered on what you have read, broadly called the text. *Text* is a term that includes items as diverse as photos, advertisements, online postings, and movies as sources for *text-based writing*, but in this book, we are concerned specifically with writing about reading, hence our use of the term *reading-based writing*.

For instruction in this book, reading-based writing comes in three forms: summary, reaction, and two-part response. In writing a summary, you use your own words to restate the main ideas in what you have read. In writing a reaction, you comment critically on what you have read, while giving credit for the ideas and words you borrow. In composing a two-part response, you write both a summary and a reaction, but you separate them to show your instructors that you know the difference between the two forms.

The Reading Component

Reading-based writing can also make you a better reader. When you are reading for a writing assignment, you concentrate more because you are thinking about how you will be using the content. When you are writing, your mind reflects back on what you have read, running ideas critically by your windows of experiences and knowledge. Reading-based writing represents the complete *you* as a thinking, feeling person in relation to what you have read.

56

⌒ Reading-Based Writing and Other Approaches in Writing

Reading-based writing will serve you well in classrooms across your campus and also in your career. Of course, *At a Glance: Essays* contains a range of writing approaches that may or may not make use of reading-based writing, including those called *personal experience, individual perspective, cross-curricular,* and *career-related.* All of those approaches are offered with instruction, examples, exercises, and suggested topics and prompts. Some approaches overlap, but each has a main thrust with variations imposed by particular writing objectives.

Reading-based writing is presented in this early chapter because most of the writing instruction in this book involves reading in some way. The abundant student and professional readings were selected to stimulate thought and discussion, to provide content for writing, and to inform writing by strong examples of techniques and forms. Even reading-based writing has its own different forms, and reading itself has its own special techniques. Those techniques and forms are shown here in a concise outline of the instruction that covers the remainder of this chapter:

I. Reading techniques
   A. Underlining
   B. Annotating
   C. Outlining
   D. Taking notes

II. Reading-based writing forms
   A. Summary
   B. Reaction
   C. Two-part response

⌒ Reading Techniques

Underlining

Imagine you are reading a chapter of several pages and you decide to underline and write in the margins. Immediately, the underlining takes you out of the passive, television-watching frame of mind. You are engaged. You are participating. It is now necessary for you to discriminate, to distinguish more important from less important ideas.

Perhaps you have thought of underlining as a method designed only to help you with reviewing. That is, when you study the material the next time, you will not have to reread all of it; instead, you can review only the most important—those that are underlined—parts. However, even while you are underlining, you are benefiting from an imposed concentration, because this procedure forces you to think, to focus. Consider the following guidelines for underlining:

1. Underline the main ideas in paragraphs. The most important statement, the topic sentence, is likely to be at the beginning of the paragraph.
2. Underline the support for those main ideas.
3. Underline answers to questions that you bring to the reading assignment. These questions may have come from the end of the chapter, from subheadings that you turn into questions, from your independent concerns about the topic, or from questions posed by your instructor.
4. Underline only the key words. You would seldom underline all the words in a sentence and almost never a whole paragraph.

Do these guidelines fit your approach to underlining? Possibly not. Most students, in their enthusiasm to do a good job, overdo underlining.

The trick is to figure out what to underline. You would seldom underline more than about 30 percent of a passage, although the amount would depend on your purpose and the nature of the material. Following these guidelines will be useful. Learning more about the principles of sentence, paragraph, and essay organization in the preceding chapters will also be helpful.

Annotating

Annotating, writing notes in the margins, is a practice related to underlining. You can do it independently, although it usually appears in conjunction with underlining to record your understanding and to extend your involvement in reading.

Writing in the margins represents intense involvement because it turns a reader into a writer. If you read material and write something in the margin as a reaction to it, then in a way you have had a conversation with the author. The author has made a statement and you have responded. In fact, you may have added something to the text; therefore, for your purposes, you have become a coauthor or collaborator. The comments you make in the margin are of your own choosing according to your interests and the purpose you bring to the reading assignment. Your response in the margin may merely echo the author's ideas, it may question them critically, it may relate them to something else, or it may add to them.

The comments and marks on the following essay will help you understand the connection between writing and reading. Both techniques—underlining to indicate main and supporting ideas and annotating to indicate their importance and relevance to the task at hand—will enhance thinking, reading, and writing.

Total Institutions

Seymour Feshbach and Bernard Weiner

Total institution encompasses individual (thesis)

1   A total institution completely encompasses the individual, forming a barrier to the types of social intercourse that occur outside such a setting. Monasteries, jails, homes for the aged, boarding schools, and military academies are a few examples of total institutions.

1. Individual activities in same setting

2   Total institutions have certain common characteristics. First, the individuals in such environments must sleep, play, and work within the same setting. These are generally segmented spheres of activity in the lives of most individuals, but within a total institution one sphere of activity overlaps with others.

2. All life within group

Second, each phase of life takes place in the company of a large group of others. Frequently, sleeping is done in a barracks, food is served in a cafeteria, and so on. In such activities everyone is treated alike and must perform certain essential tasks.

3. Activities tightly scheduled

Third, activities in an institution are tightly scheduled according to a master plan, with set times to rise, to eat, to exercise, and to sleep. These institutional characteristics result in a bureaucratic society, which requires the hiring of other people for surveillance. What often results is a split in the groups within an institution into a large, managed group (inmates)

Managed groups and staff at distance

and a small supervisory staff. There tends to be great social distance between the groups, who perceive each other according to stereotypes and have severely restricted communications.

Two worlds—inside and outside 3   The world of the inmate differs greatly from the outside world. When one enters a total institution, all previous roles, such as father or husband, are disrupted. The individual is further depersonalized by the issuance of a uniform, confiscation of belongings, and gathering of personal information, as well as by more subtle touches like doorless toilets, record keeping, and bedchecks. The effects

Personality altered   of an institutional setting are so all-encompassing that one can meaningfully speak of an "institutional personality": a persistent manner of behaving compliantly and without emotional involvement.

4   Of course, there are individual differences in adaptation to the situation. They can be as extreme as psychosis, childlike regression, and depression or as mild as resigned compliance. Most

Becomes psychotic, childlike, or depressive   individuals do adjust and build up a system of satisfactions, such as close friendships and cliques.

5   But because of these bonds and the fact that the habits needed to function in the outside world have been lost, inmates face great problems upon leaving an institution. A shift from

Individuals adjust but have trouble later on street   the top of a small society to the bottom of a larger one may be further demoralizing.

Outlining

After reading, underlining, and annotating the piece, the next step could be outlining. If the piece is well-organized, you should be able to reduce it to a simple outline so that you can, at a glance, see the relationship of ideas (sequence, relative importance, and interdependence).

The essay on total institutions can be outlined very easily:

Total Institutions

I. Common characteristics
   A. All activities in the same setting
   B. All phases of life within a larger group
   C. Activities scheduled according to a master plan
      1. Bureaucratic society
      2. Social distance between inmates and staff

II. Adjusting to the world inside
    A. Individual depersonalized
        1. Wears uniform
        2. No personal belongings
        3. No privacy
    B. Adaptation
        1. Negative
            a. Psychosis
            b. Regression
            c. Depression
        2. Positive
III. Problems upon release outside
    A. Adjusting to a different system
    B. Encountering shock of going to the bottom of a new order

Exercise 1 Underlining, Annotating, and Outlining

Underline and annotate this passage. Then complete the outline that follows.

Effective E-Mail Practices

Use short lines and short paragraphs. A short line length (perhaps 50 to 60 characters) is much easier to read than the 80-character line of most text editors. Similarly, short paragraphs (especially the first and last paragraph) are more inviting to read. Avoid formatting a long message as one solid paragraph.

Don't shout. Use all-capital letters only for emphasis or to substitute for italicized text (such as book titles). Do NOT type your entire message in all capitals: It is a text-based form of *shouting* at your reader and is considered rude (not to mention being more difficult to read).

Proofread your message before sending it. Do not let the speed and convenience of e-mail lull you into being careless. Although an occasional typo or other surface error will probably be overlooked by the reader, excessive errors or sloppy language creates an unprofessional image of the sender.

Use a direct style of writing and think twice; write once. Put your major idea in the first sentence or two. If the message is so sensitive or emotionally laden that a more indirect organization would be appropriate, you should reconsider whether e-mail is the most effective medium for the message. Because it is so easy to respond immediately to a message, you might be tempted to let your emotions take over. Such behavior is called "flaming" and should be avoided. Always assume the message you send will never be destroyed but will be saved permanently in somebody's computer file.

—Adapted from Scot Ober, *Contemporary Business Communication*

I. Short lines; short paragraphs
   A. _____
   B. _____

II. No shouting
   A. No entire message in capital letters
   B. Causes problems
      1. _____
      2. _____

III. Proofread message before sending

   A. Resist temptation to send without checking

   B. Errors create unprofessional image

IV. Direct style with deliberation

   A. _____

   B. _____

Taking Notes

Taking notes for reading-based writing in this book consists of underlining and annotating passages in reading selections and jotting down the relevant points for support in your outline as you organize your summary, reaction, or two-part response. While writing, you will use those notes for support as you refer directly to what you have read and use some quotations from it. You will also give credit to the source(s) you are reading, and—if your instructor requires you to do so—you will use documentation, including page numbers and identification of your source(s) for those ideas and words you borrow.

If you were doing a longer writing based on numerous sources outside this book, you would consult page 229 in Chapter 13, "The Research Paper," which presents a well-organized system for using cards that group and coordinate borrowed ideas in relation to a basic outline of the ground you expect to cover. Of course, as you carefully and critically read sources in this book, you will naturally underline significant passages (often only a few words at a time) and annotate your reactions to what you read. Those annotations will vary according to your audience, their interests and background, and the nature of your topic. The sooner you settle on a topic and its natural divisions, the better, because only then will you be able to take those relevant notes.

If you already have at least a general topic before you read, you can easily formulate some basic questions to help you focus. Most reading-based writing prompts at the ends of Chapters 5 through 12 divide topics into parts that can serve as divisions for your outline. Reading some of the prompts before you read the selections will also be useful in helping you concentrate.

Here is an example of a reading-based writing prompt for the essay "Low Wages, High Skills" by Katherine S. Newman. "Transferable skills" is the operative phrase in organizing the response.

Low Wages, High Skills [title of Newman's essay]

Write a two-part response to the essay. Concentrate your critical thinking on Newman's idea that those who work at Burger Barn have transferable skills. Relate those specific skills to what you have experienced in a low-pay service job. Use direct references to and quotations from the essay. Agree or disagree with Newman.

Putting together a simple outline in advance and allowing some writing space between lines will provide you with room to pencil in references and quotes, with page numbers. Then when you write your outline or reaction, you can just incorporate your notes without having to refer back to the reading(s).

Here is an example of how you can place notes inside outlines. It is an excerpt from student Alex Mylonas's reading-based reaction to the short story "The Use of Force" by William Carlos Williams. During his first reading, Mylonas underlined and annotated freely; later he selected phrases as support in his outline, which he submitted with his assignment. His reaction appeared in a previous edition of this book.

I. The surface conflict
   A. Doctor-patient relationship
   B. Physical struggle
      1. Girl won't cooperate
      2. Doctor uses force to examine her throat

II. The inner conflict
   A. Doctor versus himself
      1. Wants to be professional
      2. Loses self-control
         "attractive little thing," p. 333
         "damned little brat," p. 333
      3. Loses sight of objective
         "got beyond reason," p. 334
   B. Emotional (brutal) side wins
      "It was a pleasure to attack her," p. 335
      "blind fury," p. 335

⁓ Reading-Based Writing Forms

Summary

The **summary**, the purest form of reading-based writing, is a rewritten, shortened version of a source in which you use your own wording to express the main ideas. Learning to summarize effectively will help you in many ways. Summary writing reinforces comprehension skills in reading, because it requires you to discriminate among the ideas in the target reading passage. Summaries are usually written in the form of a well-designed paragraph or set of paragraphs. Frequently, they are used in collecting material for research papers and in writing conclusions to essays.

The following rules will guide you in writing effective summaries.

1. Cite the author and title of the text.
2. Reduce the length of the original by about two-thirds, although the exact reduction will vary, depending on the content of the original.
3. Concentrate on the main ideas and include details only infrequently.
4. Change the original wording without changing the idea.
5. Do not evaluate the content or give an opinion in any way (even if you see an error in logic or fact).
6. Do not add ideas (even if you have an abundance of related information).
7. Do not include any personal comments (that is, do not use *I*, referring to self).
8. Use quotations only infrequently. (If you do use quotations, however, enclose them in quotation marks.)
9. Use some author tags ("says York," "according to York," or "the author explains") to remind the reader(s) that you are summarizing the material of another writer.

Exercise 2 Evaluating a Summary

Apply the rules of summary writing to the following summary of "Total Institutions," page 59. Mark the instances of poor summary writing by using rule numbers from the preceding list.

Total Institutions

A total institution completely encompasses the individual.

Total institutions have certain common characteristics.

Institutions provide the setting for all rest, recreation, and labor.

Residents function only within the group. And residents are directed by a highly organized schedule, which, I think, is what they need or they wouldn't be there. There residents are depersonalized by being required to wear a uniform, abandon personal items, and give up privacy. Some adapt in a negative way by developing psychological problems, but most adapt in a positive way by forming relationships with other residents. Several popular movies, such as *The Shawshank Redemption*, show how prison society works. Once outside the total institution, individuals must deal with the problem of relearning old coping habits. They must also withstand the shock of going from the top of a small society to the bottom of a larger one. Society needs these total institutions, especially the jails.

The following is an example of an effective summary.

A Summary of "Total Institutions"
Michael Balleau

In "Total Institutions," Seymour Feshbach and Bernard Weiner explain that a total institution encompasses the lives of its residents, who share three common traits: The residents must do everything in the same place, must do things together, and must do things according to the institution's

schedule. The institution takes away the
residents' roles they had in society, takes
away their appearance by issuing uniforms,
takes away their personal property by
confiscation, and takes away their privacy by
making life communal. The authors say that
some residents adapt negatively by developing
psychological problems, but most form
relationships and new roles within the
institution. Upon release, these residents
must learn to function in the free world all
over again, as they start at the bottom of
society. This shift "may be further
demoralizing."

Reaction

The reaction statement is another kind of reading-based writing,
one in which you incorporate your views. Some reactions require
evaluation with a critical-thinking emphasis. Some focus on simple
discussion of the content presented in the reading and include summary material. Others concentrate on the writer's experience as related directly to the content of the passage.

The following paragraph is student Tanya Morris's reaction
statement to "Total Institutions." She could have expanded her
ideas to write an essay. Her instructor did not require her to provide
page-number locations of her references and quotations.

Institutions Always Win
Tanya Morris

The short essay "Total Institutions," by
Seymour Feshbach and Bernard Weiner, is a
study of conflicts in controlled
environments. The common characteristics of
such places are in personal combat with the
individual, in which the resident is stripped
of his or her choices and made to "sleep,

play, and work within the same setting." The resident who tries to assert his or her uniqueness is controlled by a master plan. That plan is enforced by personnel who become the masters of surveillance, set up social barriers, and maintain control over their underlings. The result is "a bureaucratic society." Cut off from the free world, the resident is in conflict with significant matters of newness—clothes, facilities, regulations, and roles. The authors explain that almost always the institution wins, sometimes converting the resident into a disturbed person or an amiable robot among other inmates. But at some point after that conversion, the institutionalized person may be returned to the free world. There a new conflict arises for the inmate, who goes from "the top of a small society to the bottom of a larger one." The authors of this essay are very clear in showing just how comprehensive these institutions are in waging their war, regardless of the motives, against individuality. After all, they are "total." As such, they should be, whenever possible, avoided.

Two-Part Response

As you have seen, the reaction response includes a partial summary or is written with the assumption that readers have read the original piece. However, your instructor may prefer that you separate the forms—for example, by presenting a clear, concise summary followed by a reaction. This format is especially useful for critical examination of a text or for problem-solving assignments because it requires you to understand and repeat another's views or experiences before responding. The most comprehensive reading-based writing form, the two-part response also helps you avoid the common problem of writing only a summary of the text when your instructor wants you to both summarize and react.

Total Institutions: A Summary and a Reaction

Michael Balleau

Part I: Summary

In "Total Institutions," Seymour Feshbach and Bernard Weiner explain that a total institution encompasses the lives of its residents, who share three common traits: The residents must do everything in the same place, must do things together, and must do things according to the institution's schedule. The institution takes away the residents' roles they had in society, takes away their appearance by issuing uniforms, takes away their personal property by confiscation, and takes away their privacy by making life communal. The authors say that some residents adapt negatively by developing psychological problems, but most form relationships and new roles within the institution. Upon release, these residents must learn to function in the free world all over again as they start at the bottom of society. This shift "may be further demoralizing."

Part 2: Reaction [Page-number documentation was not required.]

The basic ideas in "Total Institutions" gave me an insight into the behavior of my older cousin. Let's call him George. He spent almost five years in prison for a white-collar crime he committed at the bank where he worked. Before George was incarcerated, he was an individual, almost to the extreme of being a rebel. When he got out, he was clearly an institutionalized person. Following the pattern of institutionalized behavior laid out in "Total Institutions," George had become a group person without knowing it. Many of "the habits needed to function in the outside world [had] been lost." Even at home after he returned, he had to be around people. He wanted some of us to be with him all the time, and he liked the noise of a radio or television. When we went out, he found it difficult to make decisions, even in buying a simple item, such as a shirt, or ordering food in a restaurant. Once when he was driving, we were stopped by a police officer because his car's taillight was out, and George became transformed into someone who was on automatic pilot in answering questions. It was his "institutional personality." Minutes later, he seemed hostile and had bad, unwarranted things to say about the officer. Altogether, George did five years in prison, and it took him about three more to adjust before he seemed like sort of what he was before. He was certainly never the same. As the authors say, every person reacts differently to "total institutions," and some institutions are more extreme than others, but each one has a profound effect on the resident's individuality.

∼ Kinds of Support for Reading-Based Writing

In your reading-based writing assignments, you are likely to use three methods in developing your ideas: explanations, direct references to the reading selection, and quotations from the reading selection.

- Your explanations will often be expressed in patterns, such as causes and effects, comparison and contrast, definition, and exemplification. These forms are presented with others in depth in Chapters 5 through 12.
- Your references will point your reader(s) directly toward original ideas in sources. The more specific the references, the more helpful they will be to your readers.
- Your quotations will be words borrowed from sources and credited to those sources. You will use quotation marks around those words, which will appear as sentences or as partial sentences blended with your own words.

These concepts are important in all reading-related writing, but they are especially important in the reading-based writing you will be doing in Chapters 5 through 12 of this textbook.

∼ Basic Formal Documentation in Reading-Based Writing

Borrowing words or ideas without giving credit to the originator is called **plagiarism** and is not acceptable scholarship, regardless of whether it is unintentional. As you use sources from your textbook, your instructor will ask you to document the ideas of others formally or informally. Informally, you will credit a source by title or author's name. Formally, you will indicate the precise location of all the original ideas you have borrowed according to a system. (See "Plagiarism" in Chapter 13, pages 230–231, for more details.)

Citations

Documenting sources for papers based on written material is systematic. Most English instructors use MLA (Modern Language Association) style with the 2009 Update, the system used in this chapter and explained further in Chapter 13, "The Research Paper." Mainly, you need to remember that when using material from a source, you must give enough information so that the reader will recognize it or be able to find it in its original context. Here are the most common principles of documentation that can be used for textbook or other restricted sources, whether it is quoted, paraphrased (restated), or summarized.

If you use the author's name in introducing a quotation, then usually give only the page number.

> EXAMPLE: Suzanne Britt says that "neat people are bums and clods at heart" (255).

If you use the author's name in introducing a borrowed idea, then usually give only the page number.

> EXAMPLE: Suzanne Britt believes that neat people are weak in character (255).

If you do not use the author's name to introduce a quotation or an idea, then usually give both the author's name and the page number:

> EXAMPLE: Music often helps Alzheimer's patients think more clearly (Weiss 112).

Works Cited

Works Cited lists the sources used, meaning those that appear in citations, as shown in the previous section. Each kind of publication has its own order of parts and punctuation. You need not memorize them. They are given in detail in Chapter 13, on pages 220–228, and some can be found on the Internet by Googling "MLA Form with the 2009 Update."

Here is an example of a Works Cited entry. Other examples can be found at the end of the next student work and on page 224 of Chapter 13, under "A Work in an Anthology or Textbook with Readings." Note the punctuation between parts and the order of those parts: author's name (last, first), title of composition (quotation marks for a short work, italics for a long work), name of the anthology, editor(s) of the anthology, edition, place of publication, publisher, date of publication, pages on which the selection appears, and medium of publication.

Work Cited

Blaylock, Richard. "More Than the Classroom."
*Paragraphs and Essays with Integrated
Readings.* Ed. Lee Brandon and Kelly
Brandon. 10th ed. Boston: Houghton, 2008.
228. Print.

◠ An Example of Student Reading-Based Writing

Your reading-based paragraph or essay may include ideas from newspapers, magazines, online sources, or books. To make classwork simpler for you here, most of the reading-based assignments relate to selections included in this book. When you are writing about something you have read, just write as you usually would, but bring in ideas and quotations from that source. You may also want to refer to more than one source.

Student (partial) Essay with Documentation

This excerpt from Lydia Hsiao's essay illustrates how to incorporate ideas and document them. More extensive instruction is presented in Chapter 13.

Struggling Against Silence

Lydia Hsiao

Maxine Hong Kingston and I both come
from a strict Chinese background and were
taught that "a ready tongue is an evil"
(Kingston 252). We were also taught to keep
to ourselves. We were never taught to
communicate with those outside our culture.
This background may have caused my self-
consciousness and my paralyzing fear of being
embarrassed. During my first year in the
United States, I attended middle school in

Riverside, California. I was constantly teased about my Chinese accent, even though initially I felt certain I did not have one, for I had attended an American school in Taiwan. Perhaps my fellow students reacted as they did because I was the only Chinese girl in school. Nevertheless, as a result of this treatment, I became silent whenever possible, and if I mispronounced a word during class, I could not help but be disgusted by my own mistake, causing me even greater embarrassment. Kingston says, "[They] scared the voice away" (254). The result was that, like Kingston, my potential was for years undiscovered.

In the same way Kingston allowed silence to "[paint] layers of black over [her life]" (254), silence continued to create a thicker darkness in *my* life. It first embarrassed me; then it soon robbed me of my self-esteem. As Kingston says, "[Talking] takes up that day's courage" (252). It was almost as if silence was more than a curtain. It seemed to grow its own body and walk beside me. That silence became my sinister friend, taking advantage of my willingness to accept this cruel school life, tricking me into believing that home was the only place I could find my voice. The monster silence kept me quiet.

Work Cited

Kingston, Maxine Hong. "Silence." *The Woman Warrior*. In *Rereading America*. Ed. Gary Colombo, Robert Cullen, and Bonnie Lisle. New York: Bedford/St. Martin's, 1998. 252-55. Print.

Writer's Guidelines at a Glance: Reading for Thinking, Discussion, and Writing

1. **Underlining** helps you to read with discrimination.

   - Underline the main ideas in paragraphs.
   - Underline the support for those ideas.
   - Underline answers to questions that you bring to the reading assignment.
   - Underline only the key words.

2. **Annotating** enables you to actively engage the reading material.

   - Number parts if appropriate.
   - Make comments according to your interests and needs.

3. **Outlining** the passages you read sheds light on the relationship of ideas, including the major divisions of the passage and their relative importance.

4. **Taking notes** for reading-based writing in this book consists of underlining and annotating passages in reading selections and jotting down the relevant points for support, with page numbers, in your outline as you organize your summary, reaction, or two-part response.

5. **Summarizing** helps you concentrate on main ideas. A summary

   - cites the author and title of the text.
   - is usually shorter than the original by about two-thirds, although the exact reduction will vary depending on the content of the original.
   - concentrates on the main ideas and includes details only infrequently.
   - changes the original wording without changing the idea.
   - does not evaluate the content or give an opinion in any way (even if the original contains an error in logic or fact).
   - does not add ideas (even if the writer of the summary has an abundance of related information).
   - does not include any personal comments by the writer of the summary (therefore, no use of *I*, referring to self).
   - seldom contains quotations (although, if it does, only with quotation marks).

- includes some author tags ("says York," "according to York," or "the author explains") to remind the reader(s) that it is a summary of the material of another writer.

6. Two other types of reading-based writing are

- the reaction, which shows how the reading relates to you, your experiences, and your attitudes; also, it is often a critique of the worth and logic of the piece.
- the two-part response, which includes a summary and a reaction that are separate.

7. Most ideas in reading-based papers are developed in one or more of these three ways:

- explanation
- direct references
- quotations

8. **Documenting** is giving credit to borrowed ideas and words.

- Informal documentation gives credit to sources as directed by your instructor.
- Formal documentation gives credit to sources according to published guidelines, such as those provided by the MLA (Modern Language Association) with the 2009 Update.

9. Consider using CLUESS for revising and COPS for editing.

5

Descriptive Narration: Moving Through Time and Space

∿ A Natural Combination of Narration and Description

As patterns of writing, description and narration go together like peanut butter and jelly. You would almost never describe something without relating it to something else, especially to a story or a narrative. And you would seldom narrate something (tell a story) without including some description. A narrative moves through time; a description moves mainly through space.

∿ The Narrative Pattern

In our everyday lives, we tell stories and invite other people to do so by asking questions such as "What happened at work today?" and "What did you do last weekend?" We are disappointed when the answer is "Nothing much." We may be equally disappointed when a person doesn't give us enough details or gives us too many and spoils the effect. After all, we are interested in people's stories and in the people who tell them. We like narratives.

What is a narrative? A **narrative** is an account of an incident or a series of incidents that make up a complete and significant action. A narrative can be as short as a joke, as long as a novel, or anything in between, including the essay. Each narrative has five properties: Situation, Conflict, Struggle, Outcome, and Meaning.

Situation

Situation is the background for the action. The situation may be described only briefly, or it may even be implied. ("To celebrate my seventeenth birthday, I went to the Department of Motor Vehicles to take my practical test for my driver's license.")

Conflict

Conflict is friction, such as a problem in the surroundings, with another person(s), or within the individual. The conflict, which is at the heart of each story, produces struggle. ("It was raining and my appointment was the last one of the day. The examiner was a serious, weary-looking man who reminded me of a bad boss I once had, and I was nervous.")

Struggle

Struggle, which need not be physical, is the manner of dealing with the conflict. The struggle adds action or engagement and generates the plot. ("After grinding on the ignition because the engine was already on, I had trouble finding the windshield wiper control. Next I forgot to signal until after I had pulled away from the curb. As we crept slowly down the rain-glazed street, the examiner told me to take the emergency brake off. All the while I listened to his pen scratching on his clipboard. 'Pull over and park,' he said solemnly.")

Outcome

Outcome is the result of the struggle. ("After I parked the car, the examiner told me to relax, and then he talked to me about school. When we continued, somehow I didn't make any errors, and I got my license.")

Meaning

Meaning is the significance of the story, which may be deeply philosophical or simple, stated or implied. ("Calmness promotes calmness.")

These components are present in some way in all the many forms of the narrative. They are enhanced by the use of various devices such as the following:

- **Description** (the use of specific details to advance action, with images to make readers see, smell, taste, hear, and feel)

  the *rain-glazed street*

  listened to his *pen scratching*

- **Dialogue** (the exact words of the speakers, enclosed in quotation marks)

  "Pull over and park," he said solemnly.

- **Transitional words** (words, such as *after*, *finally*, *following*, *later*, *next*, *soon*, and *when*, that move a story forward, for narratives are usually presented in chronological order)

  Next I forgot to
  After I parked the car

Most narratives written as college assignments have an expository purpose (that is, they explain a specified idea). Often the narrative will be merely an extended example. Therefore, the meaning of the narrative is exceedingly important and should be clear, whether it is stated or implied.

⌒ The Descriptive Pattern

Description is the use of words to represent the appearance or nature of something. Often called a **word picture**, description attempts to present its subject for the mind's eye. In doing so, it does not merely become an indifferent camera; instead, it selects details that will depict something well. Just what details the descriptive writer selects will depend on several factors, especially the type of description and the dominant impression in the passage.

Types of Description

On the basis of treatment of subject material, description is customarily divided into two types: objective and subjective.

Effective **objective description** presents the subject clearly and directly as it exists outside the realm of feelings. If you are explaining the function of the heart, the characteristics of a computer chip, or the renovation of a manufacturing facility, your description would probably feature specific, impersonal details. Most technical and scientific writing is objective in that sense. It is likely to be practical and utilitarian, making little use of speculation and poetic technique while focusing on details of sight.

Effective **subjective description** is also concerned with clarity and it may be direct, but it conveys a feeling about the subject and sets a mood while making a point. Because most expression involves personal views, even when it explains by analysis, subjective description (often called **emotional description**) has a broader range of uses than objective description.

Descriptive passages can have a combination of objective and subjective description; only the larger context of the passage will reveal the main intent.

Imagery

To convey your main concern effectively to readers, you will have to give some sensory impressions. These sensory impressions, collectively called **imagery**, refer to that which can be experienced by the senses—what we can see, smell, taste, hear, and touch.

Subjective description is more likely to use more images and words rich in associations than is objective description. But just as a fine line cannot always be drawn between the objective and the subjective, a fine line cannot always be drawn between word choice in one and in the other. However, we can say with certainty that whatever the type of description, careful word choice will always be important.

General and Specific Words

To move from the general to the specific is to move from the whole class or body to the individual(s); for example:

General	Specific	More Specific
food	pastry	Twinkie
mess	grease	oil slicks on table
drink	soda	mug of root beer
odor	smell from grill	smell of frying onions

Abstract and Concrete Words

Words are classified as abstract or concrete depending on what they refer to. **Abstract words** refer to qualities or ideas: *good, ordinary, ultimate, truth, beauty, maturity, love*. **Concrete words** refer to substances or things; they have reality: *onions, grease, buns, tables, food*. The specific concrete words, sometimes called **concrete particulars**, often support generalizations effectively and convince the reader of the accuracy of the account.

Dominant Impression

Never try to give all of the details in description; instead, be selective, picking only those that you need to make a dominant impression, always taking into account the knowledge and attitudes of your readers. Remember, description is not photographic. If you wish to describe a person, select only the traits that will project your intended dominant impression. If you wish to describe a landscape, do not give all the details that you might find in a picture; just pick the details that support what you want to say. That extremely important dominant impression is directly linked to your purpose and is created by the choosing and arranging of images, figurative language, and revealing details.

Useful Procedure for Writing Description

Description is seldom static. The framework usually includes some narrative pattern, as shown here.

What is your subject? (school campus during summer vacation)
What is the dominant impression? (deserted, reminding you of different times)
What is the situation? (Note the natural entry of the narrative: You are walking across campus in early August.)
What details support the dominant impression? (silence, dust on water fountain, bare bulletin boards)
What is the movement (order) as you present details? (movement through time and space)

∿ Order for Descriptive Narration: Time and Space

All the details of the descriptive narration must have some order, some sequence. Although the two patterns blend, time is the primary factor for telling a story, and space is the primary factor for describing an object or a scene. The following words will help you order time and space.

Transitional Words for Improving Coherence

- **FOR DESCRIPTION: Space:** *above, over, under, below, nearby, near, across, beyond, among, to the right, to the left, in the background, in the foreground, further, beside, opposite, within sight, out of sight*

- **FOR NARRATION: Time:** *after, before, later, earlier, initially, soon, recently, next, today, tomorrow, yesterday, now, then, until, currently, when, finally, not long after, immediately, (at) first, (at) last, third, previously, in the meantime, meanwhile*

~ Career-Related Writing: Workplace Reports

At the workplace, numerous reports fit the pattern of narrative writing: trip reports, status reports (from investigation or development of something such as a program or product), or incident reports (one of the most universal from industry to industry).

In most instances the incident report denotes problems. Something unforeseen has occurred and it must be documented: an accident, a theft, a disturbance, a dangerous condition, a lost child, an act of vandalism, an equipment failure, or a health emergency other than one caused by an accident. A report on one of these incidents is likely to be written as an important record. It may be the essential information on which law enforcement acts, equipment is replaced, clients are served, safety is assured, security is established, or the physical plant is protected.

These reports are sometimes dictated, but they are more often written by the person most directly related to an incident. Your ability to write an effective report will aid your company and reflect well on you as an intelligent, educated employee. Although the procedure and the form of these incident reports will vary, there are some principles that can be applied to all; these principles follow the basic narrative form.

> **Situation:** Identify the kind of problem.
> **Conflict:** Indicate when and where it occurred.
> **Struggle and outcome:** Provide an account of what happened.
> **Meaning:** If appropriate, write a recommendation for what could be done to avoid a repetition of such an incident if it is appropriate to do so.

Follow these guidelines in writing an incident report:

- Write in the first person (*I*), for you are the one who is writing the report.
- Start with the date, time, and your reason for involvement.
- If you use the words of anyone reporting on the incident, enclose them in quotation marks and acknowledge the source of those words.
- Use facts, not opinions.
- Do not step outside your work expertise and become a psychologist, philosopher, physician, or moralist. If you do, should this report make its way to a court case, what you say will be discredited.

- Use past tense; you are writing about something that has already happened.
- Use mostly active voice. For example, write, "Mills made the report," not "The report was made by Mills."
- Identify those involved. Drop the titles, such as Mr., Mrs., Dr., and so on. After the first reference to the person in the report, use only the surname or the first initial and the surname.

See pages 93–95 for an example of an incident report.

◠ Practicing Patterns of Descriptive Narration

Exercise 1 Completing Patterns

Fill in the blanks in the following outline to complete the descriptive narration.

Topic: last-minute shopping for a present

I. _____ (a certain department in a mall store)

    A. Other shoppers

        1. _____ (appearance)

        2. _____ (behavior)

    B. Condition and arrangement of merchandise (describe with appropriate details of imagery: sight, sound, taste, smell, and touch)

        1. _____

        2. _____

        3. _____

II. Can't find a particular item

    A. Search and search

    B. Start getting frustrated

    C. Meet an old friend (perhaps the person you are shopping for)

        1. _____ (description of friend)

        2. _____ (more description, perhaps adding person in action)

III. _____ (whatever the friend does to help)

    A. _____

    B. _____

IV. _____ (what you purchase or what you decide to do)

⌢ Examining Essays of Descriptive Narration

Student Writing

Not Invulnerable

Charles C. Ortiz

College student and cadet police officer Charles C. Ortiz entered law enforcement with unwarranted confidence and a feeling of invulnerability. Then one calm summer night, only an hour into a routine patrol, eight gunshots put him more in touch with reality.

1   I had always considered myself invulnerable when I was riding in a police unit. I was a knight, a Rambo, a centurion. I was sure that there was nothing I couldn't handle. I had been with the sheriff's department for almost three years, and I was certain that I was ready for anything. Who would have guessed that that mentality would almost cost me my life?

2   On January 16, I was assigned to work 55 Frank, which was a South El Monte crime unit. Because it was my first time working this car, I felt nervous, but at the same time I was also excited. Strangely, although this wasn't my first time on patrol, I still felt somewhat apprehensive. I was sure this night was different, yet I didn't know why.

3   Our shift started out pretty slowly. All we did for the first three hours was write

out traffic citations. Once the traffic began
to slacken, we proceeded with our routine
patrol checks of the homes and businesses in
our area. On a check of Santa Anita Avenue, a
man began to flag us down. As we approached
him, I noticed he was staggering and yelling
at the top of his lungs. He insisted that we
take him to jail. Once I had explained his
options, he agreed to be taken to our station
to begin his sobering-up process. I cuffed
him and put him in the back of the unit. This
was routine stuff.

4   But as we headed toward the station, a
distress call blared over the radio:
"Attention, all units in the vicinity of
South El Monte. 55 Adam is requesting backup.
He has five at gunpoint. All units
responding, go Code 3!" Because we were a
minute away, we responded. As we took off, my
adrenaline started to rise, causing me to
feel anxious. Upon arriving at the scene, I
grabbed the shotgun, got out of the car, and
pointed the shotgun toward the vehicle in
question. The first suspect was called out.
As he emerged in front of us, he reached into
his waistband, pulled out a gun, and pointed
it in my direction. In a moment, he fired two
shots at me. I hit the ground. At the same
time a fear of dying took over my body. I
didn't know if I was hit, if I was dying, or
what. I was in a state of shock.

5   After I discovered that the shots had
missed me and the situation was under
control, I rose somewhat slowly. I looked
toward the suspect and saw him lying dead in

a pool of blood. He had been shot six times by the deputies at the scene. The other four suspects were arrested for grand theft auto. Even though the incident was secured, I was able to see what "real" fear was. I understood that policing is not a game; it is life-and-death reality. Walking in a cop's shoes is not something that everyone can handle.

6   Facing my most horrible fear has truly shown me how important my life is. It's not something to be taken for granted. I also now know personally what deputies face when they encounter someone who is armed and possibly dangerous. I have found a new sense of respect for all police officers, for I have now experienced law enforcement from their view. Furthermore, I feel a lot older and a lot wiser now. Going into the streets thinking "I'm invulnerable" is the wrong kind of attitude.

Exercise 2 Discussion and Critical Thinking

1. What conflicting ideas does the author present in the first two paragraphs that attract reader interest and create suspense?

2. Dramatically, what is the effect of the minor conflict in paragraph 3?

3. How does Ortiz's attitude about police work change?

4. To which other parts of the essay does the last line relate?

5. Underline the thesis and use annotation to mark the situation, conflict, struggle, outcome, and meaning in this essay.

Professional Writing

No Tears for Frankie

Gina Greenlee

Freelance writer Gina Greenlee recalls a bully from her childhood, his death, and his funeral, which she attended. This article was first published in the "Lives" section of the New York Times Magazine.

1   I was in the fifth grade when Frankie died. It was 1971. My whole class planned to attend the funeral, since we knew him. My father thought going might give me nightmares, but I insisted. I had never seen a dead person before. Most of all, I wanted to be sure that the little creep would never touch me again.

2   Frankie lived in Lower Manhattan where run-down tenements along Avenues A, B and C were on the verge of becoming the crack houses of the '80s. At the time, I lived nearby. Then in 1970 my family moved into an apartment in Coop Village on Grand Street and F.D.R. Drive. It was only three blocks—and a world—away from the projects to a predominantly white middle-class community on the East River. Overnight at school, I became "that black girl who lives in the rich Jew buildings." Or at least that's what Frankie and my other African-American classmates thought I was. It became a familiar chant of theirs as I made my way through my old neighborhood to get to school.

3   Frankie and I were in the same grade, but I was 10 and he was 12 because he had been left back twice. He tormented all of the girls in our class. But Frankie relished singling me out—the only black girl in a sea of Jewish girls dotted with Latinas—and he had done so since I first arrived from another school in third grade.

4   He never did any schoolwork. Instead, for the first three periods Frankie's curriculum was mayhem; by fourth period he was usually in the principal's office; and by the fifth, he was back in class unremorseful and pumped to do it again. He only got worse in that working-class, urban-blight panacea, the after-school program. It was a nice idea: children whose parents were unavailable at 3 o'clock because they were working stayed after school to study, improve skills and tackle extra-credit projects. I spent those afternoons trying to stay alive.

5   Frankie and his crew would grab my breasts, genitals and buttocks when the teachers weren't looking. Their hands, quick as filthy street rats, darted across my private parts in assembly

line, during dance rehearsals and yard processions. They would leave scrawled notes in my book bag that read, "I'm gonna beat you up after school," or "I'll get you in the stairwell."

6   One spring afternoon, I had made it through another harrowing two hours after school, only to be cornered on the stairs by the whole nasty lot. They taunted me to walk down ahead of them. I managed each step as if it were my first, balancing myself on the chalk-blue shellacked handrail as I peered through the landing divider reminiscent of a wire cage, hoping to see another student, teacher, anyone. Frankie shoved me, and I tumbled one full flight, landing on my knees, my favorite brown plaid dress above my ears, easy-pickings for the tiny vultures who cackled obscenities while snatching at my body, punching and kicking me. That day, I understood the depth of Frankie's perversity.

7   When I told a friend that our classroom emptied out at 3 p.m., leaving me alone with Frankie's boys, without having to share another detail, she said, "Come to my house after school." I had enjoyed two afternoons of baking cookies and doll playing when I let slip that my parents thought I was in class. My friend's mother welcomed me to play at her home anytime as long as my parents knew. "Why were you at Amy's and not in the after-school program?" my father asked me later that night. I didn't tell him because I didn't think he could help me. His interventions would only inspire retaliations and spiral me deeper into the mess.

8   I did try to tell my teachers, but nobody believed me. They chuckled and said, "Frankie just has a crush on you." That's what I told my father 15 years after the attacks, when he asked me if I had told my teachers. I guess in their world, 12-year-old boys don't sexually attack 10-year-old girls. What world did they come from, anyway? What world was I in, and how could I fix it so Frankie would disappear?

9   One morning when my teachers had stepped away from the classroom, Frankie and his boys shoved me into the coat closet and held the door shut while I was alone with Frankie. It was dark. As he kept touching me, I tried to push him away and screamed to be let out. But Frankie's friends held steadfast until the teachers arrived; then they scrambled to their seats. None of the other kids said a word. But in front of them all, I told Frankie that I hated his guts and hoped he would die.

10   Quite accommodating, he lay in a casket later that year. I didn't
shed a tear. My heart was hardened, though. As usual, Frankie was
up to no good—tampering with public property with the boys—
when he got himself electrocuted. I was 10, and I was glad.

Exercise 3 Discussion and Critical Thinking

1. Write a phrase to indicate each part of this narrative:

   Situation
   Conflict
   Struggle
   Outcome
   Meaning

2. Why didn't Gina Greenlee shed a tear?

3. Is this an essay that only a person who has been bullied dread-
fully can understand, or can it be appreciated by anyone? Explain.

4. What would you say to people who would have forgiven Frankie
in his casket?

The Jacket

Gary Soto

> *Gary Soto was born in Fresno, California, in 1952 to working-
> class Mexican American parents. In his youth he worked in the
> neighborhood and in nearby fields. Later he would discover his
> talent for writing, attend Fresno City College and California State
> University at Fresno, and become a prominent author of poetry,
> short stories, essays, and novels. His books include* Living Up the
> Street, Nickel and Dime, Taking Sides, *and* Baseball in April and
> Other Stories.

1   My clothes have failed me. I remember the green coat that I
wore in fifth and sixth grades when you either danced like a
champ or pressed yourself against a greasy wall, bitter as a
penny toward the happy couples.

2   When I needed a new jacket and my mother asked what
kind I wanted, I described something like bikers wear: black
leather and silver studs with enough belts to hold down a small
town. We were in the kitchen, steam on the windows from her

cooking. She listened so long while stirring dinner that I thought she understood for sure the kind I wanted. The next day when I got home from school, I discovered draped on my bedpost a jacket the color of day-old guacamole. I threw my books on the bed and approached the jacket slowly, as if it were a stranger whose hand I had to shake. I touched the vinyl sleeve, the collar, and peeked at the mustard-colored lining.

3   From the kitchen Mother yelled that my jacket was in the closet. I closed the door to her voice and pulled at the rack of clothes in the closet, hoping the jacket on the bedpost wasn't for me but my mean brother. No luck. I gave up. From my bed, I stared at the jacket. I wanted to cry because it was so ugly and so big that I knew I'd have to wear it a long time. I was a small kid, thin as a young tree, and it would be years before I'd have a new one. I stared at the jacket, like an enemy, thinking bad things before I took off my old jacket whose sleeves climbed halfway to my elbow.

4   I put the big jacket on. I zipped it up and down several times, and rolled the cuffs up so they didn't cover my hands. I put my hands in the pockets and flapped the jacket like a bird's wings. I stood in front of the mirror, full face, then profile, and then looked over my shoulder as if someone had called me. I sat on the bed, stood against the bed, and combed my hair to see what I would look like doing something natural. I looked ugly. I threw it on my brother's bed and looked at it for a long time before I slipped it on and went out to the backyard, smiling a "thank you" to my mom as I passed her in the kitchen. With my hands in my pockets I kicked a ball against the fence, and then climbed it to sit looking into the alley. I hurled orange peels at the mouth of an open garbage can and when the peels were gone I watched the white puffs of my breath thin to nothing.

5   I jumped down, hands in my pockets, and in the backyard on my knees I teased my dog, Brownie, by swooping my arms while making bird calls. He jumped at me and missed. He jumped again and again, until a tooth sunk deep, ripping an L-shaped tear on my left sleeve. I pushed Brownie away to study the tear as I would a cut on my arm. There was no blood, only a few loose pieces of fuzz. Damn dog, I thought, and pushed him away hard when he tried to bite again. I got up from my knees and went to my bedroom to sit with my jacket on my lap, with the lights out.

6   That was the first afternoon with my new jacket. The next day I wore it to sixth grade and got a D on a math quiz. During

the morning recess Frankie T., the playground terrorist, pushed me to the ground and told me to stay there until recess was over. My best friend, Steve Negrete, ate an apple while looking at me, and the girls turned away to whisper on the monkey bars. The teachers were no help: They looked my way and talked about how foolish I looked in my new jacket. I saw their heads bob with laughter, their hands half-covering their mouths.

7   Even though it was cold, I took off the jacket during lunch and played kickball in a thin shirt, my arms feeling like braille from goose bumps. But when I returned to class I slipped the jacket on and shivered until I was warm. I sat on my hands, heating them up, while my teeth chattered like a cup of crooked dice. Finally warm, I slid out of the jacket but a few minutes later put it back on when the fire bell rang. We paraded out into the yard where we, the sixth graders, walked past all the other grades to stand against the back fence. Everybody saw me. Although they didn't say out loud, "Man, that's ugly," I heard the buzz-buzz of gossip and even laughter that I knew was meant for me.

8   And so I went, in my guacamole jacket. So embarrassed, so hurt, I couldn't even do my homework. I received Cs on quizzes, and forgot the state capitals and the rivers of South America, our friendly neighbor. Even the girls who had been friendly blew away like loose flowers to follow the boys in neat jackets.

9   I wore that thing for three years until the sleeves grew short and my forearms stuck out like the necks of turtles. All during that time no love came to me—no little dark girl in a Sunday dress she wore on Monday. At lunchtime I stayed with the ugly boys who leaned against the chainlink fence and looked around with propellers of grass spinning in our mouths. We saw girls walk by alone, saw couples, hand in hand, their heads like bookends pressing air together. We saw them and spun our propellers so fast our faces were blurs.

10   I blame that jacket for those bad years. I blame my mother for her bad taste and her cheap ways. It was a sad time for the heart. With a friend I spent my sixth-grade year in a tree in the alley waiting for something good to happen to me in that jacket, which had become the ugly brother who tagged along wherever I went. And it was about that time that I began to grow. My chest puffed up with muscle and, strangely, a few more ribs. Even my hands, those fleshy hammers, showed bravely through the cuffs, the fingers already hardening for the coming fights.

But that L-shaped rip on the left sleeve got bigger; bits of stuffing coughed out from its wound after a hard day of play. I finally Scotch-taped it closed, but in rain or cold weather the tape peeled off like a scab and more stuffing fell out until that sleeve shriveled into a palsied arm. That winter the elbows began to crack and whole chunks of green began to fall off. I showed the cracks to my mother, who always seemed to be at the stove with steamed-up glasses, and she said that there were children in Mexico who would love that jacket. I told her that this was America and yelled that Debbie, my sister, didn't have a jacket like mine. I ran outside, ready to cry, and climbed the tree by the alley to think bad thoughts and watch my breath puff white and disappear.

11   But whole pieces still casually flew off my jacket when I played hard, read quietly, or took vicious spelling tests at school. When it became so spotted that my brother began to call me "camouflage," I flung it over the fence into the alley. Later, however, I swiped the jacket off the ground and went inside to drape it across my lap and mope.

12   I was called to dinner: Steam silvered my mother's glasses as she said grace; my brother and sister with their heads bowed made ugly faces at their glasses of powdered milk. I gagged too, but eagerly ate big rips of buttered tortilla that held scooped up beans. Finished, I went outside with my jacket across my arm. It was a cold sky. The faces of clouds were piled up, hurting. I climbed the fence, jumping down with a grunt. I started up the alley and soon slipped into my jacket, that green ugly brother who breathed over my shoulder that day and ever since.

Exercise 4   Discussion and Critical Thinking

1. Why is the jacket more of a disappointment than it would have been if Soto's mother had given it to him as a surprise?

2. What kind of jacket did Soto request?

3. How is the jacket like a person and an evil force?

4. What are some of the failures Soto attributes to his jacket?

5. Why doesn't he lose it or throw it away?

Student Career-Related Writing

Incident Report of the Falling Shoppers

Douglas Ross

Student Douglas Ross welcomed the opportunity to write a narrative about an event that occurred at work, especially one that was written up as a report or could have been. One event that stood out in Ross's mind was an accident that occurred in his presence when he worked for a regional market chain. The report had been favorably reviewed by a district manager, and Ross was promoted soon after that time to a full-time senior checker. In his writing that follows, he re-creates what he recorded on that day, using a form similar to the store template for incident reports.

Employee Report
Form 117-Incident
☒ Accident ☐ Reported theft ☐ Disturbance ☐ Dangerous condition

☐ Lost child ☐ Vandalism ☐ Health emergency ☐ Other

Business and Location: [Name and address of business omitted by student request]
Time: July 27, 2009, at 09:33 a.m.
Employee Name: Douglas Ross

Situation
Conflict
Struggle

Incident Report: At 09:33 a.m. I was working the cash register at Station 3 when I saw an elderly couple approach my empty customer slot from the nearby newspaper, book, and magazine rack. The woman was walking ahead of the man, who carried a small bag of fruit in one hand and a loaf of fresh bakery bread in the other. A younger woman with a shopping cart full of items had also spotted the open slot and headed that way. The wife started walking faster, turned to her husband, said

something I couldn't hear, and motioned for
him to follow her. He increased his pace
and followed. Then he staggered and lost
his balance and lunged forward, hitting his
wife, who had turned away from him. Thrown
off balance, she also lunged forward and
struck a display of pastries, knocking it
down as she fell to her knees. By this
time, her husband had fallen, striking his
head on the tile floor.

I came to their aid quickly, helping
the woman to her feet. The man rolled over
and sat there. I said I would call
paramedics. The woman asked the man if he
were hurt. He said he would be all right.
I got on the phone and called Supervisor
Kennedy, who was out at the loading dock.
He said I should call paramedics anyway,
because the man was still sitting on the
floor.

While we were waiting for the
paramedics, the man took an oblong loop
of stiff plastic binding material from
his foot and showed it to me. He
explained that it had apparently been
left by the magazine rack where it had
been used to tie a bundle of newspapers.
He said he had stepped on one side of it
and, when he did, the other side of it
popped up like a small hula hoop and
caught his other foot as he was about to
take another step. Then he fell and hit
his wife, who also fell.

Outcome   The paramedics came and examined the
husband and wife, Carl and Ruth Sutton

[names changed]. The paramedics asked them about abrasions and pains. They said they needed no further medical care or examination. The paramedics completed a report on the particulars, now attached to this one. Mr. and Mrs. Sutton said they would go to their family doctor.

Supervisor Kennedy took down additional information and gave them his business card. Mrs. Sutton asked me if I had witnessed what happened. I said I saw them fall. She looked at my badge and wrote my name and employee number down in her address book. I gave the loop of plastic binding to Supervisor Kennedy.

Meaning

Recommendation: When stocking the shelves with any items that are bound, the binding should be carefully disposed of. As a further precaution, it would be a good idea to clip the loops of plastic bindings so that no one could trip over them even if they were left on the floor.

～ Topics for Essays of Descriptive Narration

Reading-Based Writing Topics

For reading-based writing, include references to and quotations from the reading selection(s), and give credit to your sources. See Chapter 4 for additional discussion on reading-based writing.

"Not Invulnerable"

1. Using this essay as a model, write a descriptive narration about a time when you or someone you know did something that was dangerous but, through ignorance or preoccupation, approached the event with little or no fear. Consider a rescue or an incident at school, at work, or during recreation. Explain how Ortiz's fear and what he said about fear specifically relate to your experience. Use quotations and references.

"No Tears for Frankie"

2. Write a reaction paragraph or essay that includes an integrated summary of the text and comments on the author's behavior and feelings. Use quotations and references. Under the circumstances, would you have expected Greenlee to consider any degree of forgiveness for her deceased tormentor? What if there had been grieving family members in the audience? Although Frankie seemed to be the worst kind of bully, is there anything that might be learned about him—call on your knowledge of bullies—that might make him seem less malicious?

"The Jacket"

3. Frequently reprinted, this essay is enormously popular with student readers. Discuss the likely reasons for its popularity. Refer directly to the essay and use quotations in your discussion.

4. Write about an embarrassing article of clothing you wore as a child, an article that you thought at the time had an influence on how others felt about you and certainly how you felt about yourself. Be specific in connecting your experience with Soto's.

5. Write about an article of clothing you wore with pride as a child or one that you now wear with pride. Be specific in connecting your experience with Soto's.

6. Use your imagination to write about the jacket from the mother's point of view. You might also imagine that she is providing her viewpoint just after reading this essay by her son; therefore, she can refer to what Gary Soto said.

7. Write about the jacket from the jacket's point of view. Refer to particular incidents in the essay. Use references to the essay and quotes from it.

Cross-Curricular Topic

8. Use description in one of the following assignments.

- Agriculture: Field-trip report
- Art History: Report on a museum or a particular work of art
- Education: School-visit report
- Ecology: Field-trip report
- Geology: Field-trip report
- Sociology: Report on a field trip to an urban zone, a prison, or another institution

Career-Related Topics

9. Use the guidelines for writing incident reports on pages 82–83 for one of the following topics. For a helpful model with a standard form on a similar topic, review "Incident Report of the Falling Shoppers" on pages 93–95.

- Write a descriptive narrative account of an encounter between a customer and a salesperson. Explain what went right and what went wrong.
- Write a descriptive narrative of an employee handling a customer's troublesome complaint. Evaluate the procedure.
- Using a workplace form you are familiar with, write an incident report about an event such as an accident, a theft, or a disturbance.

10. Write a descriptive narrative account of a work-related encounter between a manager and a worker and briefly explain the significance of the event.
11. Describe a well-furnished, well-functioning office or other work area. Be specific.
12. Describe a computer-related product; give special attention to the dominant trait that gives the product its reputation.
13. Describe a person groomed and attired for a particular job or interview. Be specific in giving details pertaining to the person and in naming the place or situation. Describe yourself from a detached point of view if you like.

General Topics

Write a descriptive narration about one of the following subjects. Limit the time frame so that you can include descriptive detail.

14. A ceremony such as a graduation, funeral, or wedding
15. A time when you made a proposal of marriage (or received one) or applied for a position you wanted
16. A time when you confronted authority or had to deliver bad news
17. Your first date, first day in a new school, first public performance, or first time in love
18. The time you met (saw) a most impressive doctor, teacher, speaker, singer, irritating person, salesperson, or police officer
19. The occasion when you witnessed an accident or a natural disaster such as a tornado or flood

Writer's Guidelines at a Glance: Descriptive Narration

Narration

1. Include the following points to be sure you have a complete narration:

   Situation
   Conflict
   Struggle
   Outcome
   Meaning

2. Consider using dialogue.
3. Give details concerning action.

Description

1. In an objective description, use direct, practical language and appeal mainly to the sense of sight.
2. In an emotional description, appeal to the reader's feelings, especially through images of sight, sound, smell, taste, and touch.
3. Use specific and concrete words if appropriate.
4. Relate your details to the dominant impression of your description.

Descriptive Narration

1. All of your details must have an order or a sequence. Although the two patterns blend, time is the primary factor for telling a story, whereas space is the primary factor for description.

   - Words indicating time include *first, second, then, soon, finally, while, after, next, later, now,* and *before.*
   - Words indicating space include *next to, below, under, above, behind, in front of, beyond, in the foreground, in the background, to the left,* and *to the right.*

2. Both description and narration in college writing usually have an expository purpose; that is, they explain a specified or implied idea.

3. Consider using CLUESS for revision and COPS for editing.

6

Exemplification:
Writing with Examples

～ Writing Essays of Exemplification

Exemplification means using examples to explain, convince, or amuse. Lending interest and information to writing, exemplification is one of the most common and effective ways of developing ideas. Examples may be developed in as much as a paragraph or more, or they may be phrases or only single words, as in the following sentence: "Children like packaged breakfast foods, such as *Wheaties*, *Cheerios*, and *Rice Krispies*."

Characteristics of Good Examples

As supporting information, the best examples are vivid, specific, and representative. These three qualities are closely linked; collectively, they must support the topic sentence of a paragraph and the thesis of an essay. The **vivid** example attracts attention. Through a memorable presentation and the use of identifying names, the example becomes **specific** to the reader. A good example must also be **representative**; that is, it must be experienced as typical so that it can be the basis for a generalization.

Finally, and most important, the connection between the example and the thesis must be clear. A bizarre case of cheating may be fascinating in itself (vivid and specific), but in an essay on "the hard work of cheating," that example must also support (represent) the thesis. The reader should say, in effect, "That's interesting, convincing, and memorable. Though it's unusual, I can see that it's typical of what goes on."

Techniques for Finding Examples

Writing a good essay of exemplification begins, as always, with prewriting. The techniques you use will depend on what you are writing about. Assuming that you begin with a topic idea, one useful

100

technique is listing. Base your list on what you have read, heard, and experienced. Here is a list on the topic "the hard work of cheating":

> The two times when I cheated: copied homework, brought in a list for a biology test, felt guilty
> A person who bought a research paper
> Jess, who copied from me
> The Internet "Cheaters" source
> The two persons who exchanged identities
> More work than it's worth
> More stress than it's worth

Transitional Words for Improving Coherence

- **FOR EXEMPLIFICATION:** *for example, as an example, another example, for instance, such as, including, specifically, especially, in particular, to illustrate, as an illustration, that is, i.e. (meaning that is), e.g. (meaning for example)*

～ Practicing Patterns of Exemplification

Exercise 1 Completing Patterns

Fill in the blanks in the following outlines to add more examples that support the thesis.

1. Thesis: Some people let television watching interfere with their social lives.

   I. Watching football games at a family gathering on holidays

   II. Watching television in a _____

   III. _____

2. Thesis: Most successful movies are more concerned with action than character, and the action is violent.

   I. (Name of movie) _____

   II. (Name of movie) _____

   III. (Name of movie) _____

Examining Essays of Exemplification

Student Reading-Based Writing

Hungering for Sounds of Silence
Eileen Baylor

The assignment for student Eileen Baylor was to select an article from a list and write a brief essay of reaction to it. She was to convey the important ideas of her subject piece with direct references and quotations, but she was not to feature a summary of it. She was required to photocopy the article; underline and annotate it; and submit it along with a brief outline, a rough draft, and a typed final draft of her brief essay of reaction.

1   "Cell Phone Backlash" by Margaret Loftus is full of good examples. They are good because they support her main point and remind me of similar examples. Like many people, Loftus is sick and tired of loud secondhand cell-phone talking.

2   The worst part is that the offensive, loud talking is getting worse. She says, "Nearly 75 percent of those surveyed in our poll think mobile phone etiquette has declined over the past five years" (26). One may be inclined to distrust an "our poll," but Loftus backs hers up by referring to a *National Geographic Traveler*/Yahoo! poll concluding that 75 percent of travelers are "sometimes or frequently annoyed" (26). For airline travelers, that percentage may go up because the Federal Communications

Commission may allow companies to remove
its ban on cell-phone use during flights.

3   Some of those who are already annoyed
are very annoyed. Loftus gives several
colorful examples. One is about a
loudmouth traveler calling numerous friends
to brag about where he was staying, where
he was dining, and which limousine service
he had booked. For revenge, an annoyed
fellow traveler slipped outside and used
his own cell phone to cancel all the
reservations.

Examples   In another example, a man on a commuter
train finally had had enough of a long
secondhand conversation about a fellow
passenger's divorce, including custody
of the dog. Finally he walked across the
aisle, grabbed the phone, and smashed
it on the floor of the train. In still
another example, a person confessed he
carries an illegal "jammer that kills cell
phone conversations within a 20-foot
radius" (26).

Topic   4   Stories like that may be satisfying to
sentence
Transition   those of us who are irritated by the
noise, but those solutions are not good
ideas for the general public. Canceling
the reservations may be just punishment,

but it is the kind of punishment that can lead to retaliation. Smashing the cell phone invites a violent response. And not only is jamming the phone illegal, as mentioned, but it might prevent a call coming through about a medical emergency.

Topic sentence 5   <u>Those reservations do not mean I am pure of thought</u>. I have concocted my own unwholesome schemes during loud cell-phone conversations at restaurants, in shopping lines, and even one in a church at a **Extended example** funeral. Last week in a restaurant a nearby loudmouth had a cell-phone conversation with his wife about her purchasing a tablecloth. He told her the one she was considering was too expensive and that she should shop for a cheaper one on the Web. He even told his wife he was dining alone, though a sweet young thing sat smiling across from him. I will admit I thought up a plot of how I could blow his cover, but instead I just left without ordering dessert.

Topic sentence 6   <u>In another incident</u> I witnessed in a **Transition** <u>middle-scale restaurant, a man came in alone and sat in a booth across from me</u>. **Extended example** Almost immediately I heard static, electric ratchet wrench sounds, and

booming voices. He had brought a walkie-
talkie with him and was monitoring calls
from his nearby place of work in a large
tire store. He was a huge man, mean-looking
and sweaty. He could carry a tire in either
hand—above his head. I stared at him. He
glared back. I thought of suggesting he use
his cell phone. Politely.

7   <u>Right then</u> I concluded that Loftus was
right in her article about cell-phone
etiquette. Things are bad and getting
worse, but maybe she does not know what
<u>worse</u> is. Maybe cell phones are just a
threshold weapon in rudeness. I ordered
a dessert to go.

Work Cited

Loftus, Margaret. "Cell Phone Backlash."
     National Geographic Traveler July/
Aug. 2005: 26. Print.

Professional Writing
Who's Cheap?
Adair Lara

Adair Lara is an award-winning newspaper columnist for the San
Francisco Chronicle *and the author of five books and dozens of
magazine articles. Her best-selling memoir about raising a
teenage daughter,* Hold Me Close, Let Me Go, *was published by
Random House (2001). Her specialty is writing about her experiences in first-person point of view.*

1   It was our second date, and we had driven one hundred miles up the coast in my car to go abalone-diving. When I stopped to fill the tank at the only gas station in sight, Craig scowled and said, "You shouldn't get gas here. It's a rip-off."

2   But he didn't offer to help pay. And that night, after dinner in a restaurant, he leaned over and whispered intimately, "You get the next one." Though he was sensitive and smart, and looked unnervingly good, Craig was as cheap as a two-dollar watch.

3   This is not an ethical dilemma, you're all shouting. *Lose the guy*, and fast.

4   Lose the guy? Is this fair? My friend Jill is always heading for the john when the check comes, but I don't hear anybody telling me to lose *her*. And she's far from the only cheap woman I know. A lot of us make decent money these days, yet I haven't seen women knocking over tables in fights for the lunch tab. In fact, many women with 20/20 vision seem to have trouble distinguishing the check from the salt, pepper and other tabletop items. But if a guy forgets to chip in for gas or gloats too long over the deal he got on his Nikes, he's had it.

5   Why is this double standard so enduring? One reason is that, while neither sex has a monopoly on imperfection, there *are* such things as flaws that are much more distasteful in one sex than in the other. Women seem especially unpleasant when they get drunk, swear or even insist on pursuing an argument they'll never win. And men seem beneath contempt when they're cheap.

6   These judgments are a holdover from the days when women stayed home and men earned the money. Though that old order has passed, we still associate men with paying for things. And besides, there's just something appealing about generosity. Buying something for someone is, in a sense, taking care of her. The gesture says, "I like you, I want to give you something." If it comes from a man to whom we are about to entrust our hearts, this is a comforting message. We miss it when it's not forthcoming.

7   Then why *not* dump on cheap men?

8   Some men are just skinflints and that's it. My friend Skye broke up with her boyfriend because when they went to the movies he doled out M&M's to her one at a time. Craig, my date back at the gas station, liked to talk about how he'd bought

his car—which in California, where I live, is like buying shoes—as a special present to himself.

9   This kind of cheapness is ingrained; you'll never change it. That guy who parks two miles away to avoid the parking lot fee was once a little boy who saved his birthday money without being told to. Now he's a man who studies the menu and sputters, "Ten dollars for *pasta*?" His stinginess will always grate on you, since he is likely to dole out his feelings as parsimoniously as his dollars.

10   On the other hand, I know a wonderful man, crippled with debts from a former marriage, who had to break up with a woman because she never paid her share, and he was simply running out of money. Though she earned a lot more than he did, she couldn't expand her definition of masculinity to include "sometimes needs to go Dutch treat."

11   To men, such women seem grasping. One friend of mine, who spends a lot of money on concerts and theater and sailing but not on restaurants he considers overpriced, has evolved a strategy for women who are annoyed at the bohemian places he favors. If his date complains, he offers to donate to the charity of her choice the cost of an evening at her favorite spot. "Some women have bad values," he says, "And if the idea of spending money on a good cause, but not on her, makes her livid, I know she's one of them."

12   I had a bracing encounter with my own values when I told my friend Danny the humorous (I thought) story of a recent date who asked if I wanted a drink after a concert, then led me to the nearest water fountain.

13   Danny gave one of his wry looks. "Let's get this straight," he said, laughing. "As a woman, you are so genetically precious that you deserve attention just because you grace the planet. So, of course, he should buy you drinks. He should also drive the car, open the door, ask you to dance, coax you to bed. And then when you feel properly pampered, you can let out that little whine about how he doesn't treat you as an equal."

14   On second thought, I guess I'd rather buy my own drink.

15   So here's the deal. Before dumping a guy for ordering the sundowner dinner or the house white, better first make sure that you aren't burdening the relationship with outdated ideas of how the sexes should behave. Speaking for myself, I know that if a man looks up from the check and says, "Your share is eleven dollars," part of me remembers that, according

to my mother, *my* share was to look charming in my flow-
ered blouse.

16   Wanting the man to pay dies hard. What many of us do now
is *offer* to split the check, then let our purses continue to dangle
from the chair as we give him time to realize that the only
proper response is to whip out his own wallet.

17   Is this a game worth playing? It's up to you, but consider
that offering to help pay implies that the check is his responsibility. And this attitude can work both ways. My sister gets
angry when her husband offers to help clean the house. "Like
it's *my* house!" she snorts.

18   Like it's *his* check.

Exercise 2   Discussion and Critical Thinking

1. Lara uses examples to explain how she came to a conclusion
   on who—male, female, or both—should pay on dates. What
   does she think about the occasion of her second date with
   Craig when he does not pay for the gas or the meal?

2. What examples does she use to show that some men are just
   "skinflints"?

3. In your estimation, who is worse on the 1–10 cheapness scale,
   the one-at-a-time M&M guy or the water-fountain guy?

4. In paragraph 9, Lara says that some men have ingrained
   cheapness and that men who are stingy with money are likely
   to be stingy with feelings. She offers no other support. Do you
   agree with her generalization? Why or why not?

5. The author seems impressed by the man (in paragraph 11) who
   says he takes dates to inexpensive restaurants and if they
   complain, he offers to give the money he saved to a worthy
   cause of his date's choice. If she does not accept, he assumes
   she is just interested in having the fine meal for herself. Do
   you think that is likely a good way to discover his date's value
   system (as he believes), or is it likely that he has just devised
   a good way to avoid paying more?

6. What paragraph carries Lara's conclusion on her main question?

⌁ Topics for Essays of Exemplification

Reading-Based Writing Topics

For reading-based writing, include references to and quotations from the reading selection(s), and give credit to your sources. See Chapter 4 for additional discussion on reading-based writing.

"Hungering for Sounds of Silence"

1. Write an essay of reaction in which you disagree or agree with the main view expressed in this essay. Use some of your own examples from personal experience. If you think Baylor's view is an overreaction, explain why it is. Does age or generation have anything to do with how an individual is likely to react to secondhand cell-phone conversations? Be specific in your references, and include quotations.

"Who's Cheap?"

2. Write a reading-based essay of reaction in which you address some of the questions in Exercise 2. Agree or disagree with Adair Lara, as you examine her use of numerous examples leading to her conclusion that from now on she will pay her part of the check. Keep in mind that at the end of her essay, she knows what she'll say after the meal. She'll say, "I'll pay half," not "Let me pay half." Discuss the difference and whether it matters from your male or female perspective. Consider using some examples from your own experience.

3. In a broader sense, do you believe that one person is obliged to pay for the expenses of the date? If so, who should pay? Should the person who asked for the date pay? What if the female of a heterosexual couple asked for the date? Try to incorporate some ideas from Lara's essay into your own.

Cross-Curricular Topic

4. Use examples as supporting information in discussing a person, an event, or an issue pertaining to another class you have taken or are taking. Your explanation might focus on why someone or something was successful or unsuccessful. You might write a report about a field trip, with examples that support a dominant impression of, say, a museum exhibit. For a case study in an education or a psychology class, you could use examples from your observations in a school or another institution.

Career-Related Topics

Use specific examples to support one of the following statements as applied to business, work, or career preparation.

5. If I had been the boss at the place where I worked, I would have handled certain situations differently.
6. "Burning bridges" should be done in warfare, not in work situations.
7. In some places where I worked [or went to school], sexual harassment occurred on an almost daily basis.
8. Sometimes one does a lot of tongue-biting and pride-swallowing when dealing with irate customers.
9. The women managers I know have really had to prove their competency.

General Topics

Develop an essay mainly by using examples to support one of these thesis statements.

10. We are surrounded by people with bad manners.
11. Most of what I really like is bad for me or someone else.
12. One can tell much about people by the way they eat [or dress, talk, react to crises, and relate to their family and friends].
13. I would be happier if I could divorce some of my relatives.

Writer's Guidelines at a Glance: Exemplification

1. Use examples to explain, convince, or amuse.
2. Use examples that are vivid, specific, and representative.

   - Vivid examples attract attention.
   - Specific examples are identifiable.
   - Representative examples are typical and therefore the basis for generalization.

3. Tie your examples clearly to your thesis.
4. Draw your examples from what you have read, heard, and experienced.
5. Brainstorm a list of possible examples before you write.
6. Consider using CLUESS for revision and COPS for editing.

7

Analysis by Division: Examining the Parts

～ Writing Essays of Analysis by Division

If you need to explain how something works or exists as a unit, you will write an analysis by division. You will break down a unit (your subject) into its parts and explain how each part functions in relation to the operation or existence of the whole. The most important word here is *unit*. You begin with something that can stand alone or can be regarded separately: a poem, a heart, a painting, a car, a bike, a person, a school, a committee.

The following procedure will guide you in writing an analysis by division: Move from subject to principle, to division, to relationship.

Step 1: Begin with something that is a unit (subject).
Step 2: State one principle by which the unit can function.
Step 3: Divide the unit into parts according to that principle.
Step 4: Discuss each of the parts in relation to the unit.

You might apply that procedure to writing about a good boss in the following way:

1. Unit	Manager
2. Principle of function	Effective as a leader
3. Parts based on the principle	Fair, intelligent, stable, competent in the field
4. Relationship of parts to the unit	Consider each part in relation to the person's effectiveness as a manager.

Organization

In an essay of analysis by division, the main parts are likely to be the main points of your outline or main extensions of your cluster.

If they are anything else, reconsider your organization. A basic outline of an analysis by division might look like this:

> *Thesis:* To be effective as a leader, a manager needs specific qualities.
>
>   I. Fairness
> II. Intelligence
> III. Stability
> IV. Competence in the field

Sequence of Parts

The order in which you discuss the parts will vary according to the nature of the unit and the way in which you view it. Here are some possible sequences for organizing the parts of a unit:

- **Time:** The sequence of the parts in your paragraph or essay can be mainly chronological, or time-based (if you are dealing with something that functions on its own, such as a heart, with the parts presented in relation to stages of the function).
- **Space:** If your unit is a visual object, especially if, like a pencil, it does nothing by itself, you may discuss the parts in relation to space. In the example of the pencil, the parts of the pencil begin at the top with the eraser and end at the bottom with the pencil point.
- **Emphasis:** Because the most emphatic location of any piece of writing is the end (the second most emphatic point is the beginning), consider placing the most significant part of the unit at the end.

Transitional Words for Improving Coherence

- **FOR ANALYSIS BY DIVISION: Time or numbering:** *first, second, third, another, last, finally, soon, later, currently, before, along with, another part (section, component)*

- **Space:** *above, below, to the left, to the right, near, beyond, under, next to, in the background, split, divide*

- **Emphasis:** *most important, equally important, central to the, to this end, as a result, taken collectively, with this purpose in mind, working with the, in fact, of course, above all, most of all, especially, primarily, without question*

From the wide range of uses of analysis by division mentioned in the introduction, two are featured in this chapter: the restaurant review and the career review.

Restaurant Review

Definition

The **restaurant review** is an article that describes three elements: ambiance, service, and food.

- **Ambiance** is the atmosphere, mood, or feeling of a place. For restaurants, it may begin with landscaping and architecture (building style). Ambiance is certainly produced by what is inside, such as the furnishings, seating, style, upkeep, sounds, sights, smells, behavior of other customers, and management style—whatever produces that mood or the feeling, even if it is franchise plastic and elevator music.
- **Service** is mainly concerned with food delivery and those who do it: their attitude, manners, helpfulness, promptness, accuracy, and availability. Self-service or pickup establishments would be judged by similar standards.
- **Food** is the emphasis—its variety, quality, quantity, price, and presentation.

Writing the Review

- Use first person (*I*) as you relate your experience in a particular restaurant or chain.
- If possible, base your evaluation on more than one item. Here is a low-cost way to do that: Dine with others and ask your companions to order different foods. Then ask them if you can taste (two small bites will suffice) what they are served, thus increasing your experience. Offering to pay a portion of their check may make others more receptive to sharing their food.
- While you are dining, use a simple outline or listing to make sure you have information on ambiance, service, and food. Copy names of foods and prices from the menu. Use quotation marks around any descriptive phrases for items you copy.
- You need not separate comments on ambiance, service, and food or present them in a particular order, but be specific in your details and examples. Use quotation marks for any descriptive phrases you borrow from the menu.

An example of a professional restaurant review, "Johnny's Wiener Wagon on a Roll," begins on page 119.

Career Review

The career review is a summary of a career, which you will personalize by relating it to your background, interests, aptitude, and other relevant vocational matters.

The organization and development of your career review follow the basic procedure for writing an analysis by division as you move from unit to division to development. It is logical, systematic, and highly manageable.

- The unit for an essay is the career field and your quest of that career field.
- The parts of that unit are the parts of the career field and your quest. Those parts can be further subdivided.
- The extent of the dividing may vary, depending on your particular purpose (assignment), the expected audience, and, if applicable, your current involvement in the career field.
- Your college library has an abundance of material that will provide you with career information you can summarize in your review. Your best overall source is probably the *Occupational Outlook Handbook* by the U.S. Department of Labor. It is available in print and online, and is ideal for you to summarize selectively for your career review. Updated and published every two years, the handbook covers hundreds of career fields, providing information about earnings, prerequisites of training and education, expected job prospects, job duties, and working conditions. Of course, you should give credit to your source(s) in your Work(s) Cited at the end of your review. The following can be used for locating the source online or in the library or for giving credit in your Work(s) Cited.

     United States. Dept. of Labor. *Occupational Outlook Handbook*, 2008–09 Edition. Web. 19 Dec. 2009.

- The following main-part outline shows some useful divisions for an essay as a career review. For a shorter essay, just select the main part or parts that fit the assignment you have in mind. For an even shorter assignment of a paragraph, subdivide one of these Roman-numeral parts for basic organization of your career review.

Unit: (the career itself)
Divisions: (parts of the unit, the career itself)

    I. My background, interests, and aptitude
   II. My desired field—an overview
  III. Working conditions, pay, benefits
  IV. Requirements for employment
   V. My step-by-step plan to enter this field

See pages 122–123 for an example of a student career review in the form of an analysis by division.

〜 Practicing Patterns of Analysis by Division

Exercise 1 Completing Patterns

Fill in the blanks in the following outlines to complete each analysis by division.

1. Unit: Doctor

   I. Principle: Effective as a general practitioner

  II. Parts based on the principle:

    A. Ability to _____

    B. Knowledge of _____

    C. Knowledge of computers and other equipment

2. Unit: Newspaper

   I. Principle: Sections for readers

  II. Parts based on the principle:

    A. News

    B. _____

    C. _____

    D. _____

    E. _____

⌒ Examining Essays of Analysis by Division

Student Reading-Based Writing

Elvis Presley: King of the Twentieth Century

Emmett Davis

Emmett Davis faced an assignment in analysis by division in which he would discuss the qualities that made a person successful. He was expected to refer to at least two sources. Davis turned to the early days of rock and roll, his special interest. Almost every source he skimmed, both on the Internet and in his college library's database, contained discussion of Elvis Presley, who became his subject.

1 After having moved a decade into the twenty-first century, we still look back and revise lists of top people of the previous one hundred years. One much-discussed category is the Greatest Performers in Popular Music. Although I have trouble choosing the top person in some categories, in this one I have no problem. Of course, it's Elvis Presley. Four factors stand out and make my choice easy: he was good looking, he could sing, he had style, and he influenced the main world of popular music, which we call "rock 'n' roll."

Looks 2 As for his looks, he was darkly handsome, some would say even beautiful, with thick, unruly hair and a sneering smile that appealed to the rebellious side of young people. Dick Clark, producer and host of *American Bandstand* for four decades, said that youth "copied his style. People imitated his gestures, dressed like him, wanted to be him (or his woman)" (148). Much has been made of the young Elvis and the old Elvis. The young was the person of slender body in a leather jacket. From that image he soon morphed into his spangled-outfit phase, a reflection of his ties with country music entertainers but also becoming the model for the glitter look of numerous rock stars. Unfortunately, toward the end of his life, he put on too much weight and favored white bejeweled jumpsuits.

Voice 3 As for singing, he had a powerful, deep voice with a wide range similar to the big voices in rhythm and blues and black gospel music he had listened to and loved as he grew up in Mississippi and Tennessee. Early in his career he was sometimes criticized for not sounding more like traditional crooners. Although it was true that he did howl, wail, and shout in certain arrangements, he could sing religious songs and simple love ballads such as "Teddy Bear" and "Love Me Tender" with great clarity and warmth.

Style 4 When he was on stage, his style was personal, as he shook his hips and belted out songs like "Heartbreak Hotel" and "You Ain't Nothin' But a Hound Dog." While making the guitar respectable, he popularized the driving rhythm of rock. He made music more personal and more aggressive. His body language may look tame today, but in the 1950s it was revolutionary.

Influence   5   <u>Because he was so different and so</u>
<u>good, he influenced and inspired others</u>
<u>who would become famous artists of rock</u>
<u>'n' roll.</u> Groups like the Beatles and the
Rolling Stones gave him credit for his
innovations. His influence even extends to
academia. In 1995 the University of
Mississippi convened an international
conference titled "In Search of Elvis."
Professor Vernon Chadwick, who helped
organize the conference, said that Elvis
"is better known and in many cases more
influential than William Faulkner" (Geier
14). Though Chadwick's statement may have
upset some of his colleagues, it is well
in line with what many of his fans
believe.

6   Some fanatical fans believe Elvis
is off hiding in the witness protection
program and shopping at the K-Marts
and Wal-Marts of the world, but, to me,
he's alive in a more important way:
he's a legend—he's the Greatest Performer
in Popular Music for the Twentieth
Century.

Works Cited

Clark, Dick. "Remembering 'Presleymania.'"

   Newsweek 8 June 1998: 148. Print.

Geier, Thom. "Eggheads for Elvis." *U.S.*

   News & World Report 7 Aug. 1995: 14.

   Print.

Exercise 2 Discussion and Critical Thinking

1. Circle the thesis.

2. What is the unit being considered?

3. What is the principle for dividing the unit?

4. Indicate the paragraphs that use these devices prominently:

   Comparison and Contrast:
   Narration:
   Cause and Effect:
   Exemplification:

5. Emmett Davis has no reservation in picking his "King." Of course, this is all a matter of opinion, but would you argue for another person? If so, who and why?

Professional Writing

Restaurant Review

Johnny's Wiener Wagon on a Roll

Floyd Garrison

> *Freelance writer Floyd Garrison was not interested in exotic cuisine, a waiter in tuxedo, and Bohemian crystal. Instead, he turned to his favorite place for eats. It had tasty food, friendly service, and down-home atmosphere.*

1   More than a food stand and less than a diner, Johnny's Wiener Wagon is shaped like a giant hotdog with wheels, though it has rested on blocks for years. It once belonged to its designer, a man named Johnny, who needed a job after World War II. Since he had been an army mess sergeant, he decided that maybe he had enough on-the-job experience to run his own hotdog stand. And run it he did for decades until about fifteen years ago when he died, and the place was bought by a Korean woman who goes by the name of Sunny. Even though the owner has changed, the menu and recipes remain with the wagon, and the food is reportedly still the same—mouth-watering

hotdogs with every topping imaginable served from a giant tow-able hotdog!

2   At Johnny's, diners stand in the open air or sit outside under an awning at a counter that extends right out of the middle of the hotdog trailer, which was moved to the current location in 1958 when the new baseball stadium was built. Eight original vinyl-topped barstools are lined up next to the ancient stainless steel counter that Sunny folds out of the framework every morning at 8 a.m. after she hoses down the sidewalk.

3   Most regular customers are guys in work clothes, but increasingly some young women and men in suits have been coming in, and there's uneasy talk among the regulars that the place could become trendy. As it is, Sunny's regulars don't have much time or money for lunch; they want food that tastes good and fills them up. The crowd is often noisy with banter, and much of the talk is about sports or work, but when Sunny delivers an order of food, conversation lags momentarily as if out of envy for the lucky recipient, who is about to chow down.

4   And I do mean *chow down*. The food at Johnny's is simple and delicious—hotdogs, chips, soda, and coffee. Sunny has kept the original menu invented by Johnny, and that means hotdogs and toppings—almost every conceivable combination of toppings that I could ever think of is available. But before I get to these, let's start with the dog. Sunny uses only Vienna Beef hotdogs, and that's important because they have the natural casing that gives the hotdog that all-important snap when bitten into. Sunny always grills the dogs and burns them just a little to increase that snap on the first bite. Resting comfortably in an oversized grilled sesame roll, the dog awaits the finishing touch, and this is where the artistry comes in; this is where the cook carefully dresses the dog, not the bun, except for the combined toppings when things go all over.

5   When Johnny started planning the menu of his place, he was still thinking of the hungry soldiers' complaints about the often unvaried, bland food he had prepared out of necessity. In his new diner, he would offer every possible combination of toppings to his single menu item, thus creating variety and the illusion of even greater variety, while keeping things simple for the cook, namely, Johnny. The result is that customers can

enjoy everything from a dog in napkin for the carb-conscious, to a no-nonsense New York–style dog, to the more elaborate and eclectic Chicago style, or to the fancy and hearty Canuck served with maple syrup and Canadian bacon piled on top of the wiener. Then at the bottom of the menu board lurks the big one: the Gutbuster. You have to be serious about your eating to consume a hotdog topped with pastrami, sauerkraut, chili, cheese, and a fried egg. There are at least twenty-five different dogs available, and people love to eat them. After the eating, maybe the second best feature is the price. A hotdog, soda, and bag of chips combo is never more than six dollars.

6   The ambience is unique and the food is great, but it's Sunny who really pulls everything together, the way old-timers say Johnny did. To Sunny, the customer is family. She knows the regulars by name, and remembers little facts about their lives. "Hey, Bill, how's the truck? Got those brakes fixed, yet?" she says as she delivers a mouth-stretching Gutbuster to a young construction worker, who looks hungry enough to eat the stool he's sitting on. Sunny laughs and shouts another order back to her helper, who toils at the grill with at least ten dogs and buns down.

7   Finally I take my place at the counter, admiring the plywood menu hanging down above the grill. Within thirty seconds, Sunny has arrived, grinning as if I were a long-lost friend. "Hey, I haven't seen you for a while. Welcome back to Johnny's. What toppings do you like?" Reflecting on my more than twenty trips to Johnny's, I know which ones I like—all of them, but only one at a time, please. One fills me up every time.

Exercise 3 Discussion and Critical Thinking

1. Which paragraph covers the ambiance (meaning the special atmosphere or mood created by the environment—the design, furnishings, sound, light, smell)?

2. Which paragraphs cover the quality and price of food?

3. Which paragraphs cover the quality of the service?

4. At a minimum, how many times should a reviewer visit a restaurant before evaluating it?

5. Is one part of a review—ambiance, food, service—most important to you? If so, why?

6. Using a five-star rating system, rank the quality of this review. Explain your reasons for the ranking.

Student Career-Related Writing

Air Traffic Control as a Career

Roger Myers

One of the suggested assignments was to write an essay about a career choice. The entire process would be analyzed. That satisfied the interests of student Roger Myers, who had recently chosen a career field, following several years of changing his intention.

Since my senior year in high school, I have changed my career goals several times. I was set on being a pilot, an anthropologist, and a teacher. At one time I even made plans to move to Alaska and work in construction and outdoor recreation. After exploring those careers by reading, talking to people in those fields, and taking some courses, I expanded my search and decided on my career for good. Now my short-range and long-range career goals are in place. I intend to be an air traffic controller.

I discovered the field when I was taking college aeronautics courses. One was in navigation and communication. On a field trip, we visited a local airport and went into the control tower to watch landings and take-offs. I was fascinated by the way tower operators directed traffic. I signed up for an introductory course in air traffic control, which included more firsthand observations in the same tower.

The outline that follow covers the middle part of the report. To read the entire report, go online to the Cengage *At a Glance: Essays* Student Companion Site.

I. Nature of the Work
II. Working Conditions, Benefits, Pay, and Retirement
III. Training, Employment, and Job Outlook
IV. My Final Approach

```
            Although I could take the examination for
   the FAA Academy and probably do well because
   I have a good basic knowledge of the career
   field and have passed similar tests for my
   private pilot's license, I intend to complete
   two years at my community college and enlist
   in the United States Air Force. I have talked
   to recruiters who have assured that I can be
   guaranteed entrance to the military school for
   air traffic controllers. In the service, I can
   learn on the job and, upon being discharged in
   four years, be in an almost certain position
   to move into the FAA program. It is possible
   that I will enjoy military life and remain in
   the service as an air traffic controller.
```

Work Cited

United States. Dept. of Labor.

Occupational Outlook Handbook.

2010-11 Edition. Web. 19 Aug. 2010.

Exercise 4 Discussion and Critical Thinking

1. What is the unit for analysis by division?

2. What are the divisions?

3. What is the principle on which the division is based?

4. What paragraph discusses that principle?

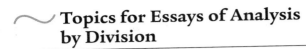 Topics for Essays of Analysis by Division

Reading-Based Writing Topics

For reading-based writing, include references to and quotations from the reading selection(s), and give credit to your sources. See Chapter 4 for additional discussion on reading-based writing.

"Elvis Presley: King of the Twentieth Century"

1. Write a reaction in which you generally agree or disagree with Emmett Davis's view. Discuss Elvis's qualities: Are these divisions the right ones? Is Elvis the greatest in these divisions collectively? Refer directly to the essay and use quotations. Should Davis have discussed other factors such as Elvis's sales of recordings and his movie career?

2. If you believe some other performer is greater than Elvis and deserves to be called "King," then write a reaction to argue your point by referring to Davis's essay, by using quotations from his essay, and by introducing other factors that should be considered.

"Johnny's Wiener Wagon on a Roll"

3. Write a two-part response in which you first summarize and then react to Garrison's restaurant review. Be specific. Discuss the parts—ambiance, service, and food—by pointing out the usefulness and the shortcomings of his discussion of each part. Refer to the review and use quotations.

Cross-Curricular Topic

4. For an essay topic pertaining to a current or former class other than English, select a unit that can be divided into parts. Consult your textbook(s) for ideas on that subject. Talk with your instructor(s) in other fields, especially those that relate to your major field of study. Your writing instructor may require you to photocopy a page or more of your source material if your work is largely summary. Following are a few examples from various disciplines:

   - Art History: Points for analyzing a painting or other work of art
   - Music History: Points for analyzing a musical composition or the performance of a musical composition

- Agriculture: Points for judging livestock
- History: Characteristics that made a historical figure great
- Government: Basic organization of the United Nations
- Biology: Working parts of an organ or organism
- Physical Education: Parts of a football team in a particular offensive or defensive formation
- Business: Structure of management for a particular business
- Law Enforcement: Organization of a specific precinct

Career-Related Topics

5. Write an analysis by division of your own career field or a career field that interests you. Include these parts that are relevant to your quest: your background and aptitude, an overview of the field, working conditions and benefits, requirements for employment, or your plan for entering the field. For a helpful model on a similar topic, see "Air Traffic Control as a Career" on pages 122–123. For directions and a reference to good source material, see "Career Review" on pages 114–115.

6. If you have worked as a food server in a restaurant, analyze a party of more than four you have served. Use three or more parts for your analysis, such as behavior and politeness, cleanliness and neatness, and fairness and generosity in tipping.

7. Explain how the parts of a particular product function as a unit.

8. Explain how each of several qualities of a specific person— intelligence, sincerity, knowledgeability, ability to communicate, manner, attitude, appearance—makes that individual an effective salesperson, manager, or employee.

General Topics

9. Using Garrison's review as a model (see pages 119–121) and instructions for writing a restaurant review by discussing ambiance, service, and food (see page 113), write a review of your own experience at a local restaurant or fast-food place. Include a five-star rating and explain your reasons.

10. Using Garrison's review as a model, write a review of your campus cafeteria or snack bar. Include useful information by specifying the appearance, freshness, quality, and pricing of food; by giving examples of good or bad service at the serving line (hint: ask some questions) and at the checkout station; and by giving descriptive details about the atmosphere, including such matters as exterior and interior features (architecture, landscaping, painting,

tile, lighting, furniture, and decorations), tidiness (cleanliness of tables, windows, and floor), and music or the absence of it. Consider using a five-star ranking for each aspect. Include a five-star rating and explain your reasons.

Some of the following topics are too broad for an essay and should be narrowed. For example, the general "a wedding ceremony" could be narrowed to the particular "José and Maria's wedding ceremony." Divide your focused topic into parts and analyze it.

11. An organ in the human body
12. A ceremony—wedding, graduation
13. A holiday celebration, a pep rally, a sales convention, or a religious revival
14. A family, a relationship, a gang, a club, a sorority, or a fraternity
15. A movie, a television program, or a video game
16. Any well-known person—an athlete, a politician, a criminal, or a writer

Writer's Guidelines at a Glance: Analysis by Division

Almost any unit can be analyzed by division— for example, how the parts of the ear work in hearing, how the parts of the eye work in seeing, or how the parts of the heart work in pumping blood throughout the body. Subjects such as these are all approached with the same systematic procedure.

1. This is the procedure:

   - Step 1: Begin with something that is a unit.
   - Step 2: State the principle by which the unit can function.
   - Step 3: Divide the unit into parts according to that principle.
   - Step 4: Discuss each of the parts in relation to the unit.

2. This is the way you might apply that procedure to writing about a good boss.

   - Step 1: Unit   Manager
   - Step 2: Principle of function   Effective as a leader
   - Step 3: Parts based on the   Fair, intelligent, stable,
     principle   competent in the field

- Step 4: Discussion   Consider each part in relation to the person's effectiveness as a manager.

3. This is how a basic outline of analysis by division might look:

   Thesis: To be effective as a leader, a manager needs specific qualities.

       I. Fairness
      II. Intelligence
    III. Stability
    IV. Competence in the field

4. Consider using CLUESS for revision and COPS for editing.

Thesis: There are { only / Perhaps / exactly / approx. } { # } { Types / sorts / groups } of ___

(Class:)

8

Process Analysis: Writing About Doing

~ Writing Essays of Process Analysis

If you have any doubt about how frequently we use process analysis, just think about how many times you have heard people say, "How do you do it?" or "How is [was] it done?" Even when you are not hearing those questions, you are posing them yourself when you need to make something, cook a meal, assemble an item, take some medicine, repair a toy, or figure out what happened. In your college classes, you may have to discover how osmosis occurs, how a rock changes form, how a mountain was formed, how a battle was won, or how a bill goes through the legislature.

If you need to explain how to do something or how something was (is) done, you will write a paper of **process analysis**. You will break down your topic into stages, explaining each so that your reader can duplicate or understand the process.

Two Types of Process Analysis: Directive and Informative

The questions "How do I do it?" and "How is (was) it done?" will lead you into two different types of process analysis—directive and informative.

Directive process analysis explains how to do something. As the name suggests, it gives directions and tells the reader how to do something. It says, for example, "Read me, and you can bake a pie [tune up your car, solve a math problem, write an essay, take some medicine]." Because it is presented directly to the reader, it usually addresses the reader as "you," or it implies the "you" by saying something such as "First [you] purchase a large, fat wombat, and then [you]. . . ." In the same way, this textbook addresses you or implies "you" because it is a long how-to-do-it (directive process analysis) statement.

Informative process analysis explains how something was (is) done by giving data (information). Whereas the directive process analysis tells you what to do in the future, the informative process analysis tells you what has occurred or what is occurring. If it is something in nature, such as the formation of a mountain, you can read and understand the process by which it emerged. In this type of process analysis, you do not tell the reader what to do; therefore, you do not use the words *you* or *your*.

Working with Stages

Preparation

In the first stage of writing directive process analysis, list the materials or equipment needed for the process and discuss the necessary setup arrangements. For some topics, this stage will also provide technical terms and definitions. The degree to which this stage is detailed will depend on both the subject itself and the expected knowledge and experience of the projected audience.

Informative process analysis may begin with background or context rather than with preparation. For example, a statement explaining how mountains form might begin with a description of a flat portion of the earth made up of plates that are arranged like a jigsaw puzzle.

Steps

The actual process will be presented here. Each step must be explained clearly and directly, and it must be phrased to accommodate the audience. The language, especially in directive process analysis, is likely to be simple and concise; however, avoid dropping words such as *and*, *a*, *an*, *the*, and *of*, and thereby lapsing into "recipe language." In directive process analysis the steps may be accompanied by explanations about why certain procedures are necessary and how not following directions carefully can lead to trouble. In informative process analysis the steps should appear in a logical progression within a sequence.

Order

The order will usually be chronological (time-based) in some sense.

Transitional Words for Improving Coherence

- **FOR PROCESS ANALYSIS:** Certain transitional words are commonly used to promote coherence. The order will usually be chronological (time-based) in some sense: *first, second, third, then, soon, now, next, finally, at last, therefore, consequently,* and—especially for informative process analysis—words used to show the passage of time, such as hours, days of the week, and so on.

Basic Forms

Consider using this form for **directive process analysis** (with topics such as how to cook something or how to fix something):

I. Preparation
   A.
   B.
   C.
II. Steps
   A.
   B.
   C.
   D.

Consider using this form for **informative process analysis** (with topics such as how a volcano functions or how a battle was won):

I. Background or context
   A.
   B.
   C.
II. Change or development (narrative)
   A.
   B.
   C.
   D.

Career-Related Writing as Process Analysis

Arguably, no form is more common for career-related writing than process analysis. Almost all tasks at the workplace involve an understanding of how things work and about how one performs tasks.

Both the understanding and the performance pertain to procedure. Many of those procedures, in turn, involve much learning and training, meaning a lot of how-to-do-it and how-it-was-done. There will be training sessions after training sessions as companies restructure and workers change employment and even change career fields. Skills in thinking and writing can be applied to different situations. With these skills, you will be more versatile and adaptable.

When you are new on the job, you will be expected first to learn. Knowing the techniques for process analysis will help you master the subject material more easily. At some point, you will probably be expected to train others. The training you do may require you both to talk and to write. Even if you are expected only to talk about a process, you will probably write it out first, at least in rough form. Regardless of the occasion or the method of communication, the organizational pattern, with some modification for your audience and subject, will be either Preparation and Steps or Background and Steps.

Knowing how to write a clear, logical, correct process analysis will be an asset for you as you look for employment or workplace advancement. Fortunately for you, the twin organizations of process analysis provide structures in this chapter as basic outlines. Remembering these outline patterns will serve you well in writing the process analysis. It will also serve you well in your oral presentation. If you use PowerPoint, imagine your outline as an overview and then as chronological development. Keep in mind that these techniques for writing process analysis in your current class differ little from what you will be doing at work. The essay "The Skinny on Working for a Dermatologist" on pages 132–136 explains one procedure of the writer's job. The outline form could be used to indicate the main and supporting points in a PowerPoint presentation.

⁓ Practicing Patterns of Process Analysis

Exercise 1 Completing Patterns

Using directive process analysis, fill in the blanks in the following outline for replacing a flat tire with the spare. Work in a group if possible.

I. Preparation

   A. Park car.

   B. _____

C. Obtain car jack.

D. _____

E. _____

II. Steps

A. Remove hub cap (if applicable).

B. Loosen lug nuts a bit.

C. _____

D. _____

E. Remove wheel with flat tire.

F. _____

G. _____

H. Release jack pressure.

I. _____

⁓ Examining Essays of Process Analysis

Student Career-Related Writing

The Skinny on Working for a Dermatologist

J. Kim Birdine

After having traveled a long way from a Korean orphanage to the United States, J. Kim Birdine is still on the move. In writing this essay of process analysis, she demonstrates the same intellectual qualities she uses so well in her role as an assistant to a doctor, both in the office and in the operating room.

Author's role
Double underlining indicates the use of transitional devices.

1   As a medical assistant for a dermatologist, I am actively involved in every aspect of the practice, recommending products, doing laser treatments for veins, and administering skin peels. The

younger patients generally see the doctor to correct their skin problems, whether they're suffering from a persistent dry patch, uneven skin tone, or a bout with acne. A good number of the patients come in for cosmetic reasons, wanting their wrinkles smoothed out or their dark

Thesis blotches lasered off. <u>The most important</u> <u>part of my job, though, is to prepare</u> <u>surgical trays for the patients with skin</u> <u>cancer and to assist the doctor through</u> <u>the procedure.</u>

I. Preparation 2 My <u>initial concern</u> when <u>setting up a</u> <u>surgical tray</u> is that everything is

1 <u>sterile</u>. This means that all the <u>metal</u> <u>instruments, gauze,</u> and <u>applicators</u> (Q-Tips) are <u>put through</u> an <u>Autoclave</u>

2 (steam sterilizer), to ensure sterilization.

Order **by time** Once everything is sterile, <u>I begin</u> <u>setting up</u> my <u>surgical tray by placing</u> <u>a sterile field on a tray</u>, which has long legs and wheels at the base so that it can be rolled. The <u>tray</u> should <u>stand</u> about <u>waist high</u> so that the physician can reach the instruments easily. The sterile field is a large white tissue that I carefully take out of a sealed pack, touching it only at the corners to unfold it to its

full size. It serves as a base on which to
place all the instruments.

3 3   Next all of the metal instruments are
placed on the tray with a long-handled

Details: "pick-up." The necessary instruments are a
Specific words
scalpel, a skin hook, large forceps, small
forceps, straight scissors, curved
scissors, a large needle holder, and a
small needle holder. All are placed with
handles facing toward me, except the small
needle holder and the straight scissors.
These two should be positioned at a corner
away from me with the handles facing out.

Why   The position of all of the instruments is
procedure
is important   important so that the doctor can reach
them with ease. The ones placed in the
corner are for me to use while assisting
with suturing. A surgical tray is not
complete without a small stack of gauze
(large) and about twenty applicators. The
entire tray is covered with another
sterile field exactly like the one placed
initially on the tray.

4 4   Just prior to surgery, I set up
extras. I place on the counter anesthesia--
a 3cc syringe of lidocaine with
epinephrine--and a disinfectant skin
cleanser, along with two pairs of surgical

gloves, one for the doctor and one for me.

5   I turn on the hyfrecator, which is a cauterizer used to stop bleeding by burning the tissue. I prepare a specimen

6   bottle indicating on its label the patient's name, the date, the doctor's name, and the area of the body from which the specimen is taken. I remove the

7   sterile field on top of the instruments and place the sutures requested by the doctor and a different kind of sterile field, which has a hole in the middle of

Reason for procedure   it, on the tray. This field enables the doctor to place the hole directly over the surgery site, exposing the area to be worked on and covering the surrounding areas.

II. Steps 5   During surgery, once the doctor removes the section that needs to be

1   tested, I place it in the specimen jar, seal the lid on it, and place it on the counter. I have to be attentive to the surgery at this point to assist in

2   reducing the bleeding. My job is to apply gauze or applicators wherever bleeding occurs and to ready the hyfrecator in case the doctor needs it. When bleeding is minimized, the doctor begins suturing.

3   At this point I use the small needle

holder to grab the tip of the needle after

the doctor inserts it through the skin, to

pull it through for her. This makes her

job easier. I use the straight scissors to

cut the suture once she is finished with

4   knotting. Sometimes she does some internal

suturing for the tissue under the skin,

with dissolvable thread, and knots each

turn. This is when I cut directly on top

of the knot. The surface suturing is

usually knotted at the beginning and

at the end of the line of sutures and

needs cutting down to one-quarter of

an inch.

5   6   After surgery, I use peroxide to clean

the patient's surgical site. I apply

either a pressure bandage or a plain Band-

Aid with antibiotic ointment. The pressure

bandage is applied usually when there is a

concern of more bleeding post surgery. I

6   explain to the patient how to take care of

the surgical area and when to come back to

have the sutures removed. This makes my

Concludes   job complete, until it is time for another
essay and
reflects   set-up, when I will repeat the same
back on
introduction   process of ensuring a sterile environment

for the patient.

Professional Writing

Binding Decisions

Joan Gould

> *With a reputation for penetrating insight and almost detached honesty, Joan Gould is a freelance author of numerous essays and books with major publishers. In reviewing her acclaimed book* Spirals: A Woman's Journey Through Family Life *(Random House, 1988), Publishers Weekly referred to her style as "exquisitely simple, unsentimental and powerfully moving." Here we have an account of how a respectable young woman of the early 1950s dressed for a date and why she did so.*

1   I'm out of the bathtub. I'm ready to get dressed for my date tonight, which is a blind date, serious business in this year of 1950 for any girl who's over 20 and still single. I'm 22. No matter how much money I may earn in my job, I'll never be allowed to have an apartment of my own; I'll never pay an electric bill or buy a bedspread or spend a night away from home without my parents; in fact, I'll never be a grown-up as long as I remain single.

2   How shall I dress? I want to look sexy enough to attract this unknown man, so that he'll call and ask me for another date next week. (Needless to say, I won't call him, even if my life depends on it.) On the other hand, I don't want to hide the fact that I'm what's known as a Nice Girl, addicted to Peter Pan collars and velvet hats and white gloves, which means that I'm good wife material, and also makes it clear that he'll get nothing more than a goodnight kiss from me tonight.

3   And so I dress carefully. Every single item that I put on not only is complicated in itself but carries an even more complicated message.

4   My girdle comes first. Here's the badge, the bind, the bondage of womanhood. Here's the itch of it. This is the garment that tells me I'm not a little girl anymore, who wears only underpants, but neither am I middle-aged like my mother, who wears a real corset with bones that dig into her diaphragm and leave cruel sores there. I can get away with either a panty girdle or a two-way stretch, both of which are made of Lastex with a panel of stiff satin over the abdomen. The basic difference is that a panty girdle, unlike a two-way stretch, covers the crotch, which was considered a shocking—indeed obscene—idea when first introduced. Victorian women were obliged to wear half a

dozen petticoats at a time to be respectable, but never, never would they put on anything that slipped between their thighs, like a pair of pants.

5   But why should I be bothering with this sausage casing when I weighed a grand total of a hundred and two pounds?

6   I bother because being thin has nothing to do with it. A girdle is a symbolic garment, and unless I wanted to be regarded as a child or a slut I have to put it on. When I go out with girlfriends in the daytime I may choose to be more comfortable in only a garter belt, a device with four long, wiggly elastics that dangle down my thighs like hungry snakes lunging at my stockings. When I'm with a boy, however, it would be unthinkable— it would be downright indecent—to let him see my rear end jiggle or let him notice it has two halves. (All males are called "boys," no matter what their age, so long as they're single.) My backside is supposed to be molded in a rigid piece that divides into two legs, like a walking clothespin.

7   Besides, if I don't wear a girdle every day, the older girls warn me, I'm going to "spread." Spreading is somehow related to letting my flesh hang loose, which is in turn related to the idea of the "loose" woman, and none of us wants to be considered loose. A man doesn't buy a cow if he can get milk for free, our mothers tell us in dire tones. We don't point out that we're not cows, and we don't fight against girdles, which apparently do a good job of discouraging wandering hands, since most of the single girls I know are virgins.

8   But which girdle should I wear? If I pick the panty girdle, I'll need 10 minutes' advance notice before going to the toilet. If I wear the two-way stretch, it will ride up and form a sausage around my waist. Either way, my flesh will be marked with welts and stripes when, at that delirious moment in my bedroom, I can strip off my clothes and scratch and scratch.

9   I pick the two-way stretch but, born compromiser that I am, put underpants over it.

10   Next comes the bra. I don't dare look at myself in the mirror as I put it on. This is the era of the pinup girl, the heyday of Lana Turner and Betty Grable, when breasts bubble and froth over the rims of C-cups and a flat chest is considered about as exciting as flat champagne. Not until Twiggy appears on the scene in the 1960s will thinness become acceptable in a girl,

much less desirable—but how am I supposed to survive until then? The answer is the garment I've just put on, the confession of my disgrace—a padded bra. If I wear a strapless gown, I pin foam rubber bust pads, which are known as "falsies," in place. Occasionally one of these breaks loose during a particularly ardent conga or mambo and rises above my dress like the rim of the sun peering over a hilltop.

11   At least the bra won't show under my silk slip. Silk is expensive, of course, and no male will see my underwear unless he marries me or I'm carried off to a hospital emergency room— but then, as all the mothers warn us, accidents do happen.

12   Stockings next. During World War II, just as I became old enough to wear them, our wonderful new nylons were snatched away from us in order to make parachutes for what was known as the "war effort." What were we girls supposed to do—go out on a date in socks, like little children? If there weren't any stockings around, we'd have to create them. And so we bought bottles of makeup base and painted stockings on our legs and drew seams up the back with eyebrow pencils, which was undoubtedly the last time my seams were ever straight.

13   My dress, oddly enough, is easy to choose. For a woman of my years, a skirt-and-sweater is out of the question on a date. The dress mustn't be too high-style or expensive, however, or else the young man will think that I'm spoiled, a fatal defect in a girl who might otherwise qualify as good wife material. Never mind that I earned the money to buy my own clothes; I still have to show that it won't cost much to support me once we marry and I quit my job. For the same reason, wherever we go— which is always at his expense, of course—I'll insist that we travel by bus or subway, never by taxi. If he invites me out to dinner (which doesn't happen often, because of cost, and never on a first date), I'll eat a sandwich at home before I leave, to make sure I won't be tempted to order an appetizer or dessert in the restaurant.

14   Shoes. I'd like to wear my fashionable new ones, with their ankle straps criss-crossing in back and fastening above the ankle bone, but they have 3 1/2-inch heels, and I have no idea if I'll tower over this unknown man. If I choose low heels, on the other hand, he may think that I'm condescending. I pick the high heels but hide a low-heeled pair in the hall closet, just in case. Blind dates have their special hazards.

15   I still have to put on my makeup, which includes lots of lip-stick, loose face powder and an eyebrow pencil to extend my brow line, but no eye shadow, much less liner. I also have to do my hair, which is set with heavy lotion and rollers in the beauty parlor every week. (At night I sleep in a cotton mesh hairnet that I tie around my head, in order to preserve the set for at least a week.)

16   Speeding up the pace, I rush to equip my pocketbook with a monogrammed handkerchief and some "mad money," including several nickels for phone calls or a bus, obligatory for a blind date. I run to my glove drawer and hunt up a pair in white kid, since he's invited me to a concert. I won't need a hat. He'll wear one, of course.

17   The doorbell rings. I dab Shalimar on a tuft of cotton, which I tuck inside my bra; I check my stocking seams and move toward the door. For an instant, my hand rests on the knob, while I wonder what sort of person is breathing out there, only inches away from me but still unrevealed, unex-plored. And then I open the door, and I see his face and hear his voice, because he's already in mid-sentence. As a matter of fact, he's in mid-story, as if it's inconceivable that anyone could be less than fascinated with what he's saying, which hap-pens to be true, or as if he's my husband already and has waited all day, or maybe all his life, to tell me what happened to him that afternoon.

18   A box of Kleenex is tucked under his arm, because he has a cold, and he lays the box down on the hall table with the as-surance of the rightful prince stepping into his kingdom at last. This one I'll marry or I'll marry no one, I say to myself an hour later.

19   Three dates—which means three weeks—later, he proposes. "Wait I have to tell you something first," I declare in distress. He waits. I'm in turmoil. I'm risking everything on candor, and candor isn't a virtue in which I've much practice. I've never said anything like this out loud before. "You have a right to know," I announced. "I wear a padded bra."

20   He says he imagines he can handle that.

21   We were married three months later. I wonder, if he hadn't proposed so promptly, how much longer it would have been be-fore he discovered my secret for himself.

Exercise 2 Discussion and Critical Thinking

1. Is this essay directive (telling the reader how to do something) or informative (telling the reader how something occurred or is occurring)?

2. This essay is written in the present tense ("And so I dress carefully. . . ."; paragraph 3) except for the last paragraph, which is in the past tense ("We were. . . ."). What does the author accomplish by using the present tense for what she has to say here?

3. Does Gould see particular "rules" of dressing for a date in 1950 as a matter of wrong attitudes or just cultural differences?

4. Which paragraphs occupy the background (the situation that will be discussed in stages) part of this process analysis?

5. List the paragraph numbers and the words that mark the beginning of the first three stages of Gould's dressing.

6. Looking back on 1950, we are likely to see quaintness, foolishness, and unfairness mixed with innocence and sweetness. Do you think any aspects of current behavior—especially regarding dating and dressing in relation to values, intentions, and mating strategy—might be regarded in, say, sixty years, as quaint or even misguided?

⌇ Topics for Essays of Process Analysis

Reading-Based Writing Topics

For reading-based writing, include references to and quotations from the reading selection(s), and give credit to your sources. See Chapter 4 for additional discussion on reading-based writing.

"Binding Decisions"

1. Write a two-part response (separate summary and reaction) to this essay. In your reaction, evaluate the author's personal views on how she now regards what it was necessary for her to do with her "binding decisions." Refer to and quote from the essay.

2. Write a two-part response (separate summary and reaction) to this essay. In your reaction, relate Gould's decisions to the ones that might be made by either a female or a male of your generation in dressing for a date. Remember that each decision is made for a reason, and the reasons are sometimes more interesting than the choices.

Cross-Curricular Topics

3. Write an essay about a procedure you follow in your college work in a science (chemistry, biology, geology) lab. You may explain how to analyze a rock, how to dissect something, how to operate something, or how to perform an experiment.
4. Write an essay about how to do something in an activity or performance class, such as drama, physical education, art, or music.

Career-Related Topics

5. Imagine that you are about to leave a job after giving only a one-day notice to your employer. That employer kindly asks you to write a paragraph or short essay (actually as a process analysis) about how you fulfill your job description for a certain task. This information will be studied by your successor tomorrow. Do not attempt to provide a complete job description; just explain the task. For a useful model of form and workplace content, review "The Skinny on Working for a Dermatologist" on pages 132–136.
6. Explain how to perform a service or how to repair or install a product.
7. Explain the procedure for operating a machine, a computer, a piece of equipment, or another device at the workplace.
8. Explain how to manufacture, construct, or cook something at the workplace.

General Topics

Most of the following topics are directive as they are phrased. However, each can be transformed into a how-it-was-done informative topic by personalizing it and explaining stage by stage how you, someone else, or a group did something. For example, you could write either a directive process analysis about how to deal with an obnoxious person or an informative process analysis about how you or someone else dealt with an obnoxious person. The two types of process analysis are often blended, especially in the personal approach. Many of the following topics will be more interesting to you and your readers if they are personalized.

Select one of the following topics and write a process-analysis essay about it. Most of the topics require some narrowing to be treated in an essay. For example, writing about playing baseball is too broad; writing about how to bunt may be manageable.

9. How to end a relationship without hurting someone's feelings
10. How to pass a test for a driver's license
11. How to get a job at _____
12. How to eat _____
13. How to perform a magic trick
14. How to repair _____
15. How to assemble _____
16. How to learn about another culture
17. How to approach someone you would like to know better
18. How to make a videotape of a particular event

Writer's Guidelines at a Glance: Process Analysis

1. Decide whether your process analysis is mainly directive or informative, and be consistent in using pronouns and other designations.

   - Use second person for the directive analysis as you address the reader (use *you, your*).
   - Use first person for the informative analysis; do not address the reader (use *I*).
   - Use third person for the informative analysis; do not address the reader (use *he, she, it, they, them, individuals*, the name of your subject).

2. Consider using this form for the directive process analysis (with topics such as how to cook something or how to fix something):

   I. Preparation
      A.
      B.
      C.

II. Steps
   A.
   B.
   C.
   D.

3. Consider using this form for the informative process analysis (with topics such as how a volcano functions or how a battle was won):

   I. Background or context
      A.
      B.
      C.
   II. Change or development (narrative)
      A.
      B.
      C.
      D.

4. In explaining the stages and using technical terms, take into account whether your audience will be mainly well informed, moderately informed, or poorly informed.

5. Use transitional words indicating time or other progression (such as *finally, at last, therefore, consequently*, and—especially for the informative process analysis—words showing passage of time, such as hours, days of the week, and so on).

6. Avoid recipe language; do not drop *the, a, an*, or *of*.

7. Consider using CLUESS for revision and COPS for editing.

9

Cause and Effect:
Determining
Reasons
and Results

∼ Writing Essays of Cause and Effect

Causes and effects deal with reasons and results; they are sometimes discussed together and sometimes separately. Like other
forms of writing to explain, writing about causes and effects is
based on natural thought processes. The shortest, and arguably the
most provocative, poem in the English language—"I/Why?"—is
posed by an anonymous author about cause. Children are preoccu-
pied with delightful and often exasperating "why" questions. Daily
we encounter all kinds of causes and effects. The same subject may
raise questions of both kinds.

> The car won't start. *Why?* (cause)
>
> The car won't start. *What now?* (effect)

At school, from the biology lab to the political-science classroom,
and at work, from maintaining relationships to changing procedures,
causes and effects are found everywhere.

Organizing Cause and Effect

One useful approach to developing a cause-and-effect analysis is
listing. Write down the event, situation, or trend you are concerned
about. Then, on the left side of the page list the causes and on the
right side list the effects. Here is an example.

145

Causes	Event, Situation, or Trend	Effects
Low self-esteem		Life of crime
Drugs		Drug addiction
Tradition	*Joining*	Surrogate family relationship
Fear	*a gang*	Protection
Lacking family		Ostracism
Needs protection		Restricted vocational opportunities
Neighborhood status		

As you use prewriting techniques to explore your ideas, you need to decide whether your topic should mainly inform or mainly persuade. If you intend to inform, your tone should be coolly objective. If you intend to persuade, your tone should be subjective. In either case, you should take into account the views of your audience as you phrase your ideas. You should also take into account how much your audience understands about your topic and develop your ideas accordingly.

Composing the Thesis

Now that you have organized your ideas under causes and effects, you are ready to focus on the causes, on the effects, or, occasionally, on both.

Your controlling idea, or thesis, might be one of causes: "People join gangs for three main reasons." Later, as you use the idea as a thesis in an essay, you would rephrase it to make it less mechanical, allowing it to become part of the flow of your discussion. If you wanted to personalize the work—thereby probably making it more interesting—you could write about someone you know who joined a gang. And you could use the same basic framework, the three causes, to indicate why this particular person joined a gang.

Your selection of a thesis takes you to the next writing phase: that of completing an outline or outline alternative. There you need to consider three closely related points:

- Review the kinds of causes and effects.
- Evaluate the importance of sequence.
- Introduce ideas and work with patterns.

Considering Kinds of Causes and Effects

Causes and effects can be primary or secondary, immediate or remote.

Primary or Secondary

Primary means "major" and **secondary** means "minor." A primary cause may be sufficient to bring about the situation (subject). For example, infidelity may be a primary (and possibly sufficient by itself) cause of divorce for some people but not for others, who regard it as secondary. Or if country X is attacked by country Y, the attack itself, as a primary cause, may be sufficient to bring on a declaration of war. A diplomatic blunder regarding visas for workers may be of secondary importance and, although significant, would not be reason enough to start a war.

Immediate or Remote

Causes and effects often occur at a distance in time or place from the situation. The immediate effect of sulfur in the atmosphere may be atmospheric pollution, but the long-range, or remote, effect may be acid rain and the loss of species. The immediate cause of the greenhouse effect may be the depletion of the ozone layer, whereas the long-range, or remote, cause is the use of CFCs (commonly called *Freon*, found in such items as Styrofoam cups). Even more remote, the ultimate cause may be the people who use the products containing Freon. Your purpose will determine the causes and effects appropriate for your essay.

Evaluating the Importance of Sequence

The sequence in which events occur(red) may or may not be significant. When you are dealing with several sequential events, determine whether the sequence of events has causal connections; that is, does one event bring about another?

Consider this sequence of events: Joe's parents get divorced, and Joe joins a gang. We know that one reason for joining a gang is to gain family companionship. Therefore, we may conclude that Joe joined the gang to satisfy his need for family companionship, which he lost when his parents divorced. But if we do so, we may have reached a wrong conclusion, because Joe's joining the gang after the family breakup does not necessarily mean that the two events are related. Maybe Joe joined the gang because of drug dependency, low self-esteem, or a need for protection.

In each case, examine the connections. To assume that one event is *caused* by another just because it *follows* the other is a logical error called a *post hoc* ("after this") fallacy. An economic depression may occur after a president takes office, but that does not necessarily mean the depression was caused by the new administration. It might have occurred anyway, perhaps in an even more severe form.

Order

The order of the causes and effects you discuss in your paper may be based on time, space, emphasis, or a combination:

- **Time:** If one stage leads to another, as in a discussion of the causes and effects of upper atmospheric pollution, your paper would be organized best by time.
- **Space:** In some instances causes and effects are organized best by their relation in space. For instance, the causes of an economic recession could be discussed in terms of local factors, regional factors, national factors, and international factors.
- **Emphasis:** Some causes and effects may be more important than others. For instance, if some causes of divorce are primary (perhaps infidelity and physical abuse) and others are secondary (such as annoying habits and laziness), a paper about divorce could present the secondary causes first, and then move on to primary causes to emphasize the latter as more important.

In some instances, two or more factors (such as time and emphasis) may be linked; in that case, select the order that best fits what you are trying to say, or combine orders.

Transitional Words for Improving Coherence

- **FOR CAUSE AND EFFECT: Cause:** *as, because, because of, due to, for, for the reason that, since, bring about, another cause, for this reason, one cause, a second cause, another cause, a final cause*

- **Effect:** *accordingly, finally, consequently, hence, so, therefore, thus, as a consequence, as a result, resulting*

Introducing Ideas and Working with Patterns

In introducing your controlling idea—probably in an introductory paragraph—you will almost certainly want to perform two functions:

1. *Discuss your subject.* For example, if you are writing about the causes or effects of divorce, begin with a statement about divorce as a subject.
2. *Indicate whether you will concentrate on causes or effects or a combination.* That indication should be made clear early in the essay. Concentrating on one—causes or effects—does not mean you will not mention the other; it only means you will emphasize one of them. You can lend emphasis to your main concern(s), causes, effects, or a combination, by repeating key words such as *cause, reason, effect, result, consequence, and outcome.*

The most likely pattern for your work is shown in Figure 9.1.

Figure 9.1
Patterns of Cause and Effect

⁓ Cause and Effect in a Short Story Review

A short story is a brief, imaginative narrative, with numerous functional elements (all of which can be analyzed): setting, conflict, characters, plot, theme, and point of view.

The overarching element of the short story is usually the plot. In the simplest terms, the plot begins when a character in a setting experiences (with or without being aware) a conflict. The plot develops as the character deals with the conflict in a single scene or sequence of scenes. All of this narrative is related from a first-person (*I*) or a third-person (*he, she, they*) point of view. The entire presentation has a theme, the underlying generalization or fictional point.

Short stories are fiction, meaning they are not a report of what has actually happened, though they may be based squarely on an author's experience.

One theory about why we enjoy fiction—in print and film—is that we can analyze it. The events of our lives may often appear too complicated and close for us to figure out, but with fiction we can see connections more clearly. We can dissect fiction, examine the parts and their relationships, and speculate about what it all means. We can even relate fiction to our own experiences.

Like most writing, the short story review (analysis) is a combination of writing forms, but one form—analysis by division, comparison and contrast, cause and effect, or narration—may provide much of the pattern. For a short review, you will likely emphasize one aspect of the short story—setting, conflict, plot, character(s), theme, point of view—though you may touch on several. Cause and effect is often the most common form because we are concerned about why characters behave as they do (causes) and about the results of events and actions (effects). For verification of that statement, apply it to any piece of fiction you have read or film you have seen and note how often you are considering the theme, or meaning of the work.

- Develop your ideas by referring directly to the story; by explaining; and by using summaries, paraphrases, and quotations. Avoid the temptation to oversummarize.
- Use present tense in relating events in the story. For example, "Jude is trying to survive," not "Jude was trying to survive." Use quotation marks around the words you borrow and provide documentation if directed to do so by your instructor.
- Although a short story review is mainly analytical, it may include your speculation and call forth references to your personal experience.

- Two short stories are included on the *At a Glance* Student Companion Site: "The Tell-Tale Heart" and "The Cask of Amontillado." You can find others by Googling titles suggested by your instructor.

⌒ Practicing Patterns of Cause and Effect

Exercise 1 Completing Patterns

Fill in the blanks to complete first the causes outline and then the effects outline.

1. Causes for dropping out of high school

   I. Family tradition

   II. _____

   III. _____

   IV. _____

2. Effects of getting a college education

   I. Better informed

   II. _____

   III. _____

   IV. _____

⌒ Examining a Summary and an Essay on the Causes of Violence

Student Reading-Based Writing

A Summary of "Enough Is Enough"

Andrew Cossey

Student Andrew Cossey's assignment was to write a summary of a short passage on the topic of violence. The passage could come from his textbook, but if he wanted to use another source, he must photocopy and submit it with his summary. Because the source would be available to his instructor and class, he was not required to include formal documentation. His choice was to summarize "Enough Is Enough," a section from Don't Pee on My Leg and Tell Me It's Raining, *a book by Judy Schendlin and Josh Getlin. Judy Schendlin is best known as the star of* Judge Judy, *a top-rated American reality-based television court show.*

1   Judy Schendlin (popularly known as Judge Judy) has some specific observations on the causes and effects of juvenile delinquency, and she has some suggestions on what society should do. Her views come from experience. She was a family court judge for twenty-four years. She was appalled by seeing all the dysfunctional families that came before her for what were called legal problems. She says she knew otherwise. What she saw "reflected just how far we have strayed from personal responsibility and old-fashioned discipline." She and Josh Getlin discuss her perspective on this issue in their book, *Don't Pee on My Leg and Tell Me It's Raining.*

2   What she saw when she first became a judge was small-time crime, but as the decades passed, all too frequently the crimes became more vicious and "a new breed of delinquents was born." The courts and other agencies did not know what to do, and in that respect she believes little has changed.

3   She has several examples to make her argument. In one, a boy named Elmo is being charged with selling crack cocaine for the second time. Elmo has an attorney. The attorney says the boy's trouble began when his grandmother died, and he was overcome with grief. Unable to deal emotionally with the situation, the boy turned to crime. Judge Judy does not buy it. "Get a better story,"

she snaps. "Nobody goes out and sells drugs because Grandma died."

4   In the second example, a young offender named Tito has confessed to mugging an 80-year-old man. The delinquent's attorney offers a reason for this crime: the youngster's brother has just been imprisoned for murder. The attorney argues that the youngster was very close to his brother and is suffering from post-traumatic stress. That was the cause of Tito's misbehavior. "You'll have to do better than that," Judge Judy shoots back.

5   In another example, a woman with two crack-addict babies isn't reporting to her drug-rehab counselor. She says she couldn't find the address. "What do you want, a road map?" Judge Judy says to the woman.

6   Those were typical cases.

7   Judge Judy believes family courts should be run like a family. Problems should be treated with compassion, but love must sometimes be balanced with toughness. She says that we should "send a tough message to first-time offenders." Then maybe they wouldn't re-offend. After all, the first purpose of law is to protect citizens. She says that only after that is achieved should we turn to rehabilitation and help the offender. She has several ideas for "improving our juvenile system."

8   For one thing, spending public money on the children who break laws is a mistake. Most children who grow up in poverty, neglect, and abuse do not become criminals. They struggle to do the right thing. Those

are the ones who deserve help, but all too frequently the money and support go to the troublemakers. Judge Judy says she saw photos of elaborate gymnasiums built to provide recreation especially for delinquent youngsters. Those images were shown alongside photos of inner-city schools with overcrowded classrooms and decrepit buildings. "What kind of insanity is this?" she asks. The money should be going primarily to help the "good kids" who are "struggling to get by."

9	Inside the justice system, Judge Judy says that strict, no-nonsense rules should be imposed for children and parents.

10	She maintains that judges should have access to young offenders' records. The records would become sealed only after the youngsters become twenty-five and truly are rehabilitated. While they are incarcerated, they should prove that they are serious about rehabilitation. They should not be released early unless they have taken vocational programs and demonstrated good character.

11	She says that within the family, juveniles should be supervised more closely by parents. A national curfew should be mandatory for youngsters under eighteen. Parents on welfare should not receive money unless their children behave. When they don't, parents should pay for defense attorneys as they can afford to do so. Middle-class parents should not be allowed to claim income tax deductions while children are incarcerated or are not attending school.

12	Judge Judy says she has a simple message. "People create their own opportunities." She

```
is through with the "victim game. A
delinquent is responsible for his crime.
Parents are responsible for their children."
She says the practice of using social
programs to solve the juvenile crime problems
has failed. Her solution is to promote "self-
discipline, individual accountability, and
responsible conduct."
```

Exercise 2 Discussion and Critical Thinking

1. According to Judge Judy, what is wrong with our society?

2. How does she use the case of Elmo in her argument?

3. What is her reaction to the lawyer's plea that Tito's crime was caused by his post-traumatic stress?

4. How does Judge Judy feel about showing compassion to first-time offenders?

5. What is Judge Judy's economic message to parents of delinquents?

6. Do you agree with her judicial tough-love approach? Why or why not?

7. Do you agree with her view that "self-discipline, individual accountability, and responsible conduct" are the answer? Explain.

8. How would you rate this selection as a summary on a scale of 1 to 10, with 10 being perfect?

Professional Writing

The Ghetto Made Me Do It

Francis Flaherty

> *This essay by freelance author Francis Flaherty was first published in* In These Times, *a biweekly magazine from Chicago.*

1   When Felicia "Lisa" Morgan was growing up, her parents would sit down to meals with guns next to their plates. They were defending themselves—against each other.

2   "This was Lisa's dinner," explains attorney Robin Shellow. "She was seven at the time."

3   If nothing else, Lisa Morgan's childhood in a poor, inner-city Milwaukee neighborhood starkly illustrates the tragic effects of omnipresent urban violence. "Mom shot dad," Shellow says. "And Mom shot boyfriend. . . . [Lisa's] uncle, who was actually her age, was murdered. Two days later, her other uncle was murdered. Her sister's boyfriend was paralyzed from the neck down by gunfire. Her brother was shot at and injured. Her mother once had set her father on fire."

4   If this weren't enough tragedy in one young life, Lisa Morgan's mother was a drug addict and Lisa was raped at age 12.

The "Ghetto Defense"

5   So perhaps it's not too surprising that Morgan, as a teenager, committed six armed robberies and one intentional homicide in the space of 17 minutes in October 1991. The victims were girls; the stolen objects were jewelry, shoes and a coat. The dead girl was shot at point-blank range.

6   What *is* surprising—to the legal establishment, at least— is the approach Robin Shellow used in defending Morgan. In the girl's neighborhood and in her family, Shellow argued, violence is a *norm*, an occurrence so routine that Morgan's 17 years of exposure to it have rendered her not responsible for her actions.

7   This "ghetto defense" proved fruitless in Morgan's case. In court, the young woman was found both sane and guilty. Unless Shellow wins on appeal, Morgan will be behind bars well into [this] century.

8   But despite its failure for Morgan, Shellow's "cultural psychosis" or "psychosocial history" strategy has taken hold. "I've gotten hundreds of calls from interested attorneys," Shellow says. Already, the defense is being floated in courtrooms around the nation. It's eliciting both enthusiasm and outrage.

The Defense Is a Medical One

9   Technically, Shellow's defense is a medical one. She believes that Morgan suffers from post traumatic stress disorder

(PTSD) and other psychological ailments stemming from her lifelong exposure to violence.

10   Like other good lawyers, Shellow knows that the law abhors broadly applicable excuses, so she emphasizes the narrowness of her claim. Morgan belongs to a very small group of inner-city residents with "tremendous intra-familial violence," only some of whom might experience PTSD. She also stresses the unrevolutionary nature of the defense, medically and legally. PTSD has been recognized as a malady in standard diagnostic texts since 1980, she says, and it has been employed as a criminal defense for Vietnam veterans, battered wives and many other trauma victims.

11   Despite Shellow's attempts to show that her defense is neither new nor broad, the case is ringing loud alarms. For, however viewed, her strategy sets up an inflammatory equation between inner-city conditions and criminal exculpation. The implication is that if you grew up in a poor, violent neighborhood and you commit a crime, you may go scot-free.

12   Yet why not a ghetto defense? After all, if a Vietnam veteran can claim PTSD from the shock of war, why shouldn't a similar defense be available for a young black reared in the embattled precincts of Bed-Stuy [Bedford-Stuyvesant neighborhood of New York City]? Sounds sensible, no? Isn't a ghetto like a battlefield?

Compare These Neighborhoods to War Zones

13   Alex Kotlowitz, who chronicled the lives of two Chicago black boys in *There Are No Children Here*, goes even further. He says the inner city can be worse than war. "You hear constant comparisons of these neighborhoods to war zones, but I think there's some pretty significant differences," he says. "In war, there's at least a sense that someday there will be a resolution, some vision that things could be different. That is not the case in the inner cities. There is no vision. And there's no sense of who's friend and who's foe."

14   There are other analogies that make the ghetto defense seem very legitimate. For instance, despite traditional self-defense principles, a battered wife in some jurisdictions can kill her sleeping husband and be legally excused for the homicide. The reason is the psychological harm she has sustained from her life of fear and violence.

15   Why not Lisa Morgan? Hasn't her life been debilitatingly violent and fearful?

16   These arguments make some lawyers hopeful about the future of Shellow's pioneering strategy. But most observers are pessimistic. "We'll get nowhere with it," says famous defense lawyer William Kunstler.

The Poor Instead of the Powerful

17   Why? One reason is that the American justice system often favors the powerful over the poor. For generations, for instance, the bloodiest crime in the nation—drunk driving—was punished with a relative wrist slap. By contrast, a recent federal law mandates that those convicted of the new crime of carjacking get socked with a minimum and mandatory 15-year sentence.

18   What explains these disparate approaches? Simple: protection of the affluent classes. Light penalties for drunk driving protect the affluent because they often drive drunk. Harsh carjacking penalties protect the affluent because they are the usual carjacking victims. "The middle class sees carjacking [laws] as protecting them from people coming out of some poor neighborhood and just showing up in *their* neighborhood and committing a crime in which they are at risk of dying," says Professor James Liebman of Columbia University School of Law.

19   Because the ghetto defense protects the poor instead of the powerful, Kunstler and others doubt it has a bright future. Other factors further dim the strategy's chances. Fear is a main one, says Professor Liebman. The ghetto defense brings a gulp from jurors because "their first thought is, 'If he's not responsible, then none of those people are,'" he reasons. And we all know what that means: riots, mayhem, Los Angeles.

20   Social guilt raises even higher the hurdles for the ghetto defense. To allow such a defense is a tacit admission that we—society—tolerate a situation so hobbling that its victims have become unaccountable for their actions. "If it ain't them who's guilty, it's us," says Michael Dowd, director of the Pace University Battered Women's Justice Center in New York. And "it's just too horrific for us to accept responsibility, too horrific to say, 'I'm responsible for what happened in L.A.' We will be able to accept the [ghetto] defense at the same moment that we are seriously moved to eradicate the realities behind that defense."

21   What are the biggest criticisms of the ghetto defense? One focuses on the victim's identity. Battered spouses and battered children are accused of killing precisely those who hurt them. This endows the crime with a certain rough justice. But in a ghetto defense case, the victim is usually an innocent stranger.

22   Others, like Kotlowitz, worry that the ghetto defense might dislodge the cornerstone of our justice system: personal responsibility. "We have to be careful not to view people growing up in neighborhoods completely as victims; they are both victims and actors," he warns. "We can't absolve them from responsibility."

23   Lisa Morgan "went up to someone she didn't know, stole a jacket from her, and then just blew her away," he says. "There's no way as a society that we can excuse that. We can understand it, but we can't excuse it."

24   He raises a fundamental question. Everyone can point to scars from the past—alcoholic parents, tragic love, etc.—and claim exculpation. And if all are excused, who is responsible?

25   Another worry is diminished standards. "[The ghetto defense] lowers expectations," Kotlowitz continues. "It says, 'OK, I understand what you've been through, so it's OK to go out and hurt somebody.' And once you lower your expectations, particularly with kids, they will meet only those lower expectations."

A Disease Is a Disease

26   It's only fair to note that other criminal defenses also have these weaknesses. For instance, the victim of a PTSD-afflicted veteran is often an innocent passerby, and the battered-spouse doctrine certainly raises questions about personal responsibility and lowered expectations.

27   And if, as seems likely, some ghetto residents do have PTSD largely as a result of their living conditions, it's hard to see why this ailment should be exculpatory for veterans, say, but not for ghetto residents. After all, a disease is a disease, and how you got it is irrelevant.

28   How deep go the wounds from the ghetto? Here are two incidents in Morgan's life: "When Felicia was about 11, her mother put a knife to her throat and threatened to kill her," according to a psychologist's report in the case. "Felicia escaped by running into the basement, where she 'busted the lights out with my hand' so that her mother could not see her." Then, when

she was 12, the landlord attacked her. "Felicia fought him off by throwing hot grease onto him, but he finally subdued her, tied her hands to the bed, stuffed her mouth with a sock and raped her."

29   How does one live like this? Morgan gives a hint. "My ears be open," she told the psychologist, "even when I'm asleep."

30   This was a *child*. Society did nothing to stop these daily depredations upon her. While the legal propriety of the ghetto defense is an important question, the biggest question of all in this story has nothing to do with personal responsibility. It has to do with society's responsibility to poor children like Morgan. What does it say about our society that such a defense was conceived? How can things have come to this pass?

Exercise 3 Discussion and Critical Thinking

1. What writing pattern does Flaherty use in the first four paragraphs that serve as an introduction to her essay?

2. Which sentence in which paragraph contains the definition of *ghetto defense*?

3. Which sentence in which paragraph contains the best definition of *post-traumatic stress disorder* (PTSD)?

4. Does Attorney Robin Shellow argue that all poor people living in the ghetto be granted excuses for any crimes they commit? If not, what is she arguing?

5. How is Morgan's case arguably similar to and different from those of battered spouses?

6. How is Morgan's case arguably similar to those of certain Vietnam veterans with PTSD who committed homicide?

7. According to Alex Kotlowitz, how can the inner-city environment be worse than that of a war zone?

8. According to the ghetto defense, where does responsibility lie—with the person or with society?

9. What is your opinion of the ghetto defense?

10. If the ghetto defense has validity, should the concept be extended to anyone who has had extremely violent experiences—"Everyone can point to scars from the past—alcoholic parents, tragic love, etc." (paragraph 24)?

11. Imagine you were a juror judging Morgan's case. How would you have voted, and why?

Short Story

The Story of an Hour

Kate Chopin

> *The author of this famous story on love and marriage, Kate Chopin, was left a widow with six children at age thirty-two. Turning to writing seriously, she wrote stories set mainly in the Creole bayou country around New Orleans. Her independent thinking, especially about women's emotions, attracted a firestorm of critical attention to her novel* The Awakening, *and two collections of short stories,* Bayou Folk *and* A Night in Acadie, *and established her reputation.*

1   Knowing that Mrs. Mallard was afflicted with a heart trouble, great care was taken to break to her as gently as possible the news of her husband's death.

2   It was her sister Josephine who told her, in broken sentences, veiled hints that revealed in half concealing. Her husband's friend Richards was there, too, near her. It was he who had been in the newspaper office when intelligence of the railroad disaster was received, with Brently Mallard's name leading the list of "killed." He had only taken the time to assure himself of its truth by a second telegram, and had hastened to forestall any less careful, less tender friend in bearing the sad message.

3   She did not hear the story as many women have heard the same, with a paralyzed inability to accept its significance. She wept at once, with sudden, wild abandonment, in her sister's arms. When the storm of grief had spent itself she went to her room alone. She would have no one follow her.

4   There stood, facing the open window, a comfortable, roomy armchair. Into this she sank, pressed down by a physical exhaustion that haunted her body and seemed to reach into her soul.

5   She could see in the open square before her house the tops of trees that were all aquiver with the new spring life. The delicious breath of rain was in the air. In the street below a peddler was crying his wares. The notes of a distant song which some one was singing reached her faintly, and countless sparrows were twittering in the eaves.

6   There were patches of blue sky showing here and there through the clouds that had met and piled above the other in the west facing her window.

7   She sat with her head thrown back upon the cushion of the chair quite motionless, except when a sob came up into her throat and shook her, as a child who has cried itself to sleep continues to sob in its dreams.

8   She was young, with a fair, calm face, whose lines bespoke repression and even a certain strength. But now there was a dull stare in her eyes, whose gaze was fixed away off yonder on one of those patches of blue sky. It was not a glance of reflection, but rather indicated a suspension of intelligent thought.

9   There was something coming to her and she was waiting for it, fearfully. What was it? She did not know; it was too subtle and elusive to name. But she felt it, creeping out of the sky, reaching toward her through the sounds, the scents, the color that filled the air.

10   Now her bosom rose and fell tumultuously. She was beginning to recognize this thing that was approaching to possess her, and she was striving to beat it back with her will—as powerless as her two white slender hands would have been.

11   When she abandoned herself a little whispered word escaped her slightly parted lips. She said it over and over under her breath: "Free, free, free!" The vacant stare and the look of terror that had followed it went from her eyes. They stayed keen and bright. Her pulses beat fast, and the coursing blood warmed and relaxed every inch of her body.

12   She did not stop to ask if it were not a monstrous joy that held her. A clear and exalted perception enabled her to dismiss the suggestion as trivial.

13   She knew that she would weep again when she saw the kind, tender hands folded in death; the face that had never looked save with love upon her, fixed and gray and dead. But

she saw beyond that bitter moment a long procession of years to come that would belong to her absolutely. And she opened and spread her arms out to them in welcome.

14   There would be no one to live for during those coming years; she would live for herself. There would be no powerful will bending her in that blind persistence with which men and women believe they have a right to impose a private will upon a fellow-creature. A kind intention or a cruel intention made the act seem no less a crime as she looked upon it in that brief moment of illumination.

15   And yet she had loved him—sometimes. Often she had not. What did it matter! What could love, the unsolved mystery, count for in face of this possession of self assertion which she suddenly recognized as the strongest impulse of her being!

16   "Free! Body and soul free!" she kept whispering.

17   Josephine was kneeling before the closed door with her lips to the keyhole, imploring for admission. "Louise, open the door! I beg; open the door—you will make yourself ill. What are you doing, Louise? For heaven's sake open the door."

18   "Go away. I am not making myself ill." No; she was drinking in a very elixir of life through that open window.

19   Her fancy was running riot along those days ahead of her. Spring days, and summer days, and all sorts of days that would be her own. She breathed a quick prayer that life might be long. It was only yesterday she had thought with a shudder that life might be long.

20   She arose at length and opened the door to her sister's importunities. There was a feverish triumph in her eyes, and she carried herself unwittingly like a goddess of Victory. She clasped her sister's waist, and together they descended the stairs. Richards stood waiting for them at the bottom.

21   Some one was opening the door with a latchkey. It was Brently Mallard who entered, a little travel-stained, composedly carrying his grip-sack and umbrella. He had been far from the scene of accident, and did not even know there had been one. He stood amazed at Josephine's piercing cry; at Richards's quick motion to screen him from the view of his wife.

22   But Richards was too late.

23   When the doctors came they said she had died of heart disease—of joy that kills.

Exercise 4 Discussion and Critical Thinking

1. What is Mrs. Mallard's first reaction in hearing of her husband's death?

2. What is her second reaction?

3. Why hasn't she considered freedom before?

4. Did her husband love her? Did she love him?

5. Did he abuse her?

6. Is this story mainly about women's rights, freedom, or some other subject?

7. Why does Mrs. Mallard die?

∼ Topics for Essays of Cause and Effect

Reading-Based Writing Topics

For reading-based writing, include references to and quotations from the reading selection(s), and give credit to your sources. See Chapter 4 for additional discussion on reading-based writing.

"A Summary of 'Enough Is Enough'"

1. Write a reaction to Judge Judy's views in which you agree or disagree with her. You may use your own examples along with her reasoning as support of your opinions. Refer directly to the summary and use quotations.

"The Ghetto Made Me Do It"

2. In a reaction, write about one or more of the questions posed by the author:

   ▪ If under certain conditions a Vietnam veteran or a battered spouse can use post-traumatic stress disorder as a defense, then why cannot a brutalized product of the ghetto, such as Felicia Morgan, use the same or a similar defense?

- What is the role of personal responsibility in the commission of a crime, regardless of what the perpetrator has experienced?
- To what extent is society responsible when a person such as Felicia Morgan grows up under such horrific conditions?

Refer directly to the essay and use quotations from it. Evaluate the author's use of evidence, such as examples and comparisons.

Two Views on the Causes of Violence: "A Summary of 'Enough Is Enough'" and "The Ghetto Made Me Do It"

3. Write a reaction to the summary and the essay in which you include your interpretation of the views of each author and your reaction to the views. Explain why you side with the views or implied views of one author, Judge Judy or Francis Flaherty. Be specific.

"The Story of an Hour"

4. Write a two-part response. Concentrate on the main points in the story for the summary. In your separate reaction part, explain what killed Mrs. Mallard. Your interpretation may include some of the following points:

- She does not know how to reconcile freedom and marriage.
- Her emotional state regarding freedom is much more likely to be experienced by a woman than a man.
- Her husband would never have understood even if he had known her thoughts at the time of his return, and that is part of the problem.

Cross-Curricular Topic

5. From a class that you are taking or have taken, select a subject that is especially concerned with causes and effects and develop a topic. Begin by selecting an event, a situation, or a trend in the class content and make a list of the causes and effects; that procedure will almost immediately show you whether you have a topic you can discuss effectively. Class notes and textbooks can provide you with more specific information. If you use textbooks or other materials, give credit or make copies of the sources. Instructors across the campus may have suggestions for studies of cause and effect. Some areas for your search include history, political science, geology, astronomy, psychology, philosophy, sociology, business,

real estate, child development, education, fashion merchandising and design, psychiatric technician program, nursing, police science, fire science, nutrition and food, physical education, and restaurant and food-service management.

Career-Related Topics

6. Discuss the effects (benefits) of a particular product or service on the business community, family life, society generally, a specific group (age, income, interest), or an individual.
7. Discuss the needs (thus the cause of development) by individuals, families, or institutions for a particular product or type of product.
8. Discuss the effects of using a certain approach or philosophy in sales, human resources, or customer service.

General Topics

Regard each item in the following list as a subject (situation, circumstance, or trend) that has causes and effects. Then determine whether you will concentrate on causes, effects, or a combination. You can probably write a more interesting, well-developed, and therefore successful essay on a topic you can personalize. For example, a discussion about a specific young person who contemplated, attempted, or committed suicide is probably a better topic idea than a general discussion of suicide. If you do not personalize the topic, you will probably have to do some basic research to supply details for development.

9. Attending or completing college
10. Having or getting a specific job
11. Change in policy or administration
12. Change in coaches, teachers, or officeholder(s)
13. Alcoholism
14. Gambling
15. Moving to another country, state, or home
16. Passing or failing a test or course
17. Popularity of a certain television program or song
18. Teenage parenthood

Writer's Guidelines at a Glance: Cause and Effect

1. Determine whether your topic should mainly inform or mainly persuade, and use the right tone for your purpose and audience.
2. Use listing to brainstorm cause-and-effect ideas. This is a useful form:

Causes	Event, Situation, or Trend	Effects

3. Decide whether to concentrate on causes, effects, or a combination of causes and effects. Many short essays will discuss causes and effects but will use one as the framework for the piece. A typical basic outline might look like this:

> Thesis:
>
> I. Cause (or Effect) 1
> II. Cause (or Effect) 2
> III. Cause (or Effect) 3

4. Do not conclude that something is an effect merely because it follows something else.
5. Emphasize your main concern(s)—causes, effects, or a combination—by repeating key words, such as *cause, reason, effect, result, consequence,* and *outcome.*
6. Causes and effects can be primary or secondary, immediate or remote.
7. The order of causes and effects in your essay may be based on time, space, emphasis, or a combination.
8. Consider using CLUESS for revision and COPS for editing.

10

Comparison and Contrast: Showing Similarities and Differences

∿ Writing Essays of Comparison and Contrast

Comparison and contrast is a method of showing similarities and dissimilarities between subjects. Comparison is concerned with organizing and developing points of similarity; contrast has the same function for dissimilarity. Sometimes a writing assignment may require that you cover only similarities or only dissimilarities. Occasionally, an instructor may ask you to separate one from the other. Usually, you will combine them within the larger design of your paragraph or essay. For convenience, the term *comparison* is sometimes applied to both comparison and contrast, because both use the same techniques and are usually combined into one operation.

This chapter will help you find topics and choose strategies in writing comparison and contrast.

Generating Topics and Working with the 4 *P*'s

Comparison and contrast is basic to your thinking. In your daily activities, you consider similarities and dissimilarities between persons, things, concepts, political leaders, doctors, friends, instructors, schools, nations, classes, movies, and so on. You naturally turn to comparison and contrast to solve problems and to make decisions in your actions and in your writing. Because you have had so many comparative experiences, finding a topic to write

168

about is likely to be only a matter of choosing from a great number of appealing ideas. Freewriting, brainstorming, and clustering will help you generate topics that are especially workable and appropriate for particular assignments.

Many college writing assignments will specify a topic or ask you to choose one from a list. Regardless of the source of your topic, the procedure for developing your ideas by comparison and contrast is the same as the procedure for developing topics of your own choosing. That procedure can be appropriately called the "4 P's": *purpose, points, pattern,* and *presentation.*

Purpose

Purpose indicates what you want to accomplish. Are you trying just to give information about the two parts of your subject, showing how they are similar and dissimilar; or are you trying to argue that one side is better than the other, therefore, ranking the two?

For this unit of instruction, the demonstration paragraph and essay were written by Brittany Markovic when she was a student pilot in the Aeronautics Department at Mt. San Antonio College. Her English instructor provided her with a topic of comparison and contrast about two aspects of something within her intended career field. Markovic selected two training aircraft she had flown: the Piper Cherokee and the Cessna 172. Her purpose was to show that one is better than the other for the beginning pilot.

Points

After you determine your purpose, you might brainstorm by listing the points, or ideas, that can be applied somewhat equally to the two parts of your subject. From such a list, you would then select the points that would be most relevant for your purpose.

Here is Brittany Markovic's list for her topic of ranking the Piper Cherokee and the Cessna 172. Notice that she first lists possible points and then selects the ones that relate most directly to her central idea of safety inherent in the features of the two airplanes.

(power)	(design)	landing gear
cabin space	affordability	(fuel system)
air frame	communication devices	steering controls

Pattern

You will now decide on the better way to organize the points as you apply them somewhat equally to the twin parts of your topic: subject by subject or point by point. You will use the same information in each pattern, but the pattern, or organization, will be different.

The **subject-by-subject pattern** presents all of one side and then all of the other.

I. Piper Cherokee
   A. Power
   B. Design
   C. Fuel system
II. Cessna 172
   A. Power
   B. Design
   C. Fuel system

The **point-by-point pattern** shows one point in relation to the sides (subjects) one at a time. This pattern (the one chosen by Brittany Markovic) is used more frequently. In organizing her essay, she included Arabic numerals with supporting information in phrases, such as examples, details, and explanations.

I. Power
   A. Piper Cherokee
   B. Cessna 172
II. Design
   A. Piper Cherokee
   B. Cessna 172
III. Fuel system
   A. Piper Cherokee
   B. Cessna 172

Presentation

Here you would use your outline (or cluster list), to begin writing your essay. The Roman numerals in the outline usually indicate topic sentences, and, therefore, paragraphs. The Arabic numerals (details, examples, explanations) become more specific support. Brittany Markovic's essay is on pages 173–176.

Transitional Words for Improving Coherence

- **FOR COMPARISON AND CONTRAST: Comparison:** *in the same way, similarly, likewise, also, by comparison, in a like manner, as, with, as though, both, like, just as*

- **Contrast:** *but, by contrast, in contrast, despite, however, instead, nevertheless, on (to) the contrary, in spite of, still, yet, unlike, even so, rather than, otherwise*

Career-Related Writing as Comparison and Contrast

When "Either-Or" Matters

Imagine you are on a career quest and you have narrowed vocational fields to two. What is your next step? Naturally you will turn to comparing and contrasting. Or imagine you are at your workplace and you have to decide between two products, two services, two management styles, two labor issues, or two employees for advancement. What pattern of thought does your mind shift to? Of course, again it is comparison and contrast.

Using the 4 *P*'s System for Speaking and Writing

If your mind sometimes drifts around—going back and forth, up and down, sideways and other ways—as you compare and contrast, then the ideas that come out of your mouth or your computer printer will be jumbled. If, however, you have a system—say, the 4 *P*'s, with purpose, points, pattern, and presentation—you will have order, and you can avoid needless repetition, overlooked ideas, and wandering thoughts. In both the written and the oral presentation, the 4 *P*'s will provide order and a logical arrangement of ideas. The kind of outline you use in writing serves you equally well in speaking, especially as a framework for PowerPoint presentations. You need only consider your audience, organize your thoughts according to your system, and proceed to communicate. Should this be a competitive situation, you will not be the one left coughing in the winner's trail of dust.

The 4 *P*'s as an Academic Gift That Is Portable

In the example shown in the demonstration essay on pages 173–176, in which she evaluates the Piper Cherokee and the Cessna 172, student Brittany Markovic writes about aircraft she has flown in a community college aeronautics program. She may continue to fly those models when she moves into her career as a pilot. Her writing is a product comparison. It is a good model for an employee writing a comparative study for the lease or purchase of any vehicle—such as a pickup, an SUV, or a forklift. But with little modification it could be a comparison and contrast of two products that are sold or used at a workplace. Markovic was in school when she wrote her essay, but she could just as easily have been already working in aeronautics and studying the same thing concurrently in her college class.

Moreover, the 4 *P*'s system that Markovic employs can be used both in college career-related areas of study and at the workplace, because it fits so many different situations and needs. This flexible, systematic way for organizing ideas is an academic gift that just keeps on giving as you use it in the classroom, use it at your job, and perhaps use it repeatedly for training and retraining, maybe even at the same college.

The same outline used in writing an essay can be used at the workplace in a PowerPoint presentation or for bullet points in an oral presentation or a memo.

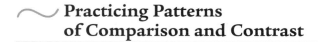

Practicing Patterns of Comparison and Contrast

Exercise 1 Practicing Patterns

Fill in the blanks in the following outlines to complete the comparisons and contrasts.

Point-by-Point Pattern

Before and after marriage

    I. Way of talking (content and manner)

        A. _____

        B. Henry: After

II. _____

   A. Henry: Before

   B. Henry: After

III. _____

   A. Henry: Before

   B. _____

Subject-by-Subject Pattern

Two SUVs: Cadillac Escalade and Toyota Sequoia (with year to be more specific)

  I. Cadillac Escalade

    A. Horsepower and gears

    B. _____

    C. Cargo area

 II. Toyota Sequoia

    A. _____

    B. Safety

    C. _____

〜 Examining Essays of Comparison and Contrast

Student Career-Related Writing

The Piper Cherokee and the Cessna 172

Brittany Markovic

As a student pilot and a student in a community college, Brittany Markovic leads a life rich in variety and excitement. She rides to school in an automobile, but her mind is in the skies where she flies training aircraft. This comparison-and-contrast assignment provided her with an opportunity to compare and contrast two aircraft often used in training student pilots for careers.

1   When most people think of an airplane,
the picture that comes to mind is likely that
of a large aircraft such as a Boeing 747.
Commercial airlines are what the public is
most familiar with, for that is what
travelers ordinarily use for long-distance
transportation. However, most business
handled by airplanes—in fact, about
80 percent of all flights—is done by small
planes in what is called general aviation.
When a student pilot thinks of an airplane,
it is probably a small training plane, the
Subject 1 Cessna 172. Later, the student's attention
may turn to another small aircraft, the Piper
Subject 2 Cherokee. Although either can be used for
Thesis and training, <u>I believe that certain features</u>
purpose <u>make the Cessna 172 the better aircraft for</u>
<u>the student</u>.

2   <u>For the student at the controls, two key</u>
Topic sentence <u>characteristics probably come to mind, all</u>
I. Power <u>related to movement, namely the power for</u>
(Point 1) <u>thrust and the landing speed</u>. In all those
Point-by-point respects, the two aircraft are similar. The
Pattern Piper Cherokee must have enough thrust to
A. Piper lift a maximum of 2,350 pounds at takeoff,
Cherokee for which it has 150 horsepower. Then in
landing, the Cherokee should come in at
B. Cessna 172 63 knots. The Cessna 172 has similar ratings:
it can lift 2,400 pounds, has 160 horsepower,
and lands at a speed between 60 and 70 knots.
All of those factors should be considered in
relation to the particular flight. The
maximum weight matters little in training
flights because they are made without extra
passengers and baggage. The landing speeds
for the two are also about the same and

nonconsequential. The only significant matter is found in the power plant, which favors the Cessna 172 by 10 horsepower, small but in some situations crucial.

3

Topic sentence
II. Design
(Point 2)
A. Piper
Cherokee

That power and speed, of course, must be seen in relation to the design of the aircraft, especially the wing placement. For the Piper Cherokee, the wing is mounted below the cockpit. That design allows for great visibility above the aircraft, which, in turn, is better for observing other aircraft and certain weather conditions. The big problem for the student pilot is that the wing-under arrangement partially blocks the pilot's view of the runway. On the contrary,

B. Cessna 172

the Cessna 172 features a wing over the fuselage, providing the new pilot with a much appreciated better view of the runway. That design allows the student pilot to more easily master the two most difficult maneuvers: taking off and landing.

4

Topic sentence
III. Fuel
System
(Point 3)
A. Piper
Cherokee

Another point to consider seriously is the fuel system, for the new pilot has enough things to take care of without having to worry about getting gas to the carburetor. In the wing-under Piper Cherokee, the tanks are in the wing, but because the wings are lower than the engine, the fuel must be pushed to the engine by a fuel pump, and a fuel pump may not work. But that possible problem does

B. Cessna 172

not exist in the high-wing Cessna 172. It also has its gas tank in the wing; however, because the wing is above the engine, gravity delivers fuel to the carburetor without need of a pump. When it comes to airplanes, less

may be more. We all know that gravity is more
reliable than a fuel pump.

5   The first features, the *power for thrust*
and the *landing speed, give* the *Cessna 172*
only a *slight edge over the Piper Cherokee.*
But the other two factors are decisive.
Better visibility for takeoffs and landings

Cessna 172 better than Piper Cherokee
afforded by the high wing and gas delivered
by gravity make the Cessna 172 the better
aircraft for student pilots.

Professional Writing

From B'wood to the 'Hood

Ryan J. Smith

> Los Angeles Times *researcher, Ryan J. Smith writes about living on the different sides of town: South Los Angeles and the West-side. His relocation is more than geography. This article was pub-lished in the* Los Angeles Times *on February 19, 2006.*

1   When I broke the news to my mother that I was moving from Brentwood to the 'hood, she immediately began praying for my protection. When I told friends and colleagues at work of my planned move toward South L.A., they would pause and whisper, "Oh." Not just any "Oh," mind you, but one freighted with "Good luck, hope you don't get shot." Strangers thought I was living out the pilgrimage of a young black man who, after a stint on the "outside," was returning to his roots.

2   That couldn't be further from the truth. I was raised by my mother in Culver City before it became "on the Westside." I at-tended UCLA and settled in Brentwood after graduation. But I needed to escape a bad roommate situation, and my father, separated from my mom, offered me his vacant apartment near Jefferson Park in the Crenshaw district.

3   At first I thought I couldn't survive a move south. I'd tried the 'hood in the early 1990s, when the movie "Malcolm X" came out and my mother decided I needed to know "my people." So I bypassed my usual summer YMCA experience for a camp close to Baldwin Village known as "the Jungles" because of the rampant gang activity nearby. I was called everything in the book.

"Why do you talk so white, white boy?" was a frequent question as I was being punched. At night, I cried, but I never told Mom about my camp experiences. One day, though, she coyly smiled and asked, "Black folks sure can be mean, can't they?"

4   Older, more culturally aware and growing ever more desperate to leave Brentwood, I decided to face my childhood demons and take my father up on his offer. The area seemed no different than other urban landscapes in Los Angeles. But adjustments needed to be made. I soon got used to the nighttime "ghetto-birds" (helicopters) that plagued the community, and the annoying chime of ice cream trucks that made their neighborhood rounds at midnight. To better fit in, I walked around with a no-nonsense 'hood face—which only made it more obvious that I was not from the neighborhood.

5   "Why did you do that, baby? You have to make sure all your doors are locked!" Aunt Cathy playfully chided me when I told her I didn't regularly lock my car. Note to self: Lock everything! My parents also reminded me of the do's and don'ts when (not if) the police pulled me over. Their advice came in handy one Halloween night when two officers cuffed me and put me in the back of a squad car while they scanned my nonexistent record. Only my embarrassing temptation to blurt out that I grew up on the Westside contained my rage.

6   More discomfiting than the dangers I have to be wary of are the conveniences I miss. I yearn for Jamba Juice and La Salsa—anything but Jack in the Box or McDonald's. A privilege I took for granted—anytime access to an ATM—ends after 10 p.m. on Crenshaw Boulevard. Nighttime jogging is also out in my new neighborhood. But the Magic Johnson Theatre at Baldwin Hills Crenshaw Plaza is as good as the Century City Cineplex. The smothered chicken and greens at Chef Marilyn's 99-Cents-and-Up Soul Food Express makes me quickly forget the lack of sushi eateries nearby. My neighbors ask how my family and I are doing, a social custom rare on the Westside.

7   I also have become reacquainted with my younger half-brother, who lives nearby. After being shot in a gang altercation, he speaks of his struggle to stay off the streets. His dreams are often tarnished by his quest to avoid jail, drugs and death—a story I hear from too many young men his age.

8   Far more consequential, my color is not what defines me. I'm not seen as a tall black guy, lanky black man or the loud black dude. No woman clutches her purse when she sees me

approaching. No walker quickens his step when I am spotted behind him. No one rushes to open a door when I walk down a hall. In my mostly black and Latino neighborhood, my race is no longer a prelude to my being.

9   I don't ache for the conveniences and glamour of my former "home." I drink coffee in Leimert Park. I cruise Crenshaw Boulevard instead of Pacific Coast Highway, enjoying the comforts of my newfound home—doors locked, of course.

Exercise 2 Discussion and Critical Thinking

1. What is Smith's subject of this comparison and contrast?

2. What is his purpose?

3. Does Smith use a point-by-point or a subject-by-subject pattern?

4. What points does he use for his comparison and contrast?

5. In his conclusion (last paragraph), does Smith seem to prefer the Westside or South Los Angeles for a home neighborhood? Discuss.

A Mixed Tex-Cal Marriage

José Antonio Burciaga

> *A distinguished publisher and writer, José Antonio Burciaga died in 1996, leaving his readers a rich legacy of poems, short stories, and essays. He was a Chicano cultural activist, muralist, humorist, and founding member of the comedy group Culture Clash. His* Undocumented Love *won the Before Columbus American Book Award for poetry in 1992. This essay, about him and his wife, is included in his book* Drink Cultura *(1993).*

1   According to Cecilia, my wife, we have a mixed marriage. She's from California, I'm from Texas. Though we have no regrets, this truly proves that love is blind.

2   When Cecilia and I first met, we thought we had a lot in common. As young, professional Chicanos in Washington, D.C., we both supported the United Farm Workers' grape and lettuce boycotts, the Coors boycott, the Gallo Wine boycott, the Farah

Pants boycott, and the Frito Bandito boycott. We still boycott some of those items, for many reasons: health, habit, nostalgia or plain, ordinary guilt if we indulged in any of these.

3   As first-generation Mexican-Americans, we both spoke *Español*, graduated from Catholic schools, and had similar politics.

4   But, as we were soon to discover, the vast desert that separates Texas and California also differentiates the culture and style of Chicanos. Because we met far from Texas and California, we had no idea at first of the severity of our differences.

5   We both liked enchiladas—the same enchiladas, I thought, until the first time Cecilia prepared them. They looked like enchiladas, and they smelled like enchiladas. And then I bit into one.

6   "These are good, *corazón*," I said. "But these are *entomatadas*. They have more tomato than chili. *Mí Mamá* used to make them all the time."

7   She threw me a piquant stare as I chewed away. "Hmmm, they're great!" I stressed through a mouthful.

8   Californians, like her parents who emigrated from the coastal state of Jalisco, Mexico, use more tomatoes than Texans like my parents, who came from the central states of Durango and Zacatecas and use more chilis.

9   Cecilia grew up with white *menudo*, tripe soup. White menudo? How could anyone eat colorless menudo? And not put hominy in it? Ours was red-hot and loaded with hominy. In Texas, we ate our menudo with bread. In California, it's with tortillas. Texas flour tortillas are thick and tasty, California flour tortillas are so thin you can see through them.

10   She didn't particularly like my Tony Lama boots or my country-western and Tex-Mex musical taste. I wasn't that crazy about Beach Boys music or her progressive, California-style country-western.

11   In California, the beach was relatively close for Cecilia. On our first date she asked how often I went to the beach from El Paso. Apparently, geography has never been a hot subject in California schools. That's understandable considering the sad state of education, especially geography, in this country. But in Texas, at one time the biggest state in the union, sizes and distances are most important.

12   In answer to Cecilia's question, I explained that to get to the closest beach from El Paso, I had to cross New Mexico, Arizona

and California to reach San Diego. That's 791 freeway miles. The closest Texas beach is 841 freeway miles to the Gulf of Mexico.

13   Back when we were courting, California Chicanos saw *Texanos* as a little too *Mexicano*, still wet behind the ears, not assimilated enough, and speaking with either thick Spanish accents or "Taxes acksaints."

14   Generally speaking, Texanos saw their *Califas* counterparts as too weird, knowing too little if any Spanish and with speech that was too Anglicized.

15   After our marriage we settled in neutral Alexandria, Virginia, right across the Potomac from the nation's capital. We lived there a couple of years, and when our firstborn came, we decided to settle closer to home. But which home, Califas or Texas? In El Paso we wouldn't be close to the beach, but I thought there was an ocean of opportunity in that desert town. There was some Texas pride and machismo, to be sure. It was a tug-of-war that escalated to the point of seeking advice, and eventually I had to be realistic and agree that California had better opportunities. In El Paso, the opportunities in my field were nonexistent.

16   The rest is relative bliss. Married since 1972, I'm totally spoiled and laid-back in Northern Califas, but I still miss many of those things we took for granted in Texas, or Washington, D.C.—the seasonal changes, the snow, the heat, heating systems, autumn colors, and monsoon rains; the smell of the desert after a rain, the silence and serenity of the desert, the magnified sounds of a fly or cricket, distant horizons uncluttered by trees, and the ability to find the four directions without any problem. I do miss the desert and, even more, the food. El Paso *is* the Mexican-food capital of this country.

17   Today, I like artichokes and appreciate a wide variety of vegetables and fruits. I even like white, colorless menudo and hardly ever drink beer. I drink wine, but it has to be a dry Chardonnay or Fume Blanc although a Pinot Noir or Cabernet Sauvignon goes great with meals. Although I still yearn for an ice cold Perla or Lone Star beer from Texas once in a while, Califas is my home now—mixed marriage and all.

Exercise 3 Discussion and Critical Thinking

1. Which sentence states the thesis most emphatically (see paragraph 1)? Copy it here.

2. In paragraphs 6 through 15, what are the three points used for comparison and contrast?

3. In paragraphs 16 and 17, Burciaga discusses how he has changed. In what ways does that imply comparison and contrast?

4. Because all of us are culturally complex, being the products of many cultures, we frequently blend and clash with others in matters of age, ethnicity, gender, sexual preferences, religion, and so on. As for the broad concept of "mixed marriage," were Cecilia and José fairly typical compared with other marriage partners you know? Do you have some examples of those more extreme and less extreme? You might also discuss this topic in connection with friendships you have or know about.

～ Topics for Essays of Comparison and Contrast

Reading-Based Writing Topics

For reading-based writing, include references to and quotations from the reading selection(s), and give credit to your sources. See Chapter 4 for additional discussion on reading-based writing.

"From B'wood to the 'Hood"

1. If you have lived in two different (culturally, economically, socially) parts of a city and struggled with your own adjustments, write about those experiences. Consider trailer-park units and townhouses, company houses and private neighborhoods, barrios and places like Smith's Westside, apartment buildings and private homes, and car or camper living and house living. For a reading-based essay, refer to and quote from the article by Smith to connect his insights with yours, in either agreement or disagreement.

2. Write a two-part response to Smith's essay. Separate your summary from your reaction in which you evaluate his views or relate them to your own experiences. Use quotations and direct references.

"A Mixed Tex-Cal Marriage"

3. Using the structural points and insights of this essay for direction, write about a marriage or relationship between two individuals who are significantly different from each other. Consider making a list of their possible differences (such as religion; education; country, regional, city, or suburban background; politics; ethnicity; and preferences for food, activities, or behavior). In your discussion, do not overlook the common characteristics that have brought and kept them together, and briefly discuss how each person has compromised. Explain how your subject couple is different from and similar to Burciaga and his wife. Use references and quotations.

4. Write a two-part response to Burciaga's essay. In your reaction, explain how Burciaga makes a powerful and colorful statement that does much to counteract the stereotyping of ethnic groups, saying in effect, "He's just like the rest of us." Document it. In your discussion consider referring to people you know.

Cross-Curricular Topics

5. In the fields of nutritional science and health, compare and contrast two diets, two exercise programs, or two pieces of exercise equipment.

6. Compare and contrast your field of study (or one aspect of it) as it existed some time ago (specify the years) and as it is now. Refer to new developments and discoveries, such as scientific breakthroughs and technological advances.

Career-Related Topics

7. Select two businesses, two pieces of work-related equipment (such as a vehicle, computer, appliance, and so on) and write an essay to show that one is better. Support should come from your experience, independent judgment, and, perhaps, from the Internet or library sources. Use points that apply somewhat equally to both sides of your comparison and contrast. You will see that those are the same kinds of points that would be used

as talking points for a PowerPoint presentation at the workplace or bulleted items for a talk or memo. For a helpful model for form, review the essay on the Piper Cherokee and the Cessna 172 on pages 173–176.

8. Compare and contrast two products or services, with the purpose of showing that one is better.

9. Compare and contrast two management styles or two working styles.

10. Compare and contrast two career fields to show that one is better for you.

11. Compare and contrast a public school and a business.

12. Compare and contrast an athletic team and a business.

General Topics

The following topics refer to general subjects. Provide specific names and detailed information as you develop your ideas by using the 4 *P*'s (purpose, points, patterns, and presentation).

13. Using Markovic's essay as a model, compare and contrast two other vehicles to show that one is better than the other for particular needs or purposes (everyday driving, certain kinds of work or recreation, making a good impression on peers). Use the Internet or library sources to collect specific information. Give credit to your source(s).

14. Using Markovic's essay as a model, compare any other two products to show that one is better or more useful for a particular need or purpose. Give specific information.

15. Musical styles

16. Romantic attachments

17. Sitcoms

18. Businesses (selling the same product)

19. Methods of disciplining children

20. Courage and recklessness

21. Relatives

22. Jobs you have held

23. Passive student and active student

24. Weddings

25. Neighborhoods

26. Actors or other performers

Writer's Guidelines at a Glance: Comparison and Contrast

1. Work with the 4 *P*'s:

   - **Purpose:** Decide whether you want to inform (show relationships) or to persuade (show that one side is better).
   - **Points:** Decide which ideas you will apply to each side.
   - **Patterns:** Decide whether to use subject-by-subject or point-by-point organization.
   - **Presentation:** Decide to what extent you should develop your ideas. Be sure to use cross-references to make connections and to use examples and details to support your views.

2. Your basic subject-by-subject outline will probably look like this:

   I. Subject 1
      A. Point 1
      B. Point 2
   II. Subject 2
      A. Point 1
      B. Point 2

3. Your basic point-by-point outline will probably look like this:

   I. Point 1
      A. Subject 1
      B. Subject 2
   II. Point 2
      A. Subject 1
      B. Subject 2

4. Consider using CLUESS for revision and COPS for editing.

11

Definition:
Clarifying Terms

~ Writing Essays of Definition

Most definitions are short; they consist of a **synonym** (a word that has the same meaning as the term to be defined), a phrase, or a sentence. For example, we might say that a hypocrite is a person "professing beliefs or virtues he or she does not possess." Terms can also be defined by **etymology**, or word history. *Hypocrite* once meant "actor" (*hypocrites*) in Greek because an actor was pretending to be someone else. We may find this information interesting and revealing, but the history of a word may be of no use because the meaning has changed drastically over the years. Sometimes definitions occupy a paragraph or an entire essay. The short definition is called a **simple definition**; the longer one is known as an **extended definition**.

Techniques for Development

Essays of definition can take many forms. Among the more common techniques for writing an essay of definition are the patterns we have worked with in previous chapters. Consider each of those patterns when you need to write an extended definition. For a particular term, some forms will be more useful than others; use the pattern or patterns that best fulfill your purpose.

Each of the following questions takes a pattern of writing and directs it toward definition.

- **Narration:** Can I tell an anecdote or a story to define this subject (such as *jerk*, *humanitarian*, or *patriot*)? This form may overlap with description and exemplification.
- **Description:** Can I describe this subject (such as *a whale* or *the moon*)?

- **Exemplification:** Can I give examples of this subject (such as naming individuals, to provide examples of *actors, diplomats,* or *satirists*)?
- **Analysis by division:** Can I divide this subject into parts (for example, the parts of a *heart, cell,* or *carburetor*)?
- **Process analysis:** Can I define this subject (such as *lasagna, tornado, hurricane, blood pressure,* or any number of scientific processes) by describing how to make it or how it occurs? (Common to the methodology of communicating in science, this approach is sometimes called the "operational definition.")
- **Cause and effect:** Can I define this subject (such as *a flood, a drought, a riot,* or *a cancer*) by its causes and effects?
- **Classification:** Can I group this subject (such as kinds of *families, cultures, religions,* or *governments*) into classes?

Subject	Class	Characteristics
A republic	is a form of government	in which power resides in the people (the electorate).

- **Comparison and contrast:** Can I define this subject (such as *extremist* or *patriot*) by explaining what it is similar to and different from? If you are defining *orangutan* to a person who has never heard of one but is familiar with the gorilla, then you could make comparison-and-contrast statements. If you want to define *patriot*, you might want to stress what it is not (the contrast) before you explain what it is: a patriot is not a one-dimensional flag waver, not someone who hates "foreigners" because America is always right and always best.

When you use prewriting strategies to develop ideas for a definition, you can effectively consider all the patterns you have learned by using a modified clustering form. Put a double bubble around the subject to be defined. Then put a single bubble around the patterns and add appropriate words. If a pattern is not relevant to what you are defining, leave it blank. If you want to expand your range of information, you could add a bubble for a simple dictionary definition and another for an etymological definition. The following bubble cluster shows how a term could be defined using different essay patterns.

Order

The organization of your extended definition is likely to be one of emphasis, but it may be space or time, depending on the subject material. You may use just one pattern of development for the

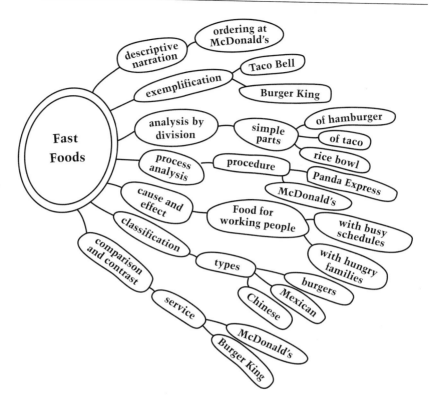

overall sequence. Use the principles of organization discussed in previous chapters.

Transitional Words for Improving Coherence

- **FOR DEFINITION:** *originates from, means, derives from, refers to, for example, as a term, as a concept, label, similar to, different from, in a particular context, in common usage, in historical context*

Introduction and Development

Consider these ways of introducing a definition: with a question, with a statement of what it is not, with a statement of what it originally meant, or with a discussion of why a clear definition is important. You may use a combination of these ways or all of them before you continue with your definition.

Development, whether in the form of sentences for the paragraph or of paragraphs for the essay, is likely to represent one or more of the patterns of narration, description, analysis (also called exposition), and argumentation.

Whether you personalize a definition depends on your purpose and your audience. Your instructor may ask you to write about a word within the context of your experience or to write about it from a detached, clinical viewpoint.

⌒ Practicing Patterns of Definition

Exercise 1 Completing Patterns

Fill in the following double bubble with a term to be defined. You might want to define culturally diverse society, educated person, leader, role model, friend, puppy love, true love, success, *or* intelligence. *Then fill in at least one more bubble on the right for each essay pattern. If the pattern does not apply (that is, if it would not provide useful information for your definition), mark it NA ("not applicable").*

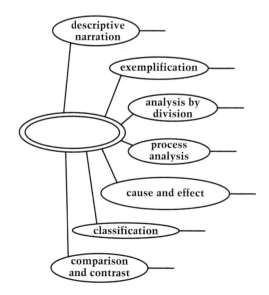

⌒ Examining Essays of Definition

Student Writing

Modern Mother

Marie Maxwell

After having read numerous articles about women who are now free to pursue careers, Marie Maxwell reflected on her own situation. Her conclusion is that her situation is more typical than those she has read about. She wishes that were not true.

Background

1   The modern mother, according to dozens of magazine articles, is a super being of incredible organization, patience, wisdom, and grooming. She is never cross with loved ones and never too tired for a game with her children. She wouldn't think of throwing a frozen dinner into the oven and calling it supper. She even has the courage (and the cleaning skills) to own a white carpet. She is a being apart, and I could never quite

Thesis

measure up. <u>I believed that, until I recently decided there were far more women like me than there were Wonder Women.</u>

2   The ideal mother featured in the magazines has a lovely home, a handsome husband, and children who at all times appear to have just stepped from the pages of a clothing catalog. Her house is always clean and ready for drop-in guests, and should these guests arrive at supper time, so much

Contrast

the better. <u>My reality is a single-parent home.</u> I have a son who I suspect is <u>colorblind</u>, judging from some of his outfits. Often when I return home from work, I must

Examples

step carefully to avoid the <u>assortment of books, clothes, and toys strewn from one room</u>

to the next. Unexpected company better not
show up! As for feeding uninvited guests—they
had better have an invitation if they expect
to be fed.

3   Unlike me, the mothers in the articles
always seem to have glamorous and exciting
jobs. Most of them receive six-figure incomes
and love their jobs (oops!) *careers.* They are
fashion designers, doctors, or managers on

Examples   their way up the corporate ladder. Every
working day is another fascinating challenge
to anticipate. I sigh wistfully as I read,
and I think how dull my secretarial duties

Contrast   are by comparison. I've received two
promotions in eight years—hardly a mercurial
rise to the top. I generally enjoy my job; it
pays the bills and a little bit more, and it

Effects   has enough variety to prevent abysmal
boredom. It's just that I feel somehow shamed
by the way I earn my living after reading an
article about the "new woman."

4   Most magazine writers choose as a subject
a mother who has also returned to school, in
addition to everything else she does. It
depresses me to read that she has usually
earned a 3.80 grade point average, seemingly
effortlessly. Her family cheers her on and
never seems to mind the time that school and
homework demand from her. Even more
disheartening is that her family members
report with pride that she was able to make
those grades without depriving them of their

Contrast   normal family life. That certainly hasn't
Example   been my experience. Algebra, for example,
demanded so much of my time and energy that
bitter words and sarcasm were routine in my

household. When I was married, my husband was supportive only as long as my classes didn't disrupt his life.

5   Some modern mothers may indeed be just as they are described in the magazines, but I feel certain that there are many more just like me. My wish would be to have a writer showcase a woman, if not with feet of clay, at least shuffling her way artlessly through a cluttered life and, at times, barely coping. I might not admire her, but I wouldn't feel inadequate, and I'm certain I could identify with her. In fact, I think I would like her.

Professional Writing

Graffiti: Taking a Closer Look

Christopher Grant

First published as a cover story in the FBI Law Enforcement Bulletin, *this article is included as general-interest material in InfoTrac, a data service provider mainly for libraries. It offers a thorough analysis, but it also takes an argumentative position. See how it compares to your own views.*

1   Not long ago, the word *graffiti* conjured images of innocent messages, such as "Tom loves Jane," or "Class of '73." Such simple and innocuous scribblings, although occasionally still seen, have become essentially messages of the past. Most of the graffiti that mars contemporary American landscape—both urban and rural—contains messages of hatred, racism, and gang warfare. Public attitudes toward graffiti tend to fluctuate between indifference and intolerance. On a national level, the criminal justice system has yet to adopt a uniform response to graffiti and the individuals who create this so-called street art. While some jurisdictions combat the problem aggressively, others do very little or nothing at all to punish offenders or to deter the spread of graffiti.

2   To a large degree, society's inability to decide on a focused response to graffiti stems from the nature of the offense. It

could be argued that graffiti falls into the grey area between crime and public nuisance. If graffiti is considered in a vacuum, such an argument could appear to have some credence. However, it is unrealistic, and ultimately foolhardy, to view such a public offense in a vacuum. There is a growing consensus in communities around the country that the problem of graffiti, if left unaddressed, creates an environment where other more serious crimes flourish and can quickly degrade once low-crime areas. At a time when law enforcement agencies nationwide are adopting more community-based policing philosophies, administrators are exploring ways to address the basic factors that lead to crime and neighborhood decline. The time has come to take a closer look at graffiti.

Wall Writing

3   **Graffiti** is a general term for wall writing, perhaps humankind's earliest art form. The crude wall writings of prehistoric times and the highly stylized street art of today's inner-city youths share one common feature: Each stems from a basic human need to communicate with others. For youths who may not be able to express themselves through other media, such as prose or music, graffiti represents an easily accessible and effective way to communicate with a large audience. Anyone can obtain a can of spray paint and "make their mark" on a highway overpass or the side of a building.

4   Modern graffiti generally falls into one of three categories— junk graffiti, gang graffiti, and tagging. **Junk graffiti** messages are not gang-related but often involve obscene, racist, or threatening themes. The line separating gang graffiti and tagging has become blurred in recent years. **Tagging**, once seen as a nonviolent alternative to more threatening gang activities, is now considered an entry level offense that can lead to more serious crimes, including burglary and assault. In addition, tagging often results in direct gang affiliation. While all types of graffiti threaten the quality of life in affected areas, tagging and graffiti tied to gang activities represent the most widespread and formidable challenges to communities around the country.

Tagging

5   Tagging as a form of graffiti first appeared in the early 1980s and has grown immensely popular in many parts of the country,

in both rural and urban areas. A tagger is someone who adopts a nickname, or tag, and then writes it on as many surfaces as possible, usually in highly visible locations. Although spray paint is the most common medium, taggers—sometimes referred to as "piecers," "writers," and "hip-hop artists"—also may use magic markers or etching tools to create their images.

6   The motivation behind tagging involves fame, artistic expression, power, and rebellion—all integral parts of what has been referred to as the hip-hop culture. Tagging may fill an even deeper void for youths without a strong sense of personal identity. Interviews with taggers reveal a deep desire simply to be known, to create an identity for themselves, and to communicate it to others. The thrill of risk taking also appears to be an underlying motivation for many taggers. While the images taggers create may not necessarily be gang-related, research shows that most taggers hope to join gangs and use tagging as a way to gain the attention of gang members. The more often their monikers appear in different locations, the more publicity they receive. Consequently, a small number of taggers can cause a disproportionate amount of property damage in a community. Tagging messages usually resemble handwriting, but may be difficult, if not impossible, to read. Taggers also have been known to invent their own letters or symbols, often adding to the confusion over the message and the author. . . .

Communication and Territoriality

7   In an article about the increase in area gang violence, a local California newspaper accurately described graffiti as a "crude but effective way for gang members to communicate among themselves, with the community, and with rival gangs." Communication is an important attribute of graffiti that law enforcement and community leaders should understand as they attempt to address the problem. While neighborhood residents and police might see graffiti simply as a blight, gang members and many taggers view it not so much as property damage but as a means to send messages understood within the gang community.

8   The expressive value of graffiti also forms an important component of gang territoriality. Gangs, and potential gang members, use graffiti to identify and mark their territory. Although the traditional perception of gang territoriality has

been altered by increased mobility via the automobile, research of a noted gang expert indicates that gangs continue to "mark, define, claim, protect, and fight over their turf." In fact, territoriality among rival gangs continues to be a major source of gang violence. Graffiti as a primary form of communication and turf identification plays a direct part in feeding this violence.

True Impact of Graffiti

9   The threat posed by graffiti to neighborhoods and society in general goes much deeper than territorial gang violence. Community leaders need only to consider the reverberating effects of graffiti to understand how a seemingly low-grade misdemeanor can threaten or destroy the quality of life in an entire community. The monetary damages attributed to graffiti speak for themselves. In one year, the City of Los Angeles spent more than $15 million on graffiti eradication. This figure does not include the volunteer time devoted to graffiti cleanup or the estimated millions of dollars spent by private businesses taking care of the problem themselves. In addition, the Southern California Rapid Transit District spent $12 million on graffiti removal during the same year. . . .

10   James Q. Wilson, UCLA criminologist and framer of the "broken windows" theory, states that signs of disorder in society—such as graffiti, abandoned cars, broken windows, and uncollected trash—frighten law-abiding citizens into avoiding public places. Those places are then left to criminals who further deface them, creating a downward spiral in which the fear of crime leads to an increase in criminal activity. The presence of graffiti discourages citizens from shopping or living in affected areas. As established businesses relocate or close, new businesses might be reluctant to move into areas where customers would feel unsafe. As property values decline and law-abiding citizens with resources move, once-thriving neighborhoods can quickly degrade into dangerous places. Thus, the seemingly trivial offense of graffiti ultimately can have devastating consequences for a community.

The Future

11   Citizens must understand that this type of behavior cannot be tolerated because its insidious nature threatens communities from within. To deter new graffiti, young people should be

taught that their actions can have far-reaching consequences. Law enforcement agencies may consider augmenting drug- and gang-prevention efforts with lessons on graffiti. Students should be advised that damaging property with graffiti is a serious crime and offenders will be punished. As part of the lesson, instructors also may suggest and encourage alternative methods of self-expression.

Conclusion

12   Like prostitution and illegal gambling, people often view graffiti as a victimless crime. But as communities around the country have learned, there is no such thing as a victimless crime. In fact, crimes that do not produce a single, identifiable victim generally have more impact on the entire community. As a highly visible offense, graffiti represents a particularly menacing threat to the quality of life in a community. The residual effects of reduced property values, lost business, increased gang territoriality, and heightened fear of crime escalate the severity of graffiti-related offenses beyond their impact as visual pollution. Communities that do not develop measures to deter and prevent graffiti now may find themselves confronting more intractable problems in the future.

Exercise 2 Discussion and Critical Thinking

1. Underline the sentence in paragraph 2 that indicates what the author is trying to do.

2. Underline the sentence in paragraph 4 that takes a clear position on graffiti and, therefore, can be called the proposition.

3. Draw vertical lines in the left margin to indicate the sentences in paragraphs 1 and 2 that tie this essay to an audience concerned with law enforcement.

4. According to Grant, what motivates taggers?

5. Why do many gang members do graffiti?

6. What is the "broken window" theory?

7. In your opinion what are the best ways to deter further graffiti?

8. Does the solution of educating young people about the problems caused by graffiti suggest that the writer has faith in human beings? Explain your answer.

9. What parts of this essay do you agree with, and what parts do you not agree with? Explain.

10. If you could add one more strong section (or strengthen one), what would it be? Discuss.

⌒ Topics for Essays of Definition

Reading-Based Writing Topics

For reading-based writing, include references to and quotations from the reading selection(s), and give credit to your sources. See Chapter 4 for additional discussion on reading-based writing.

"Modern Mother"

1. Using this essay as a model, define one of the following terms (the one you select should apply to you or to people you know): *modern mother, modern father, modern grandmother, modern grandfather, modern wife, modern husband, modern parents, modern kid)*. Relate your observations to Maxwell's essay by using references and/or quotes, and give appropriate credit to Maxwell.

"Graffiti: Taking a Closer Look"

2. Write a reaction to Grant's definition of *graffiti* in which you take issue with some of his views and definitions. Use quotations from and references to his essay.
3. Write a reaction that is generally in agreement with Grant's view, citing his definitions and using your own examples to refer to neighborhoods or towns damaged by graffiti.
4. If you know people who do or have done graffiti, interview them with questions framed around Grant's argument. Then

write an essay that accepts or rejects their views. Use quotations and references, and give credit for what you borrow.

Cross-Curricular Topics

Define one of the following terms in an essay.

5. History and government: socialism, democracy, patriotism, capitalism, or communism
6. Philosophy: existentialism, free will, determinism, ethics, or stoicism
7. Education: charter schools, school choice, gifted program, ESL (English as a second language), paired teaching, or digital school
8. Music: symphony, sonata, orchestra, or tonic systems
9. Health science: autism, circulatory system, respiratory system, thyroid, cancer, herbal remedies, or acupuncture
10. Marketing: depression, digitalization, discretionary income, electronic commerce, globalization, marketing channel, free trade, telemarketing, or warehouse clubs

Career-Related Topic

11. Define one of the following terms by using the appropriate pattern(s) of development (such as exemplification, cause and effect, descriptive narration, comparison and contrast, analysis by division, process analysis, and classification): *total quality management, quality control, downsizing, outsourcing, business ethics, customer satisfaction,* or *cost effectiveness.*

General Topics

Write an essay of extended definition about one of the following terms:

12. Terrorism
13. Depression
14. Political correctness
15. "Wannabe" (surfer, gangster, cool, tough guy, athlete, sexy, intellectual, parent, or student)
16. A good coach, doctor, clergy, teacher, or police officer
17. Domestic violence
18. Addiction (perhaps concentrating on one substance or activity, such as alcoholism, smoking tobacco, or gambling)

Writer's Guidelines at a Glance: Definition

1. Use clustering to consider other patterns of development that may be used to define your term. See page 187 for an example.
2. The organization of your extended definition is likely to be one of emphasis, but it may be space or time, depending on the subject material. You may use just one pattern of development for the overall organization.
3. Consider these ways of introducing a definition: with a question, with a statement of what it is not, with a statement of what it originally meant, or with a discussion of why a clear definition is important. You may use a combination of these ways before you continue with your definition.
4. Whether you personalize a definition depends on your purpose and your audience. Your instructor may ask you to write about a word within the context of your own experience or to write about it from a detached, clinical viewpoint.
5. Consider using CLUESS for revision and COPS for editing.

12

Argument: Writing to Influence

∼ Writing Essays of Argument

Persuasion and Argument Defined

Persuasion is a broad term. When we write persuasion, we try to influence people to think in a certain way or to do something. **Argument** is persuasion on a topic about which reasonable people disagree. Argument involves controversy. Whereas exercising appropriately is probably not controversial because reasonable people do not dispute the idea, an issue such as gun control is controversial. In this chapter, we will be concerned mainly with the kind of persuasion that involves argument.

Techniques for Developing Essays of Argument

Statements of argument are informal or formal in design. An opinion column in a newspaper is likely to have little set structure, whereas an argument in college writing is likely to be tightly organized. Nevertheless, the opinion column and the college paper have much in common. Both provide a proposition, which is the main point of the argument, and both provide support, which is the evidence or the reasons that back up the proposition.

For a well-structured college essay, an organization plan is desirable. Consider these elements—background, proposition, qualification of proposition, refutation, and support—when you organize an essay of argument, and ask yourself the following questions as you develop your ideas:

- **Background:** What is the historical or social context for this controversial issue?

199

- **Proposition** (the **thesis** of the essay): What do I want my audience to believe or to do?
- **Qualification of proposition:** Can I limit my proposition so that those who disagree cannot easily challenge me with exceptions? For example, if I am in favor of using animals for scientific experimentation, am I concerned only with medical experiments or with any use, including experiments for the cosmetics industry?
- **Refutation** (taking the opposing view into account, mainly to point out its fundamental weakness): What is the view on the other side, and why is it flawed in reasoning or evidence?
- **Support:** In addition to sound reasoning, can I use appropriate facts, examples, statistics, and opinions of authorities?

Components of Your Essay

The basic form for an essay of argument includes the proposition (the thesis of the essay), the refutation, and the support, although the refutation is often omitted. The support sentences are, in effect, *because* statements; that is, the proposition is valid *because* of the support. Your organization should look something like this:

> *Proposition (thesis)*: It is time to pass a national law restricting smoking in public places.
>
> I. Discomfort of the nonsmoker (support 1)
> II. Health of the nonsmoker (support 2)
> III. Cost to the nation (support 3)

Kinds of Evidence

In addition to sound reasoning generally, you can use the following kinds of evidence, or support:

1. **Facts.** Martin Luther King Jr. was killed in Memphis, Tennessee, on April 4, 1968. Because an event that has happened is true and can be verified, this statement about King is a fact. But that James Earl Ray acted alone in killing King is to some a questionable fact. That King was the greatest of all civil rights leaders is also opinion because it cannot be verified.

   Some facts are readily accepted because they are general knowledge—you and your reader know them to be true because they can be or have been verified. Other "facts" are based on personal observation and are reported in various publications but may be false or questionable. You should always be concerned about the reliability of the source for both the information you use and the information used by those with other viewpoints. Still other so-called facts are genuinely debatable because of their complexity or the incompleteness of the knowledge available.

2. **Examples.** You must present a sufficient number of examples, and the examples must be relevant.

3. **Statistics.** Statistics are facts and data of a numerical kind that are classified and tabulated to present significant information about a given subject.

   Avoid presenting a long list of figures; select statistics carefully and relate them to things familiar to your reader. The millions of dollars spent on a war in a single week, for example, become more comprehensible when expressed in terms of what the money would purchase in education, highways, or urban renewal.

   To test the validity of statistics, either yours or your opponent's, ask: Who gathered them? Under what conditions? For what purpose? How are they used?

4. **Evidence from, and opinions of, authorities.** Most readers accept facts from recognized, reliable sources—governmental publications, standard reference works, and books and periodicals published by established firms. In addition, they will accept evidence and opinions from individuals who, because of their knowledge and experience, are recognized as experts.

   In using authoritative sources as proof, keep these points in mind:

   - Select authorities who are generally recognized as experts in their field.
   - Use authorities who qualify in the field pertinent to your argument.
   - Select authorities whose views are not biased.
   - Try to use several authorities.
   - Identify the authority's credentials clearly in your essay.

Transitional Words for Improving Coherence

- **FOR ARGUMENT:** *it follows that, as a result, causes taken collectively, as a concession, even though, of course, in the context of, in the light of, in the final analysis, following this, further, as additional support, moreover, consequently, according to, in support of, contrary to, therefore, naturally*

Career-Related Writing:
Proposals for the Workplace

In the workplace, the proposal is the purest expression of persuasion. Although it does not have a precise form, there are different kinds of proposals and different situations from which proposals arise. In this chapter, we will attempt to summarize the main forms and purposes of the proposal, but we will not try to teach how to write a long, complicated one that requires extensive research. Learning to work with the basic form will give you useful practice in this kind of writing. On the job, you will experience the many ways of framing proposals.

Notice the remarkable similarities between conventional college writing assignments and workplace proposals.

Paragraph or Essay of Persuasion (or Argument)	Proposal
Background (placing the issue into a social or historical perspective)	Background (indicating the problem or the need, emphasizing the urgency)
Proposition, with possible qualification	Solution to the problem, or need, stated concisely
Possible refutation	Possible explanation of why other solutions are inadequate
Support (reasoning and evidence)	In detail, what you can do
Support (reasoning and evidence)	How you can do it
Support (reasoning and evidence)	When you can do it
Support (reasoning and evidence)	What it will cost
Conclusion (clinching statement)	Conclusion (emphasizing the problem and solution)

The body of your proposal will usually have the parts shown in the proposal list. You will be able to determine what is necessary. For example, if you are proposing a change in procedure for an internal solution to a problem such as miscommunication, the cost may not be mentioned. As for order, the sequence shown in the list is common, but you can easily change the sequence to fit your needs. An outline of the proposal can be useful for PowerPoint presentations.

Longer and highly technical proposals often begin with an executive summary, a statement that carries the major ideas but not the explanations. Such a component would be read by executives, who would depend on others to evaluate and report on the remaining parts of the extensively detailed proposal.

◯ Practicing Patterns of Argument

Exercise 1 Completing Patterns

Fill in the blanks in the following outlines with supporting statements for each proposition. Each outline uses this pattern:

Proposition
   I. Support
   II. Support
   III. Support

A. Proposition: Medically assisted suicide for the terminally ill should be illegal.

   I. _____

   II. Better pain management offered

   III. Could be misused by unscrupulous doctors or patients' relatives

B. Proposition: Medically assisted suicide for the terminally ill should be legal.

   I. _____

   II. The expense of care for the terminally ill

   III. The pain and suffering of the dying person

◯ Examining Essays of Argument

Student Reading-Based Writing

Teaching Our Kids to Shoot 'Em Up

Tina Sergio

Tina Sergio's instructor had directed her to write an essay that included ideas from at least three newspaper, magazine, or journal sources. She was to document the ideas she incorporated into the content of her essay and submit photocopies of the works she cited. (See Chapter 13 for MLA style of citation.) A suggested writing

topic about the negative effects of media on youth intrigued her.
The issue was something that most people of her generation could
relate to as they reflected on their childhood: the confusing blur of
fact and fantasy in all media but especially in video games and in
television cartoons, sitcoms, dramas, and news.

1

Background

Why is it that if video games or
television shows contain any type of nudity,
many parents become outraged and forbid
their children from involvement; however,
when video games and television shows
feature shooting and killing, these parents
don't bat an eye? What does absorbing all
this violence teach children? A Surgeon

**Authority's
view**

General's special report has told us that
viewing violence on the media can teach
aggressive attitudes and behaviors, and can
desensitize feelings ("Media Violence" 78).
It is now a matter of responsibility for all
parties involved. Parents need to monitor

**Proposition
and thesis**

their children's consumption of media, and
video-game manufacturers, and television
networks need to reduce the amount of
violence they display.

2

**Authority's
view**

Media have become a central force in
children's lives. Educator Donald J. Graff
points out that children now average 35 hours
per week watching television and playing
video games (22). A majority of that time is
spent watching cartoons, and cartoons can
sometimes be more violent than cop shows on
prime-time television. Studies have shown
that prime-time action shows stage three to
five violent acts per hour, whereas violence
in Saturday morning children's programming

Statistics

ranges between 20 and 25 violent acts per
hour (Graff 22). According to psychologist

Richard Lieberman of Cornell University, we're seeing an especially high-risk population for lethal violence in the 10- to 14-year age group because developmentally their concept of death is still magical. Children think of death as temporary ("Death Doesn't Count" 33). For instance, in the **Example** cartoon *South Park*, there's a character named Kenny who gets killed in every episode but always reappears in the next episode. Although *South Park* is an adult cartoon, some parents allow their children to watch it, mainly because it is a cartoon.

3   Video games are another major contributor to media violence, and kids are spending more and more time playing them. Over the years, video-game action has become much more graphic and grizzly. For example, in the game called **Example** *Doom*, the players wander through corridors blasting the guts out of their enemies. What effects do these games have on children when day after day they sit in front of the screens pretending to shoot and kill? Arguably some may lose touch with reality, maybe even lose respect for life. Because video games are not yet rated by the Federal Communications Commission, parents don't realize that video games such as *Doom* are not meant for children.

4   Unfortunately, violent entertainment survives on television because the audience has been conditioned to expect the harsher realities. The kind of show that contains both of these components—entertainment and violence—is the news. The ratings soar with live coverage of such events as a car chase

Example

down a freeway and a man shooting his brains out. It is scary the way the media cover tragedies like the massacre at Columbine High School, where two kids kill their classmates and themselves. Surely the nonstop pictures and commentary sometimes give desperate and troubled kids ideas about ways to get attention on network news. It is time for the news media to take some responsibility for what to show and to whom.

5

Restated proposition

Violence in the media has become a public-health issue that affects us all. Parents should stop using video games and cartoons as babysitters, and Americans should be a little less hung up on nudity in the media and a little more worried about the violence their children are absorbing. The media and video producers need to exercise concern and restraint. If all parties were to show responsibility, legislation would be unnecessary.

Works Cited

"Death Doesn't Count." *Newsweek* 21 Feb. 1999: 33. Print.

Graff, Donald J. "Violence in the Media." *Business First* 28 Apr. 1997: 22. Print.

"Media Violence." *Pediatrics* 1 June 1995: 78-79. Print.

Professional Writing

Shouldn't Men Have "Choice" Too?

Meghan Daum

Meghan Daum is the author of The Quality of Life Report *and the essay collection* My Misspent Youth *and writes a weekly column for the* Los Angeles Times. *Known for her humor and acute cultural observations, she has inspired controversy over a range of topics, including social politics and class warfare.*

1   For pro-choicers like myself, Supreme Court nominee Samuel A. Alito Jr.'s position regarding spousal consent for abortion seems like one more loose rock in the ongoing erosion of Roe vs. Wade. Even those of us who are too young to remember the pre-Roe era often see any threat to abortion rights as a threat to our very destinies. We are, after all, the generation that grew up under Title IX, singing along to "Free to Be You and Me" (you know, the 1972 children's record where Marlo Thomas and Alan Alda remind us that mommies can be plumbers and boys can have dolls). When it comes to self-determination, we're as determined as it gets.

2   But even though I was raised believing in the inviolability of a woman's right to choose, the older I get, the more I wonder if this idea of choice is being fairly applied. Most people now accept that women, especially teenagers, often make decisions regarding abortion based on educational and career goals and whether the father of the unborn child is someone they want to hang around with for the next few decades. The "choice" in this equation is not only a matter of whether to carry an individual fetus to term but a question of what kind of life the woman wishes to lead.

3   But what about the kind of life men want to lead? On December 1, Dalton Conley, director of the Center for Advanced Social Science Research at New York University, published an article on the Op-Ed page of the *New York Times* arguing that Alito's position on spousal consent did not go far enough. Describing his own experience with a girlfriend who terminated a pregnancy against his wishes, Conley took some brave steps down the slippery slope of this debate, suggesting that if a father is willing to assume full responsibility for a child not wanted by a mother, he should be able to obtain an injunction stopping her from having an abortion—and he should be able to do so regardless of whether or not he's married to her. Conley freely acknowledges the many obvious caveats in this position— the most salient being the fact that regardless of how "full" that male responsibility might be, the physical burden of pregnancy and childbirth will always put most of the onus on women. But as much as I shudder at the idea of a man, husband or not, obtaining an injunction telling me what I can or cannot do with my own body, I would argue that it is Conley who has not gone far enough.

4   Since we're throwing around radical ideas about abortion rights, let me raise this question: If abortion is to remain legal and relatively unrestricted—and I believe it should—why shouldn't men have the right during at least the first trimester of pregnancy to terminate their legal and financial rights and responsibilities to the child?

5   As Conley laments, the law does not currently allow for men to protect the futures of the fetuses they help create. What he doesn't mention—indeed, no one ever seems to—is the degree to which men also cannot protect their own futures. The way the law is now, a man who gets a woman pregnant is not only powerless to force her to terminate the pregnancy, he also has a complete legal obligation to support that child for at least 18 years. In other words, although women are able to take control of their futures by choosing from at least a small range of options—abortion, adoption or keeping the child—a man can be forced to be a father to a child he never wanted and cannot financially support. I even know of cases in which the woman absolves the man of responsibility, only to have the courts demand payment anyway. That takes the notion of "choice" very far from anything resembling equality.

6   I realize I've just alienated feminists (among whose ranks I generally count myself) as well as pro-lifers, neither of whom are always above platitudes such as "You should have kept your pants on." But that reasoning is by now as reductive as suggesting that a rape victim "asked for it." Yes, people often act irresponsibly and yes, abortion should be avoided whenever possible. But just as women should not be punished for choosing to terminate a pregnancy, men should not be punished when those women choose not to.

7   One problem, of course, is that the child is likely to bear the brunt of whatever punishment remains to be doled out. A father who terminates his rights, although not technically a deadbeat dad, has still helped create a kid who is not fully supported. And (in case you were wondering) there are dozens of other holes in my theory as well: What if a husband wants to terminate his rights—should that be allowed? What if a father is underage and wants to terminate, but his parents forbid him? Should a father's decision-making time be limited to the first trimester? Should couples on first dates discuss their positions on the matter? Should Internet dating profiles let men check a box saying

"will waive parental rights" next to the box indicating his astrological sign?

8   There's also the danger that my idea is not just a slippery slope but a major mudslide on the way to Conley's idea. If a man can legally dissociate himself from a pregnancy, some will argue, why couldn't he also bind himself to it and force it to term? That notion horrifies me, just as my plan probably horrifies others. But that doesn't mean these ideas aren't worth discussing. Though it may be hard to find an adult male who's sufficiently undiplomatic to admit out loud that he'd like to have the option I'm proposing, let alone potentially take it, I know more than a few parents of teenage boys who lose sleep over the prospect of their sons' landing in the kind of trouble from which they'll have no power to extricate themselves.

9   And although the notion of women "tricking" men into fatherhood now sounds arcane and sexist, we'd be blind not to recognize the extent to which some women are capable of tricking themselves into thinking men will stick around, despite all evidence to the contrary. Allowing men to legally (if not always gracefully) bow out of fatherhood would, at the very least, start a conversation for which we haven't yet found the right words.

10   Actually, there's one word we've had all along: choice. We just need to broaden its definition.

Exercise 2 Discussion and Critical Thinking

1. Which paragraph contains Daum's thesis?

2. How does Daum introduce her proposition?

3. What qualified support does she offer in paragraph 3?

4. Which paragraph contains the rebuttal?

5. If you were to support Daum's proposition, how would you answer the questions Daum poses in paragraph 7?

6. In paragraph 8, Daum says males might be reluctant to admit publicly that they agree with her proposition. How do you think most men would respond? most women?

7. Daum has redefined the word *choice*. Use your own words to write her proposition.

8. Do you agree with the proposition? Why or why not?

Student Career-Related Writing as a Proposal

Abolish Homework in Elementary School

Emily Lucero

While attending college part-time, Emily Lucero is already working in the field in which she intends to advance: She is a paid teacher's aide. She also has a child in elementary school and two children in middle school. This assignment had special appeal to her:

> *Write a proposal to the manager or managers of an organization or establishment for whom you are working or have worked, or for an organization or establishment with whom you have done business. Explain the problem, discuss its increasing urgency, and propose a solution. Your solution may be the modification, replacement, or removal of a practice or procedure that is having a bad effect on the clients it is intended to serve.*

Lucero knew just what she wanted to propose. For her class, she wrote a proposal about her work situation. It was a proposal she wanted to send to officials in the school district where she was employed. For now, she would submit it to her English instructor. It would give her practice in developing her writing skills and in crafting a formal proposal.

Lucero's essay is annotated to indicate these aspects of a proposal: proposal statement, background, solution, inadequate solution, how to do it, when it can be done, what it will cost, and conclusion.

1   As a former room mother for a year on five occasions, a lifetime PTA member, a paid teacher's assistant, and a student on my way to becoming a teacher, I have come to a conclusion that heretofore would have been

Proposal/ unacceptable, and even shocking, to me. But
solution here it is: It is time to abolish homework in

Inadequate solution

elementary school. Less drastic suggestions by parents and teachers to cut back on assignments have failed because an unchallenged pressure for increasing homework comes from people who do not see the bad effects of it.

2

Background

I have reached this position because all my experiences tell me that the current situation is bad and getting worse. Even in kindergarten, students do homework, and expectations are unrealistically high. I have seen children actually wet their pants upon receiving their homework assignments. Parents will tell you that their children routinely lose sleep time and are deprived of a relaxed family relationship because of homework assignments that all too frequently are lengthy and unclear. Seeing their children struggle with projects, these parents try to teach and often do the work themselves. Teachers and aides struggle to evaluate huge stacks of material each day and to explain to the students and parents what went right and wrong. Academic competition within schools and between schools turns assignments into an escalating homework war. Everywhere we see students getting burned out, dropping out of other activities, and becoming sluggish and overweight.

3

How

Therefore, I propose that homework be abolished. Instead of doing homework, students would be encouraged to read, visit museums, participate in community youth activities, and enjoy their families. Relieved of evaluating homework, instructors would teach an additional approximately

thirty minutes each day, with the exact time
to be agreed to by district management and
the teacher's union. The extra time each day
could be class work directed by teachers and
supported by teachers' aides and parents
volunteering as tutors. This program could

When   be drawn up during summer workshops, piloted
during the fall semester, and introduced
campus-wide during the spring semester. The

Cost   cost to the school district would be the pay
for teachers in workshops and whatever
salary adjustments might be necessary, as
agreed to by management and faculty
negotiators.

4   Abolishing homework would return formal

Conclusion education to the schools, relieve pressures
at home, and restore childhood to our
children.

Exercise 3 Discussion and Critical Thinking

1. Do you generally agree or disagree with Lucero's proposal? Explain.

2. What would you add to or delete from her proposal?

3. Do you think Lucero should or should not submit this to the school principal where she works? Why or why not?

⌒ Topics for Essays of Argument

Reading-Based Writing Topics

For reading-based writing, include references to and quotations from the reading selection(s), and give credit to your sources. See Chapter 4 for additional discussion on reading-based writing.

"Teaching Our Kids to Shoot 'Em Up"

1. Write a two-part response in which you first summarize and then, in a separate reaction, either agree with or disagree with Sergio's views. Include your own experiences if they are relevant.

"Shouldn't Men Have 'Choice' Too?"

2. Rely on what you have witnessed and experienced and on what you believe to write a reaction to Daum's argument. Be sure to refer directly to her essay and use quotations. Your reaction should be an answer to the question posed in the essay title.

3. Write a two-part response in which you summarize Daum's view and then react with answers to the question in the title and the questions in paragraph 7.

Cross-Curricular Topic

4. From a class you are taking or have taken, or from your major area of study, select an issue on which thoughtful people may disagree, and write an essay of persuasion or argument. It could be an interpretation of an ambiguous piece of literature for an English class; a position on global warming, public land management, or the Endangered Species Act for a class in ecology; a paper arguing about the effectiveness of a government program in a political-science class; a view on a certain kind of diet in a food-science class; a preference for a particular worldview in a class on philosophy; or an assertion on the proper role of chiropractors as health-care practitioners in a health-science class.

Career-Related Topics

Write a proposal to solve a problem in your family, neighborhood, school, or workplace. The problem is likely to be the purchase or modification of something, the introduction or modification of a procedure, or the introduction of a service. For this assignment, use basically the same form regardless of the location or circumstances of the problem. You can use a basic pattern, background, solution (as a proposition), support (how it can be done, when it can be done, what it will cost, if anything). The problem that you are proposing to alleviate or eliminate can be based on your experiences or it can be purely fictional. If you are suggesting the purchase of an item or items to solve a problem, the Internet can provide you with prices and specifications. Those data could be integrated into your proposal or photocopied and attached, with references.

For a useful model of form for a brief proposal, review "Abolish Homework in Elementary School" on pages 210–212.

Following are a few specific topic suggestions:

5. Home
   a. Contracting with a gardener or a housekeeper
   b. Dividing the chores
   c. Respecting the privacy and space of others

6. Neighborhood
   a. Limiting noise
   b. Dealing with dogs—vicious, wandering, barking
   c. Parking recreational vehicles out front

7. College
   a. Parking
   b. Enrollment and registration
   c. Classroom procedure
   d. Safety

8. Workplace
   a. Time-saving equipment
   b. Doing your job (or part of it) at home rather than at the workplace
   c. Fringe benefits
   d. Evaluation procedures
   e. Staggering lunch hours and work breaks
   f. Communication between workers on different shifts

General Topics

Write an essay of argument on one of the following broad subject areas. You will have to limit your focus for an essay of argument. You may modify the topics to fit specific situations.

9. Homeschooling
10. Sex education
11. Sexual harassment
12. Juvenile justice
13. State-run lotteries
14. Cost of illegal immigration

15. Change in (your) college registration procedure
16. Curfew for teenagers
17. Laws keeping known gang members out of parks

Writer's Guidelines at a Glance: Argument

1. Ask yourself the following questions. Then consider which parts of the formal argument you should include in your essay.

   - **Background:** What is the historical or social context for this controversial issue?
   - **Proposition** (the **thesis** of the essay): What do I want my audience to believe or to do?
   - **Qualification of proposition:** Can I limit my proposition so that those who disagree with me cannot easily challenge me with exceptions?
   - **Refutation** (taking the opposing view into account, mainly to point out its fundamental weakness): What is the view on the other side, and why is it flawed in reasoning or evidence?
   - **Support:** In addition to sound reasoning, can I use appropriate facts, examples, statistics, and opinions of authorities?

2. The basic pattern of an essay of argument is likely to be in this form:

   Proposition (thesis)
   I. Support 1
   II. Support 2
   III. Support 3

3. Consider using CLUESS for revision and COPS for editing.

13

The Research Paper

⌒ The Research Paper Defined

The **research paper** is a long documented essay based on a thorough examination of your topic and supported by your explanations and by both references to and quotations from your sources. The traditional research paper in the style of the Modern Language Association, typically called MLA style (**here with 2009 MLA Update**), includes a title page and an outline (if your instructor requires them), a thesis, a documented essay (text), and a list of sources (called "Works Cited," referring to the works used specifically in the essay).

This chapter presents ten steps for writing a research paper. Don't be apprehensive; if you can write an effective essay, you can write an effective research paper. Pick a feasible topic and stay on schedule. (The two main problems for students working on research papers are [1] they select topics that are too broad or too narrow and [2] they fall behind schedule.) The form for documentation is shown in Step 3. Completing a research paper using the following ten steps will give you practice in finding sources in your school library and on the Internet, and it will give you experience in writing a longer, more complicated essay. It will help you master skills so that you can communicate better.

Although specific aims and methods may vary from one research activity to another, most nonexperimental, objective research tasks depend on ten basic steps. See the following explanation and then review the student work for illustration. A partial, annotated student final draft follows this discussion.

⌒ Ten Steps to Writing a Research Paper

Step 1   Select a Topic

Select a topic and make a scratch outline. Then construct a thesis as you did for writing an essay by choosing what you intend to

216

write about (subject) and by deciding how you will limit or narrow your subject (focus). Your purpose will be either to inform (explain) or to persuade (argue). For persuasive issues, see General Topics on page 214.

- Your topic should interest you and be appropriate in subject and scope for your assignment.
- Your topic should be researchable through library and other relevant sources, such as the Internet. Avoid topics that are too subjective or are so new that good source material is not available.

To write a focus for your subject, you may need to scan a general discussion of your topic area so that you can consider it in perspective and begin to see the parts or aspects on which you will want to concentrate. Relevant sections of encyclopedias and comprehensive books, such as textbooks, are often useful in establishing the initial overview. At this point, the closer you can come to a well-defined topic with a functional scratch outline of its divisions, the more likely you are to make a smooth, rapid, effective journey through the process. Try to divide your thesis into its functional parts.

Student Example

Tentative thesis: Despite some valid criticism, <u>the zoo as an</u>
subject
<u>institution</u> <u>will probably survive because of its roles in</u>
focus
<u>entertainment, education, and conservation.</u>

  I. Entertainment
     A. Money
     B. Problems
 II. Education
     A. General public
     B. Students
III. Conservation
     A. Science
     B. Breeding
 IV. Criticism
     A. Pro
     B. Con
  V. Zoos of future
     A. Education
     B. Conservation

Step 2   Find Sources

Find sources for your investigation. With your topic and its divisions in mind, use the resources and the electronic databases available in your college library and on the Internet to identify books, articles, and other materials pertaining to your topic. The list of these items, called the **bibliography**, should be prepared on cards in the form appropriate for your assignment (MLA style is used in this text). Seek different kinds of materials, different types of source information (primary, meaning coming from direct study, participation, observation, involvement; and secondary, meaning coming from indirect means—usually reporting on what others have done, observed, or been involved in), and credible writers (authorities and relatively unbiased, reliable reporters on your topic).

The main parts of the library pertaining to most research papers are the book collection and the periodical collection. Books are arranged on shelves by subject according to the Library of Congress system or the Dewey Decimal system. Periodicals, including newspapers, are stored in a variety of ways: in unbound form (very recent editions), in bound form, on microfilm, in databases, and in online computer systems.

Printed Material Other Than Books

For the typical college research paper, the main printed nonbook sources are periodicals, such as newspapers, magazines, and journals. Various indexes will provide you with information for finding the source material you need. Depending on the library and the publication, periodicals are listed in indexes printed on paper or in electronic form. The most common index in bound volumes is the *Readers' Guide to Periodical Literature* (now also computerized). It indexes more than 200 popular magazines such as *Time* and *Newsweek*, which means it is useful for basic research but not for more scholarly studies. The *New York Times* and numerous other metropolitan newspapers are also covered by indexes. For more academic searches, check with a reference librarian for indexes in specific fields such as anthropology or art. Indexes are usually kept in one area of the reference section. The figure on page 220 shows three sample entries from the *Readers' Guide*.

Books

Today most academic and municipal libraries provide information about books online, with databases accessible by author, title, subject, or other key words. Usually a printout of sources is available.

As with the Internet, selecting key words and their synonyms is crucial. A combination of words will help you focus your search. In the following sample printout on the topic *animal?* and *conservation*, the user has keyed in the topic and then clicked to the title to check for location and availability:

```
BOOK - Record 1 of 20 Entries Found                            Brief View
- - - - - - - - - - - - - - - - - - - - - - - - - - - - - - - - - - - - - - - - - -
Title:          The atlas of endangered species
Published:      New York : Macmillan : Toronto : Maxwell Macmillan Canada,
                1991.
Subjects:       Endangered species.
                Endangered plants.
                Nature conservation.
                Rare animals.
                Rare plants.
                Wildlife conservation.
                Environmental protection.
- - - - - - - - - - - - - - - - - - - - - - - - - - - - - - - - - - + Page 1 of 2 - - - - - - - - - -
Search Request: K=ANIMAL? AND CONSERVATION        MS<ENTER>=Book catalog
BOOK - Record 1 of 20 Entries Found                            Brief View
- - - - - - - - - - - - - - - - - - - - - - - - - - - - - - - - - - - - - - - - - -
Title:          The atlas of endangered species
- - - - - - - - - - - - - - - - - - - - - - - - - - - - - - - - - - - - - - - - - -
LOCATION:               CALL NUMBER             STATUS:
REFERENCE SHELVES       333.9516 At65           Not checked out
(Non-Circulating)
```

Computerized Indexes and Other Online Services

Computerized indexes, such as *InfoTrac*, *Periodical Abstracts*, and *Newspaper Abstracts Ondisc*, can be accessed in basically the same way as the online book catalogs, using key words and word combinations. They provide source information, perhaps with printouts. Some indexes include short abstracts (brief summaries) of the individual entries. Some indexes even provide the full text of material. One such index is *LexisNexis*, an online service that can help you find sources and then provide the text of the original source material, all of which can be printed out.

An online essay originally published in, say, *Time* magazine usually will be published without illustrations and in a different format. Therefore, it is important that you give full bibliographical information about your particular source (source citation instructions appear in Step 3).

Government publications, pamphlets, and other materials are cataloged in several ways. Procedures for searching all electronic indexes and sources routinely are posted alongside terminals, and librarians are available for further explanations and demonstrations. Many libraries also have pamphlets listing the periodicals they carry, their arrangements with other libraries for sharing or borrowing materials, access to the Internet, databases stored on CD-ROMs, and various online services.

Search engines, such as Google, Windows Live, and Yahoo!, will yield an abundance of material on your topic. Just key in your subject and choose among sources with discrimination. As with all sources, credibility depends on the expertise of the writer(s). You should ask the following questions: What are the qualifications of the author? What is the reputation of the publication? How reliable is the support? When was the material published?

Step 3   List Sources

List tentative sources in a preliminary bibliography.

Bibliography and Works Cited, MLA Style (with 2009 MLA Update)

You will list source material in two phases of your research paper project: the preliminary bibliography and the Works Cited list.

The 2009 MLA Update makes only a few major style changes.

- It replaces underlining with italics.
- It uses URLs only when they are requested or needed for finding sources.

- It uses abbreviations (*N.p.* for *no publisher, n.d.* for *no date,* and *n. pag.* for *no page*).
- It specifies the medium of publication (e.g., Print, Web, Performance, or Television).
- These changes are shown in examples in this chapter. For more obscure changes, consult the *MLA Handbook for Writers of Research Papers,* 7th edition, or use your search engine on your computer.

When you begin your research, make a list of works that may provide useful information on your topic. At this time, do not stop to make a careful examination and evaluation of each entry, although you should keep in mind that your material usually should come from a variety of sources and that those sources ideally should be objective, authoritative, and current. For various reasons, some sources may not find their way into your research paper at all. As you read, you may discover that some sources are superficial, poorly researched, overly technical, off the topic, or unavailable. The preliminary bibliography is nothing more than a list of sources to consider and select from.

The sources that you actually use in the paper—meaning those that you refer to by name or quote—become part of the Works Cited list at the end of the final draft. Whether you use cards, sheets of paper, or computer files, become familiar with the form you will use in writing your paper and take care in recording the detailed information you will need for documentation.

The MLA research paper form is commonly used for both the preliminary bibliography and the list of works cited. This format is unlike the formats used in catalogs and indexes. The following examples show the difference between printout forms from library files and the MLA research paper forms.

Periodicals

Printout Form

```
Author:    Ormrod, Stefan A.
Title:     Boo for zoos.
Source:    New Scientist v. 145 (Mar. 18 '95) p. 48
```

MLA Research Paper Form

```
Ormrod, Stefan A. "Boo for Zoos." New Scientist
    18 Mar. 1995: 48. Print.
```

Books

Printout Form

```
Author:        DiSilvestro, Roger L.
Title:         The African elephant: twilight in Eden
Published:     New York: Wiley. © 1991.
```

MLA Research Paper Form

Titles of longer works are italicized.

> DiSilvestro, Roger L. *The African Elephant: Twilight in Eden*. New York: Wiley, 1991. Print.

Form for Printed Sources

Articles

Article in a Journal

> Butterick, George. "Charles Olson's 'The Kingfishers' and the Poetics of Change." *American Poetry* 6.2 (1989): 28-59. Print.

Article in a Weekly or Biweekly Magazine: Author Unknown, Known

> "How the Missiles Help California." *Time* 1 Apr. 1996: 45. Print.
> Keizer, Garret. "How the Devil Falls in Love." *Harper's* Aug. 2002: 43-51. Print.

Article in a Newspaper: Author Unknown, Known

> "A Steadfast Friend on 9/11 Is Buried." *New York Times* 6 June 2002: B8. Print.
> Franklin, Deborah. "Vitamin E Fails to Deliver on Early Promise." *New York Times* 2 Aug. 2005, late ed.: F5. Print.

Article or Other Written Selection in an Anthology or Textbook

> Brownmiller, Susan. "Let's Put Pornography Back in the Closet." *Take Back the Night: Women on Pornography.* Ed. Laura Lederer. New York: Morrow, 1980. 252-55. Rpt. in *Conversations: Readings for Writing.* Ed. Jack Selzer. 4th ed. New York: Allyn, 2000. 578-81. Print.

Editorial in a Newspaper or Magazine: Author Unknown, Known

```
Gergen, David. "A Question of Values." Editorial. US
    News and World Report 11 Feb. 2002: 72. Print.
"It's Subpoena Time." Editorial. New York Times 8 June
    2007, late ed.: A28. Print.
```

Books

A Book by One Author

```
Adeler, Thomas L. In a New York Minute. New York:
    Harper, 1990. Print.
```

An Anthology or a Textbook

List the name(s) of the editor(s), followed by a comma, a space, and "ed." or "eds."

```
Grumet, Robert S., ed. Northeastern Indian Lives.
    Amherst: U of Massachusetts P, 1996. Print.
```

Two or More Books by the Same Author

```
Walker, Alice. The Color Purple: A Novel. New York:
    Harcourt, 1982. Print.
---.Meridian. New York: Harcourt, 1976. Print.
```

A Book by Two or Three Authors

```
Current, Richard Nelson, Marcia Ewing Current,
    and Louis Fuller. Goddess of Light. Boston:
    Northeastern UP, 1997. Print.
```

Use *et al.*, or you may use all names, for four or more authors.

```
Danziger, James N., et al. Computers and Politics: High
    Technology in American Local Governments. New York:
    Columbia UP, 1982. Print.
```

A Book with a Corporate Author

```
Detroit Commission on the Renaissance. Toward the
    Future. Detroit: Wolverine, 1989. Print.
```

A Work in an Anthology or Textbook with Readings

Booth, Wayne C. "The Scholar in Society." *Introduction
    to Scholarship in Modern Languages and Literatures.*
    Ed. Joseph Gibaldi. New York: MLA, 1981. 116-43.
    Print.

An Article in an Encyclopedia

Cheney, Ralph Holt. "Coffee." *Collier's Encyclopedia.*
    1993 ed. Print.

Government Publications

United States. Dept. of Transportation. National
    Highway Traffic Safety Admin. *Driver Licensing Laws
    Annotated 1980.* Washington: GPO, 1980. Print.

Citations from the *Congressional Record* require only a date and
page number.

Cong. Rec. 11 Sept. 2008: 12019-24. Print.

Proceedings

Treat particular presentations in proceedings as you would pieces in
a collection.

Wise, Mary R. "The Main Event Is Desktop Publishing."
    *Proceedings of the 34th Annual International
    Technical Communication Conference,* Denver, 10-13
    May 1987. San Diego: Univet, 1987. Print.

A Lecture, a Speech, or an Address

Kern, David. "Recent Trends in Occupational Medicine."
    AMA Convention. Memorial Hospital, Pawtucket,
    2 Oct. 1997. Address.

A Personal Interview

Thomas, Carolyn. Personal interview. 5 Jan. 2009.

Films, Filmstrips, Slide Programs, and Videotapes

It's a Wonderful Life. Dir. Frank Capra. Perf. James
    Stewart, Donna Reed, Lionel Barrymore, and Thomas
    Mitchell. RKO, 1946. DVD.

Form for Electronic Sources

Formats vary widely in electronic media because of rapidly changing systems and terms. The information you provide in your bibliography and works cited will inform your reader about such matters as the subject of each source, who has worked on it, where it came from originally, when it was first written and last changed, when you found it, where you found it, and how you found it. Be sure that you give enough information. If you cannot find directions for citing a source, you should identify a form used for similar content as a model, improvise if necessary, and be as consistent as possible. Usually the URL is unnecessary.

Do not be intimidated by the length and seeming complexity of the citations. Every part is reasonable and every part is necessary. If you are not certain whether to include some information, you probably should. As you present an orderly sequence of parts in your entries, you must take great care in attending to detail, for a single keystroke can leave your source concealed in cyberspace with no electronic map for your reader.

The examples in this section follow MLA style from the 2009 MLA Update. More details can be found at *www.mlahandbook.org.* Because the nature of electronic sources and references to them are constantly evolving, if you must include a URL, check each Web site for changes and updates.

This is the basic form for Internet and World Wide Web sources for your bibliography and Works Cited entries:

- Author's [editor's, compiler's, translator's, director's, narrator's, performer's] last name, first name, middle initial
- "Title of article or other short work" or *Title of Book*
- Title of the overall Web site
- Version or edition used
- Publisher or sponsor of the site
- Publication date
- Medium of publication
- Date of access to the source

Online Services—Library and Personal

Library Subscription Services (database with full texts)
Online library subscription services provide databases mainly of articles in journals, magazines, and newspapers. They are accessed either at a library terminal or by the student's computer. They

often include hundreds of publications and enable students to find and print out entire texts rapidly. Although most have complete printed versions, the illustrations are usually omitted, page numbers are changed or not given, and some material may be reformatted. For brief documented papers, instructors sometimes ask their students to include copies of the printouts with the final submission. Content ranges from works intended for the general reader to those written for scholarly purposes. Some are listed as "juried," which means that the selections have been evaluated for credible content by a group of experts in the field. Library online services include ProQuest Direct, LexisNexis, and EBSCOhost.

The basic form for citing sources is author, title, publication information, database, medium of publication, and date of access. Include the URL of the service in angle brackets only if the reader needs it to find the source.

Here are three examples:

> Meyer, Greg. "Answering Questions About the West Nile Virus." *Dayton Daily News* 11 July 2002: Z3-7. *LexisNexis.* Web. 17 Feb. 2003.
>
> Folks, Jeffrey J. "Crowd and Self: William Faulkner's Sources of Agency in *The Sound and the Fury.*" *Southern Literary Journal* 34.2 (2002): 30+. *EBSCO.* Web. 6 June 2003.
>
> Taylor, Steven J. "Caught in the Continuum: A Critical Analysis of the Principle of the Least Restrictive Environment." *Research and Practice for Persons with Severe Disabilities* 29.4 (2004): 218-30. *ERIC.* Web. 3 Mar. 2009.

Personal Subscription Services (databases with full texts supplied by companies such as AOL)
Typically indicate author, title, publication information (if any), name of service, medium of publication, date of access, and the *Keyword* you used or the *Path* (sequence of topics) you followed in locating the source.

> "Cloning." *BioTech's Life and Science Dictionary.* 30 June 1998. Indiana U. *America Online.* 4 July 1998. Path: Research and Learning; Science; Biology; Biotechnology Dictionary.
>
> "Tecumseh." *Compton's Encyclopedia Online.* Vers. 3.0. 1998. *America Online.* Web. 8 Apr. 2000. Keyword: Compton's.

Professional Site

The Purdue OWL Family of Sites. The Writing Lab and OWL,
at Purdue and Purdue U, 2008. Web. 9 Sept. 2009.

Personal Site

Gladwell, Malcolm. Home page. N.p., 8 Mar. 2005.
Web. 2 Mar. 2009.

Web Log (blog)

Cuthbertson, Peter. "Are Left and Right Still Alright?"
Conservative Commentary. N.p., 7 Feb. 2005.
Web. 18 Feb. 2005.

Poem Online

Hampl, Patricia. "Who We Will Love." Woman Before an
Aquarium. Pittsburgh: U of Pittsburgh P, 1978: 27-28.
A Poem a Week. Rice University. Web. 13 Mar. 1998.

Article in a Journal Online

DeKoven, Marianne. "Utopias Limited: Post-Sixties
and Postmodern American Fiction." Modern Fiction
Studies 41.1 (1995): 75-97. Web. 20 Jan. 2005.

Article in a Magazine Online

Keillor, Garrison. "Why Did They Ever Ban a Book This
Bad?" Salon.com. Salon Media Group, 13 Oct. 1997.
Web. 14 Oct. 1997.

Article in a Newspaper Online

"Tornadoes Touch Down in S. Illinois." New York Times.
New York Times, 16 Apr. 1998. Web. 20 May 1998.

Newspaper Editorial Online

"The Proved and the Unproved." Editorial. New York
Times. New York Times, 13 July 1997. Web. 13 July
1997.

Review Online

Ebert, Roger. Rev. of Star Wars: Episode I—The Phantom
Menace, dir. George Lucas. Chicago Sun-Times.
Digital Chicago. 8 June 2000. Web. 22 June 2000.

Government Publication Online

Cite an online government publication as you would cite a print version; end with the information required for an electronic source.

> United States. Dept. of Justice. Office of Justice
>   Programs. *Violence Against Women: Estimates from*
>   *the Redesigned National Crime Victimization Survey.*
>   By Ronet Bachman and Linda E. Saltzman. Aug. 1995.
>   *Bureau of Justice Statistics.* Web. 10 Jan. 2008.

Newspaper Article in an Online Database

> Weeks, Linton. "History Repeating Itself; Instead of
>   Describing Our Country's Past, Two Famous Scholars
>   Find Themselves Examining Their Own." *Washington*
>   *Post.* 24 Mar. 2002: N. pag. *LexisNexis.* Web.
>   3 Aug. 2005.

Journal or Magazine Articles in an Online Database

> Fabel, Robin F. A. "The Other War of 1812: The Patriot
>   War and the American Invasion of Spanish East
>   Florida." *Alabama Review* 57.4 (2004): 291-92.
>   *ProQuest.* Web. 8 Mar. 2005.
> Priest, Ann-Marie. "Between Being and Nothingness: The
>   'Astonishing Precipice' of Virginia Woolf's *Night*
>   *and Day.*" *Journal of Modern Literature* 26.2
>   (2002-03): 66-80. *InfoTrac.* Web. 12 Jan. 2004.
> Suggs, Welch. "A Hard Year in College Sports."
>   *Chronicle of Higher Education* 19 Dec. 2003: 37.
>   *LexisNexis.* Web. 17 July 2004.

An Article in an Encyclopedia

Include the article's title, the title of the database (italicized), the version number (if available), the sponsor, the date of electronic publication, the publication medium, and the date of access.

> "Hawthorne, Nathaniel." *Encyclopaedia Britannica Online.*
>   Encyclopaedia Britannica, 2008. Web. 16 May 2008.

Personal E-Mail Message

> Watkins, Jack. "Collaborative Projects." Message to
>   Gabriel Mendoza. 12 Apr. 2009. E-mail.

Step 4   Take Notes

Take notes in an organized fashion. Resist the temptation to record everything that interests you. Instead, take notes that pertain to divisions of your topic as stated in your thesis or scratch outline. Locate, read, and take notes on the sources listed in your preliminary bibliography. Some of these sources need to be printed out from electronic databases or from the Internet, some photocopied, and some checked out. Your notes will usually be on cards or on your computer, with each notation indicating key pieces of the information:

A. Division of topic (usually the Roman-numeral part of your scratch outline or the divisions of your thesis)
B. Identification of topic (by author's last name or title of piece)
C. Location of material (usually by page number)
D. Text of statement as originally worded (with quotation marks; editorial comments in brackets), summarized or paraphrased (in student's own words, without quotation marks), and statement of relevance of material, if possible

Student Example of Organization on a Card

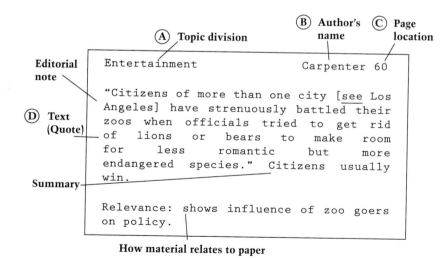

How material relates to paper

Step 5   Refine Your Thesis and Outline

Refine your thesis statement and outline to reflect more precisely what you intend to write.

Student Example

Thesis: Throughout the world, despite determined opposition, the modern zoo with a new image and compound purpose
is taking shape.

```
  I. Zoos as entertainment
     A. Attendance
     B. Income
     C. Customer preferences
 II. Captive breeding success
     A. National
     B. International
III. Scientific success
     A. Embryo transfers
     B. Artificial insemination
     C. Test-tube fertilization
     D. Storage of eggs, sperm, and tissue
     E. Computer projects
```

Step 6   Write Your First Draft

Referring to your thesis, outline, and note cards keyed to your outline, write the first draft of your research paper. Use the following guidelines to include proper MLA research-paper form in documentation.

Plagiarism

Careful attention to the rules of documentation will help you avoid **plagiarism**, the unacknowledged use of someone else's words or ideas. It occurs when a writer omits quotation marks when citing the exact language of a source, fails to revise completely a paraphrased source, or gives no documentation for a quotation or paraphrase. The best way to avoid this problem is to be attentive to the following details.

When you copy a quotation directly into your notes, check to be sure that you have put quotation marks around it. If you forget to include them when you copy, you might omit them in the paper as well.

When you paraphrase, keep in mind that it is not sufficient to change just a few words or rearrange sentence structure. You must completely rewrite the passage. One of the best ways to accomplish this is to read the material you want to paraphrase; then cover the page so that you cannot see it and write down the information as you remember it. Compare your version with the original and make any necessary changes on the note card. If you cannot successfully rewrite the passage, quote it, or part(s) of it, instead.

The difference between legitimate and unacceptable paraphrases can be seen in the following examples:

SOURCE

"What is unmistakably convincing and makes Miller's theatre writing hold is its authenticity in respect to the minutiae of American life. He is a first-rate reporter: he makes the details of his observation palpable."

UNACCEPTABLE PARAPHRASE

What is truly convincing and makes Arthur Miller's theatrical writing effective is its authenticity. He is an excellent reporter and makes his observation palpable.

LEGITIMATE PARAPHRASE

The strength of Arthur Miller's dramatic art lies in its faithfulness to the details of the American scene and in its power to bring to life the reality of ordinary experience.

The differences between the two paraphrased versions are enormous. The first writer has made some token changes, substituting a few synonyms (*truly* for *unmistakably*, *excellent* for *first-rate*), deleting part of the first sentence, and combining the two parts of the second sentence into a single clause. Otherwise, this is a word-for-word copy of the original, and if the note were copied into the paper in this form, the writer would be guilty of plagiarism. The second writer has changed the vocabulary of the original passage and completely restructured the sentence so that the only similarity between the note and the source is the ideas.

Check to see that each of your research notes has the correct name and page number so that when you use information from that note in your paper, you will be able to credit it to the right source.

Documentation: Parenthetical References, MLA Style

Although you need not acknowledge a source for generally known information such as the dates of the Civil War or the names of the ships that carried Columbus and his followers to the New World, you must identify the exact source and location of each statement, fact, or original idea you borrow from another person or work.

In the text of the research paper, MLA style requires only a brief parenthetical source reference keyed to a complete bibliographical entry in the list of works cited at the end of the paper. For most parenthetical references, you will need to cite only the author's last name and the number of the page from which the statement or idea was taken, and, if you mention the author's name in the text, the page number alone is sufficient. This format also allows you to include within the parentheses additional information, such as title or volume number, if it is needed for clarity. Documentation for some of the most common types of sources is discussed in the following sections.

References to Articles and Single-Volume Books

Articles and single-volume books are the two most common types of works you will be referring to in your research paper. When citing them, either mention the author's name in the text and note the appropriate page number in parentheses immediately after the citation or acknowledge both name and page number in the parenthetical reference, leaving a space between the two. If punctuation is needed, insert the mark outside the final parenthesis.

- *Author's Name Cited in Text*
     Marya Mannes has defined *euthanasia* as "the chosen alternative to the prolongation of a steadily waning mind and spirit by machines that will withhold death or to an existence that mocks life" (61).

- *Author's Name Cited in Parentheses*
     Euthanasia has been defined as "the chosen alternative to the prolongation of a steadily waning mind and spirit by machines that will withhold death or to an existence that mocks life" (Mannes 61).

- *Corresponding Works Cited Entry*
     Mannes, Marya. *Last Rights*. New York: Morrow, 1973. Print.

References to Works in an Anthology

When referring to a work in an anthology, either cite in the text the author's name and indicate in parentheses the page number in the anthology where the source is located or acknowledge both name and page reference parenthetically.

- *Author's Name Cited in Text*

    One of the most widely recognized facts about James Joyce, in Lionel Trilling's view, is "his ambivalence toward Ireland, of which the hatred was as relentless as the love was unfailing" (153).

- *Author's Name Cited in Parentheses*

    One of the most widely recognized facts about James Joyce is "his ambivalence toward Ireland, of which the hatred was as relentless as the love was unfailing" (Trilling 153).

- *Corresponding Works Cited Entry*

    Trilling, Lionel. "James Joyce in His Letters." *Joyce: A Collection of Critical Essays*. Ed. William M. Chace. Englewood Cliffs: Prentice-Hall, 1974. 151-59. Print.

References to Works of Unknown Authorship

If you borrow information or ideas from an article or a book for which you cannot determine the name of the author, cite the title instead, either in the text of the paper or in parentheses, and include the page reference as well.

- *Title Cited in Text*

    According to an article titled "Going Back to Booze," surveys have shown that most adult alcoholics began drinking heavily as teenagers (42).

- *Title Cited in Parentheses*

    Surveys have shown that most adult alcoholics began drinking heavily as teenagers ("Going Back to Booze" 42).

- *Corresponding Works Cited Entry*

    "Going Back to Booze." *Time* 30 Nov. 1999: 41-46. Print.

References to Internet Material

Treat Internet material as you would other material. If the author's name is not available, give the title. Consider using page and paragraph numbers if they are available; usually they are not.

References in Block Quotations

Quotations longer than four typewritten lines are indented ten spaces or one-half inch and are typed without quotation marks; their references are placed outside end punctuation.

- *Reference Cited After End Punctuation*

  > Implicit in the concept of Strange Loops
  > is the concept of infinity, since what else is
  > a loop but a way of representing an endless
  > process in a finite way? And infinity plays a
  > large role in many of Escher's drawings. Copies
  > of one single theme often fit into each other,
  > forming visual analogues to the canons of Bach.
  > (Hofstadter 15)

- *Corresponding Works Cited Entry*

  > Hofstadter, Douglas. *Gödel, Escher, Bach:*
  > *An Eternal Golden Braid.* New York: Vintage,
  > 1980. Print.

Step 7 Revise Your First Draft

Evaluate your first draft and amend it as needed (perhaps researching an area not well covered for additional support material and adding or deleting sections of your outline to reflect the way your paper has grown).

Follow the writing process guidelines, using CLUESS (**c**oherence, **l**anguage, **u**nity, **e**mphasis, **s**upport, and **s**entences) for revision and COPS (**c**apitalization, **o**missions, **p**unctuation, and **s**pelling) for editing. Before writing your final draft, read your paper aloud to discover any errors or awkward-sounding sentence structure.

Step 8 Prepare Your Works Cited Section

Using the same form as in the preliminary bibliography, prepare a Works Cited section (a list of works you have referred to or quoted and identified parenthetically in the text).

Step 9   Write Your Final Draft

Write the final version of your research paper with care for effective writing and accurate documentation. The final draft will probably include the following parts:

1. Title page (sometimes omitted)
2. Thesis and outline (topical or sentence, as directed)
3. Documented essay (text)
4. List of sources used (Works Cited)

Step 10   Submit Required Materials

Submit your research paper with any preliminary material required by your instructor. Consider using a checklist to make sure you have fulfilled all requirements. A comprehensive checklist might look like this:

Research Paper Checklist

☐ Title page (sometimes omitted, especially if the outline is not required)
☐ Thesis and outline (sometimes omitted)
☐ Documented essay (text)
   ___ Approximate total number of words
   ___ Approximate number of words quoted (Usually, more than 20 percent quoted words would be excessive.)
☐ List of sources used (Works Cited)
   ___ Number of sources used
☐ Preliminary materials, such as preliminary bibliography, note cards, and rough draft, as required
☐ Double-spaced text, one-inch margins

⁓ Student Research Paper

The following material is an excerpt from a ten-page research paper
by Michael Chung. Other parts of his assignment were shown in the
ten-step approach in the previous pages. The material here includes a
title page (which your instructor may not require), an outline (partial
only, to save space), the introduction, a sampling of body material,
the conclusion, and a Works Cited section. The material is annotated
to indicate form and technique in a well-written research paper.
Margins for the research paper are one inch at the top and bottom and
on both sides.

Title page is optional; check with your instructor.

ZOOS—AN ENDANGERED SPECIES?

Michael Chung

Professor Lee Brandon

English 1A
8 January 2010

Double-space throughout (thesis and outline section is optional;
check with your instructor).

**Heading for
all pages
starting on
the second
page of the
paper: last
name, one
space, page
number
(small Roman
numerals
for outline
pages, Arabic
for paper).**

                                                        Chung ii

Thesis statement: Throughout the world,

despite determined opposition, the modern zoo

with a new image and compound purpose is

taking shape.

   I. Zoos as entertainment (partial to save

       space)

     A. Attendance

**Align entries
in columns**
     B. Income

     C. Customer preferences

       1. Favoring certain animals

       2. Favoring animals over education

  II. Pandas for profit

     A. Criticism

     B. Benefits

       1. Money for zoo conservation projects

       2. Money back to natural habitat

 III. Captive breeding success

     A. National

     B. International

 IV. Scientific success

     A. Embryo transfers

     B. Artificial insemination

Chung 1

1" from top

Information here only if you do not use a title page

Michael Chung

Professor Lee Brandon

English 1A

8 January 2010

[Introduction]

Title

Zoos—An Endangered Species?

Uses historical perspective for introduction

Early zoos were usually little more than crude holding pens where animals, often serving dually with circuses, died off and were replaced by a seemingly unlimited supply from the wilds. In the first seven decades of the twentieth century, zoos became institutions that offered some education, a little conservation of species, and mostly entertainment. Meanwhile, many vocal critics emerged, arguing for animal rights and questioning the effectiveness and appropriateness of zoo programs. They

Basic thesis idea as question

brought into focus the question, Are zoos necessary?

Chung 2

[Excerpt from body]

In addition to the entertainment aspect of zoos is the captive breeding program. In one spectacular captive breeding success, the National Zoo in Washington, D.C., may have saved the endangered Komodo dragon from

Statistics   extinction by successfully incubating thirty eggs. This ten-foot, dangerous, ugly creature that resembles a dinosaur numbers only

Paraphrased material   somewhere around 5,000-8,000 in the wild but soon will be represented in numerous zoos

Citation   (Browne C1). Now that the incubation process is in place, the entire program offers an opportunity to restock the Komodo's habitat in Indonesia.

Not all captive breeding projects can end with a reintroduction of the species into the wild. For those species, the zoos have turned

Quotation introduced with title and author's name   to science, which has been used in a variety of ways. In "Preserving the Genetic Legacies," Karen F. Schmidt says:

Zoos are increasingly adapting the latest in human and agricultural

Chung 3

Block-indented quotation, no quotation marks

reproductive technologies to aid

beleaguered species by boosting their

numbers, increasing gene variety in

small populations and controlling

Words omitted (ellipses)

inbreeding. . . . Although still in

the early stages, embryo transfers,

artificial insemination and even test-

tube fertilization are seen by

Citation after period for long quotation

zoologists as having real or potential

application in conserving endangered

wildlife. (60)

These scientific activities began in the

1970s and now some of them are commonplace.

Female apes are on the pill and surrogate

Reference introduced with author's name

mother tigers are receiving embryos. Schmidt

reports that the Cincinnati Zoo Center for

Reproduction of Endangered Wildlife has

Blended paraphrase and quotation

frozen "eggs from a rare female Sumatran

rhino that died, hoping one day to obtain

some sperm and learn how to make test-tube

Citation after quotation marks for short quotation

rhino embryos" (60). In many zoos, eggs,

sperm, and skin for DNA storage have been

frozen in zoo labs, awaiting scientific

development by future generations.

Chung 4

[Conclusion]

The zoo of the future will almost surely be a projection of the contemporary model, one that teaches, conserves, explores, experiments, and entertains. Captive breeding cannot save thousands of creatures facing extinction, but, as Tudge points out, "Captive breeding is not an alternative to habitat protection. Increasingly, however, it is a vital backup" (51). Of course, the whole zoo operation must be monitored by those who know, appreciate, and understand animals. Nevertheless, zoos have demonstrated their value, and they have the potential to continue with their benefits.

Citation, author with two cited sources

Ends with emphasis on thesis

Works Cited

Browne, Malcolm W. "They're Back! Komodos Avoid
    Extinction." *New York Times* 1 Mar. 1994: C1, C4.
    Print.

Carpenter, Betsy. "Upsetting the Ark." *U.S. News &
    World Report* 24 Aug. 1992: 57-61. Print.

Cohn, Jeffrey. "Decisions at the Zoo." *Bioscience*
    Oct. 1992: 654-60. Print.

---. "The New Breeding Ground." *National Parks*
    Jan./Feb. 1997: 20-26. Print.

Diamond, Jared. "Playing God at the Zoo." *Discover*
    Mar. 1995: 78-86. Print.

Douglas-Hamilton, Ian, and Oria Douglas-Hamilton.
    Battle for the Elephants. New York: Viking,
    2002. Print.

Fravel, Laura. "Critics Question Zoos' Commitment
    to Conservation." *National Geographic News*.
    National Geographic Society, 13 Nov. 2003. Web.
    2 Jan. 2010.

"Not Endangered." *The Economist* 13 Apr. 1991: 55-56.
    Print.

"Project Technology." *Malaysia Elephant Satellite
    Tracking Project*, 27 Apr. 1997. Web. 2 Jan.
    2010.

Chung 6

Rainey, James. "Dogfight at the Zoo." *Los Angeles
      Times* 30 Jan. 1994: C1, C4. *Los Angeles Times.*
      Web. 2 Jan. 2010.

Schmidt, Karen F. "Preserving the Genetic Legacies."
      U.S. News & World Report 24 Aug. 1992: 60.
      Print.

Tarpy, Cliff. "New Zoos." *National Geographic* July
      1993: 6-37. Print.

Tudge, Colin. "Captive Audiences for Future
      Conservation." *New Scientist* 28 Jan. 1995: 51.
      Print.

---. *Last Animals at the Zoo: How Mass Extinction
      Can Be Stopped.* London: Hutchinson Radius, 1991.
      Print.

Writer's Guidelines at a Glance: The Research Paper

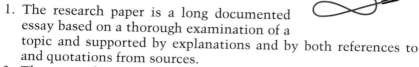

1. The research paper is a long documented essay based on a thorough examination of a topic and supported by explanations and by both references to and quotations from sources.

2. The research paper is no more difficult than other writing assignments if you select a good topic, use a systematic approach, and do not get behind with your work.

3. A systematic approach involves these ten steps:

   - Select a topic.
   - Find sources.
   - List sources.
   - Take notes.
   - Refine your thesis and outline.
   - Write your first draft.
   - Revise your first draft.
   - Prepare your Works Cited section.
   - Write your final draft.
   - Submit required materials.

4. Your library almost certainly mixes traditional and electronic indexes and sources; you should become familiar with both types of indexes.

5. MLA style for works cited differs from that used in traditional and electronic indexes.

6. You can avoid plagiarism by giving credit when you borrow someone else's words or ideas.

7. Consider using CLUESS for revision and COPS for editing.

14

Handbook

This chapter presents rules and examples for grammar, usage, punctuation, and capitalization. One good way to practice basic writing skills is to write your own examples. In working with verb tense, for example, you could write sentences (perhaps similar to the model sentences) in which you apply the appropriate patterns. In working with punctuation, you could write sentences that demonstrate your ability to use different punctuation marks correctly.

∿ Subjects and Verbs

The **subject** is what the sentence is about, and the **verb** indicates what the subject is doing or is being.

Subjects

You can recognize the **simple subject** by asking *Who?* or *What?* causes the action or expresses the state of being found in the verb.

1. The simple subject and the simple verb can be single or compound.

    My *friend* and *I* have much in common.

    My friend *came* and *left* a present.

2. Although the subject usually appears before the verb, it may follow the verb.

    From tiny acorns grow mighty *oaks.*

3. The **command**, or **imperative**, sentence has a "you" as the implied subject and no stated subject.

    (You) Read the notes.

4. Be careful not to confuse a subject with an object of a preposition.

> The *foreman* [subject] of the *jury* [object of the preposition] directs discussion.

Verbs

Verbs show action or express being in relation to the subject of a sentence.

1. **Action verbs** show movement or accomplishment of an idea or a deed.

> He *dropped* the book. (movement)
>
> He *read* the book. (accomplishment)

2. ***Being*** verbs indicate existence.

> They *were* concerned.

3. Verbs may appear as single words or as phrases.

> He *led* the charge. (single word)
>
> She *is leading* the charge. (phrase)

4. Verbs that are joined by a coordinating conjunction such as *and* and *or* are called **compound verbs**.

> She *worked* for twenty-five years and *retired*.

5. Do not confuse verbs with **verbals**, verblike words that function as other parts of speech.

> The bird *singing* [participle acting as an adjective] in the tree is defending its territory.
>
> *Singing* [gerund acting as a noun subject] is fun.
>
> I want *to eat* [infinitive acting as a noun object].

6. Do not confuse **adverbs** such as *never, not,* and *hardly* with verbs; they only modify verbs.

7. Do not overlook a part of the verb that is separated from another in a question.

> Where *had* the defendant *gone* on that fateful night?

~ **Kinds of Sentences**

On the basis of number and kinds of clauses, sentences may be classified as simple, compound, complex, and compound-complex.

Clauses

A **clause** is a group of words with a subject and a verb that functions as a part or all of a complete sentence. There are two kinds of clauses: independent (main) and dependent (subordinate).

1. An **independent (main) clause** is a group of words with a subject and a verb that can stand alone and make sense. An independent clause expresses a complete thought by itself and can be written as a separate sentence.

   I have the money.

2. A **dependent clause** is a group of words with a subject and a verb that depends on a main clause to give it meaning. The dependent clause functions in the common sentence patterns as a noun, an adjective, or an adverb.

   When I have the money

Kinds of Sentences Defined

Kind	Definition	Example
1. Simple	One independent clause	She did the work well.
2. Compound	Two or more independent clauses	She did the work well, and she was paid well.
3. Complex	One independent clause (underlined) and one or more dependent clauses (italicized)	*Because she did the work well*, she was paid well.
4. Compound-Complex	Two or more independent clauses and one or more dependent clauses	*Because she did the work well*, she was paid well, and she was satisfied.

Punctuation

1. Use a comma before a coordinating conjunction (*for, and, nor, but, or, yet, so*) between two independent clauses.

   The movie was good, *but* the tickets were expensive.

2. Use a comma after a dependent clause (beginning with a subordinating conjunction such as *because, although, when, since,* or *before*) that occurs before the main clause.

   When the bus arrived, we quickly boarded.

3. Use a semicolon between two independent clauses in one sentence if there is no coordinating conjunction.

> The bus arrived; we quickly boarded.

4. Use a semicolon before and usually a comma after a conjunctive adverb (such as *however, otherwise, therefore, on the other hand,* and *in fact*), and between two independent clauses (no comma after *then, also, now, thus,* and *soon*).

> The Dodgers have not played well this year; *however,* the Giants have won ten games in a row.

> Spring training went well; *then* the regular baseball season began.

⌒ Sentence Problems

Fragments

A correct sentence signals completeness; a **fragment** (a word or group of words without a subject, without a verb, or without both) signals incompleteness—it doesn't make sense. You would expect the speaker or writer of a fragment to say or write more or to rephrase it.

1. A **dependent clause**, which begins with a subordinating word, cannot stand by itself.

> *Because* he left.

> *When* she worked.

> *Although* they slept.

2. A **verbal phrase**, a **prepositional phrase**, and an **appositive phrase** may carry ideas, but each is incomplete because it lacks a subject and a verb.

VERBAL PHRASE	*having studied hard all evening*
SENTENCE	Having studied hard all evening, John decided to retire.
PREPOSITIONAL PHRASE	*in the store*
SENTENCE	She worked in the store.
APPOSITIVE PHRASE	*a successful business*
SENTENCE	Marks Brothers, a successful business, sells clothing.

3. Each complete sentence must have an **independent clause**, meaning a word or a group of words that contains a subject and a verb that can stand alone.

> *He enrolled* for the fall semester.

Comma Splices and Run-Ons

The **comma splice** consists of two independent clauses with only a comma between them.

The weather was disappointing, <u>*we canceled the picnic.*</u>

A comma by itself cannot join two independent clauses.

The **run-on** differs from the comma splice in only one respect: it has no comma between the independent clauses. Therefore, the run-on is two independent clauses with *nothing* between them.

The weather was disappointing <u>*we canceled the picnic.*</u>

Independent clauses must be properly connected.

Correct comma splices and run-ons by using a coordinating conjunction, a subordinating conjunction, or a semicolon, or by making each clause a separate sentence.

1. Use a comma and a **coordinating conjunction** (*for, and, nor, but, or, yet, so*).

   We canceled the picnic, *for* the weather was disappointing.

2. Use a **subordinating conjunction** (such as *because, after, that, when, although, since, how, until, unless, before*) to make one clause dependent.

   Because the weather was disappointing, we canceled the picnic.

3. Use a **semicolon** (with or without a conjunctive adverb such as *however, otherwise, therefore, similarly, hence, on the other hand, then, consequently, also, thus*).

   The weather was disappointing; we canceled the picnic.

   The weather was disappointing; *therefore,* we canceled the picnic.

4. Make each clause a separate sentence. For a comma splice, replace the comma with a period, and begin the second sentence (clause) with a capital letter. For a run-on, insert a period between the two independent clauses and begin the second sentence with a capital letter.

   The weather was disappointing. We canceled the picnic.

Sentence Combining

Coordination

If you intend to communicate two equally important and closely related ideas, you certainly will want to place them close together, probably in a **compound sentence** (two or more independent clauses).

1. When you combine two sentences by using a coordinating conjunction, drop the period, change the capital letter to a small letter, and insert a comma before the coordinating conjunction.

   He likes your home. He can visit for only three months.

   He likes your home, *but* he can visit for only three months.

2. When you combine two sentences by using a semicolon, replace the period with a semicolon and change the capital letter to a small letter. If you wish to use a conjunctive adverb, insert it after the semicolon and usually put a comma after it.

   He likes your home; he can visit for only three months.

   He likes your home; *however,* he can visit for only three months.

Subordination

If you have two ideas that are closely related but one is secondary to or dependent on the other, you may want to use a complex sentence.

   My neighbors are considerate. They never play loud music.

   Because my neighbors are considerate, they never play loud music.

1. If the dependent clause comes before the main clause, set it off with a comma.

   Before you dive, be sure there is water in the pool.

2. If the dependent clause comes *after* or *within* the main clause, set it off with a comma only if you use the word *though* or *although,* or if the words are not necessary to convey the basic meaning in the sentence.

   Be sure there is water in the pool *before you dive.*

Coordination and Subordination

At times you may want to show the relationship of three or more ideas within one sentence. If that relationship involves two or more main ideas and one or more supporting ideas, the combination can be stated in a **compound-complex sentence** (two or more independent clauses and one or more dependent clauses).

> Before he learned how to operate a computer, he had trouble
> <u>dependent clause</u>   <u>independent clause</u>
> with his typewritten assignments, but now he produces clean,
>   <u>independent clause</u>
> attractive material.

Use punctuation consistent with that of the compound and complex sentences.

Other Methods of Combining Ideas

1. Simple sentences can often be combined by using a **prepositional phrase**, a preposition followed by a noun or pronoun object.

   Dolly Parton wrote a song about a coat. The coat had many colors.

   Dolly Parton wrote a song about a coat *of many colors.*

2. To combine simple sentences, use an **appositive**, a noun phrase that immediately follows a noun or pronoun and renames it.

   Susan is the leading scorer on the team. Susan is a quick and strong player.

   Susan, *a quick and strong player*, is the leading scorer on the team.

3. Simple sentences can often be combined by dropping a repeated subject in the second sentence.

   Some items are too damaged for recycling. They must be disposed of.

   Some items are too damaged for recycling and must be disposed of.

4. Sentences can be combined by using a **participial phrase**, a group of words that includes a participle, which is a verblike word that usually ends in *-ing* or *-ed.*

   Michael rowed smoothly. He reached the shore.

   Rowing smoothly, Michael reached the shore.

⌒ Variety in Sentences

Do not bother to look for formulas in this section. Variety in sentences may be desirable for its own sake, to avoid dullness. However, it is more likely you will revise your essays for reasons that make good sense in the context of what you are writing. The following are some of the variations available to you.

Types

You have learned that all four types of sentences are sound. Your task as a writer is to decide which one to use for a particular thought. That decision may not be made until you revise your composition. Then you can choose on the basis of the relationship of ideas:

> **Simple:** a single idea
>
> **Compound:** two closely related ideas
>
> **Complex:** one idea more important than the other
>
> **Compound-complex:** a combination of compound and complex

These types were all covered earlier in this chapter (p. 248).

Order

You will choose the order of parts and information according to what you want to emphasize. Typically the most emphatic location is at the end of any unit.

Length

Uncluttered and direct, short sentences commonly draw attention. But that focus occurs only when they stand out from longer sentences. Therefore, you would usually avoid a series of short sentences.

Beginnings

A long series of sentences with each beginning containing a subject followed by a verb may become monotonous. Consider beginning sentences in different ways:

> **With a prepositional phrase:** *In the distance* a dog barked.
>
> **With a transitional connective (conjunctive adverb) such as** *then*, *however*, or *therefore*: *Then* the game was over.
>
> **With a coordinating conjunction such as** *and* or *but*: *But* no one moved for three minutes.

With a dependent clause: *Although he wanted a new Corvette,* he settled for a used Ford Taurus.

With an adverb: *Carefully* he removed the thorn from the lion's paw.

◯ Parallel Structure

Parallelism means balancing one structure with another of the same kind—nouns with nouns, verbs with verbs, adjectives (words that can describe nouns) with adjectives, adverbs (words that can describe verbs) with adverbs, and so forth.

> *Men, women,* and *children* [nouns] *enjoy* the show and *return* [verbs] each year.
> She fell *in love* and *out of love* [phrases] in a few seconds.
> *She fell in love with him,* and *he fell in love with her* [clauses].

1. Faulty parallel structure is awkward and draws unfavorable attention to what is being said.

   > *To talk* with his buddies and *eating* fast foods were his favorite pastimes. (The sentence should read *Talking . . .* and *eating* or *To talk . . .* and *to eat.*)

2. Some words signal parallel structure. All coordinating conjunctions (*for, and, nor, but, or, yet, so*) can give such signals.

   > The weather is hot *and* humid.
   > He purchased a Dodger Dog, *but* I chose Stadium Peanuts.

3. Combination words also signal the need for parallelism or balance. The most common ones are *either/or, neither/nor, not only/but also, both/and,* and *whether/or.*

   > We will *either* win this game *or* go out fighting. (verb following each of the combination words)

◯ Omissions: When Parts Are Missing

Do not omit words that are needed to make your sentences clear and logical. Of the many types of undesirable constructions in which necessary words are omitted, the following are the most common.

1. **Subjects.** Do not omit a necessary subject in a sentence with two verbs.

> ILLOGICAL The cost of the car was $12,000 but would easily last me through college. (subject of last)
> LOGICAL The cost of the car was $12,000, but the car would easily last me through college.

2. **Verbs.** Do not omit verbs that are needed because of a change in the number of the subject or a change of tense.

> ILLOGICAL The bushes were trimmed and the grass mowed.
> LOGICAL The bushes were trimmed, and the grass was mowed.
> ILLOGICAL True honesty always has and always will be admired by most people. (tense)
> LOGICAL True honesty always has been and always will be admired by most people.

3. *That* **as a conjunction.** The conjunction *that* should not be omitted from a dependent clause if there is danger of misreading the sentence.

> MISLEADING We believed Jackson, if not stopped, would hurt himself.
> CLEAR We believed that Jackson, if not stopped, would hurt himself.

4. **Prepositions.** Do not omit prepositions in idiomatic phrases, in expressions of time, and in parallel phrases.

> ILLOGICAL Weekends the campus is deserted. (time)
> LOGICAL During weekends the campus is deserted.
> ILLOGICAL I have neither love nor patience with untrained dogs. (parallel phrases)
> LOGICAL I have neither love for nor patience with untrained dogs.
> ILLOGICAL Glenda's illness was something we heard only after her recovery. (preposition omitted)
> LOGICAL Glenda's illness was something we heard about only after her recovery.

∼ Verbs

The twelve verb tenses are shown in this section. The irregular verb *drive* is used as the example. (See pp. 258–259 for a list of irregular verbs.)

Simple Tenses

Present

I, we, you, they *drive.*
He, she, it *drives.*

May imply
a continuation from
past to future

Past

I, we, you, he, she, it, they *drove.*

Future

I, we, you, he, she, it,
they *will drive.*

Perfect Tenses

Present Perfect

I, we, you, they *have driven.*
He, she, it *has driven.*

Completed recently
in the past, may con-
tinue to the present

Past Perfect

I, we, you, he, she, it, they *had driven.*

Completed prior to a
specific time in the
past

Future Perfect

I, we, you, he, she, it, they *will have
driven.*

Will occur at a time
prior to a specific
time in the future

Progressive Tenses

Present Progressive

I *am driving.*
He, she, it *is driving.*
We, you, they *are driving.*

In progress now

Past Progressive

I, he, she, it *was driving.*
We, you, they *were driving.*

In progress in the
past

Future Progressive

I, we, you, he, she, it, they *will be
driving.*

In progress in the
future

Perfect Progressive Tenses

Present Perfect Progressive

I, we, you, they *have been driving.* He, she, it *has been driving.*	In progress up to now

Past Perfect Progressive

I, we, you, he, she, it, they *had been driving.*	In progress before another event in the past

Future Perfect Progressive

I, we, you, he, she, it, they *will have been driving.*	In progress before another event in the future

Past Participles

The past participle uses the helping verbs *has, have,* or *had* along with the past tense of the verb. For regular verbs, whose past tense ends in *-ed*, the past participle form of the verb is the same as the past tense.

Following is a list of some common regular verbs, showing the base form, the past tense, and the past participle. (The base form can also be used with such helping verbs as *can, could, do, does, did, may, might, must, shall, should, will,* and *would.*)

Regular Verbs

Base Form (Present)	Past	Past Participle
ask	asked	asked
answer	answered	answered
cry	cried	cried
decide	decided	decided
dive	dived (dove)	dived
drag	dragged	dragged
finish	finished	finished
happen	happened	happened
learn	learned	learned
like	liked	liked
love	loved	loved
need	needed	needed

(continued)

Base Form (Present)	Past	Past Participle
open	opened	opened
start	started	started
suppose	supposed	supposed
walk	walked	walked
want	wanted	wanted

Whereas **regular verbs** are predictable—having an -*ed* ending for past and past participle forms—**irregular verbs**, as the term suggests, follow no definite pattern.

Following is a list of some common irregular verbs, showing the base form (present), the past tense, and the past participle.

Irregular Verbs

Base Form (Present)	Past	Past Participle
arise	arose	arisen
awake	awoke (awaked)	awaked
be	was, were	been
become	became	become
begin	began	begun
bend	bent	bent
blow	blew	blown
break	broke	broken
bring	brought	brought
buy	bought	bought
catch	caught	caught
choose	chose	chosen
cling	clung	clung
come	came	come
creep	crept	crept
deal	dealt	dealt
do	did	done
drink	drank	drunk
drive	drove	driven
eat	ate	eaten
feel	felt	felt
fight	fought	fought
fling	flung	flung
fly	flew	flown
forget	forgot	forgotten
freeze	froze	frozen

Base Form (Present)	Past	Past Participle
get	got	got (gotten)
go	went	gone
grow	grew	grown
have	had	had
know	knew	known
lead	led	led
leave	left	left
lose	lost	lost
mean	meant	meant
read	read	read
ride	rode	ridden
ring	rang	rung
see	saw	seen
shine	shone (shined)	shone (shined)
shoot	shot	shot
sing	sang	sung
sink	sank	sunk
sleep	slept	slept
slink	slunk	slunk
speak	spoke	spoken
spend	spent	spent
steal	stole	stolen
stink	stank (stunk)	stunk
sweep	swept	swept
swim	swam	swum
swing	swung	swung
take	took	taken
teach	taught	taught
tear	tore	torn
think	thought	thought
throw	threw	thrown
wake	woke (waked)	woken (waked)
weep	wept	wept
write	wrote	written

"Problem" Verbs

The following pairs of verbs are especially troublesome and confusing: *lie* and *lay*, *sit* and *set*, and *rise* and *raise*. One way to tell them apart is to remember which word in each pair takes a direct object. A direct object answers the question *whom* or *what* in connection with a verb. The words *lay*, *raise*, and *set* take a direct object.

He *raised* the window. (He *raised* what?)

Lie, *rise*, and *sit*, however, cannot take a direct object. We cannot say, for example, "He rose the window." In the following examples, the italicized words are objects.

Present Tense	Meaning	Past Tense	Past Participle	Example
lie	to rest	lay	lain	I lay down to rest.
lay	to place something	laid	laid	We laid the *books* on the table.
rise	to go up	rose	risen	The smoke rose quickly.
raise	to lift	raised	raised	She raised the *question*.
sit	to rest	sat	sat	He sat in the chair.
set	to place something	set	set	They set the *basket* on the floor.

Verb Tense

Verb tense is a word form indicating time. The rules about selecting a tense for certain kinds of writing are flexible. You should be consistent, however, changing tense only for a good reason.

Usually you should select the present tense to write about literature.

Moby Dick *is* a famous white whale.

Select the past tense to write about yourself (usually) or something historical (always).

I *was* eighteen when I *decided* I *was* ready for independence.

Subject-Verb Agreement

The basic principle of **subject-verb agreement** is that if the subject is singular, the verb should be singular, and if the subject is plural, the verb should be plural.

The *advantages* of that shoe *are* obvious.

There *are* many *reasons* for his poor work.

The *coach*, along with the players, *protests* the decision.

The *price* of those shoes *is* too high.

Voice

The **active voice** (subject, active verb, and object) is usually preferred over the **passive voice** (subject as the receiver of action, with doer unstated or at the end of a prepositional phrase).

ACTIVE   She read the book.

PASSIVE   The book was read by her.

⌇ Pronouns

A **pronoun** is a word that is used in place of a noun. **Case** is the form a pronoun takes as it fills a position in a sentence.

1. **Subjective pronouns** are *I, he,* and *she* (singular), and *we* and *they* (plural). *Who* can be either singular or plural.
   Subjective case pronouns can fill subject positions in a sentence.

   We dance in the park.

   It was *she* who spoke. (referring back to and meaning the same as the subject)

2. **Objective pronouns** are *me, him,* and *her* (singular); and *us* and *them* (plural). *Whom* can be either singular or plural.
   Objective case pronouns fill object positions.

   We saw *her* in the library. (object of verb)

   They gave the results to *us*—Maria and *me*. (object of a preposition)

3. Three techniques are useful for deciding what pronoun case to use.
   a. If you have a compound element (such as a subject or an object of a preposition), consider only the pronoun part.

   They will visit Jim and (I, me). (*Consider*: They will visit *me*.)

   b. If the next important word after *who* or *whom* in a statement is a noun or pronoun, the word choice will be *whom*; otherwise, it will be *who*. Disregard qualifier clauses such as *It seems* and *I feel*.

   The person *who* works hardest will win.

   The person *whom* judges like will win.

The person *who*, we think, worked hardest won. (ignoring the qualifier clause)

c. *Let's* is made up of the words *let* and *us* and means "you *let us*"; therefore, when you select a pronoun to follow it, consider the two original words and select another object word—*me*.

Let's you and *me* go to town.

4. A pronoun agrees with its antecedent in person, number, and gender.

a. Avoid needless shifting in person, which means shifting in point of view, such as from *I* to *you*.

INCORRECT   *I* tried, but *you* couldn't persuade her to return.

CORRECT   *I* tried, but *I* couldn't persuade her to return.

b. Most problems with pronoun-antecedent agreement involve number. The principles are simple: If the antecedent (the word the pronoun refers back to) is singular, use a singular pronoun. If the antecedent is plural, use a plural pronoun.

Ivan forgot *his* notebook.

Many students cast *their* votes today.

Someone lost *his* or *her* [not *their*] book.

c. The pronoun should agree with its antecedent in gender if the gender of the antecedent is specific. Masculine and feminine pronouns are gender-specific: *he, him, she,* and *her.* Others are neuter: *I, we, me, us, it, they, them, who, whom, that,* and *which.* The words *who* and *whom* refer to people. *That* can refer to ideas, things, and people but usually not to people. *Which* refers to ideas and things but never to people. To avoid a perceived sex bias, most writers and speakers prefer to use *he or she* or *his or her* instead of just *he* or *his*; however, many writers simply make antecedents plural.

Everyone should work until *he or she* drops.

People should work until *they* drop.

⌒ Adjectives and Adverbs

1. **Adjectives** modify (describe) nouns and pronouns and answer the questions *Which one? What kind?* and *How many?*
2. **Adverbs** modify verbs, adjectives, or other adverbs and answer the questions *How? Where? When?* and *To what degree?* Most words ending in *-ly* are adverbs.
3. If you settle for a common word such as *good* or a slang word such as *neat* to characterize something you like, you will be limiting your communication. The more precise the word, the better the communication. Keep in mind, however, that anything can be overdone; therefore, use adjectives and adverbs wisely and economically.
4. For making comparisons, most adjectives and adverbs have three different forms: the positive (one), the comparative (two), and the superlative (three or more).
   a. Adjectives
      - Add *-er* to short adjectives (one or two syllables) to rank units of two.

        Julian is *kinder* than Sam.

      - Add *-est* to short adjectives (one or two syllables) to rank units of more than two.

        Of the fifty people I know, Julian is the *kindest.*

      - Add the word *more* before long adjectives to rank units of two.

        My hometown is *more beautiful* than yours.

      - Add the word *most* before long adjectives to rank units of three or more.

        My hometown is the *most beautiful* in all America.

      - Some adjectives are irregular in the way they change to show comparison: *good, better, best; bad, worse, worst.*
   b. Adverbs
      For most adverbs, use the word *more* before the comparative form (two) and the word *most* before the superlative form (three or more).

      Carlos performed *skillfully.* (modifier)

      Sarah performed *more skillfully* than Sam. (comparative modifier)

But Sarah performed *most skillfully* of all. (superlative modifier)

5. Avoid double negatives. Words such as *no, not, none, nothing, never, hardly, barely,* and *scarcely* should not be combined.

> INCORRECT   I *don't* have *no* time for recreation.
>
> CORRECT   I have *no* time for recreation.
>
> CORRECT   I *don't* have time for recreation.

6. Do not confuse adjectives (*bad*) with adverbs (*badly*).

7. A modifier that gives information but doesn't refer to a word or group of words already in the sentence is called a **dangling modifier**.

> DANGLING   *Walking down the street,* a snake startled me.
>
> CORRECT   *Walking down the street,* I was startled by a snake.

8. A modifier that is placed so that it modifies the wrong word or words is called a **misplaced modifier**.

> MISPLACED   The sick man went to a doctor *with a high fever.*
>
> CORRECT   The sick man *with a high fever* went to a doctor.

⁓ Avoiding Wordy Phrases

Certain phrases clutter sentences, consuming our time in writing and our readers' time in reading. Watch for wordy phrases as you revise and edit.

> WORDY   *Due to the fact that* he was unemployed, he had to use public transportation.
>
> CONCISE   *Because* he was unemployed, he had to use public transportation.
>
> WORDY   *Deep down inside* he believed that the Red Sox would win.
>
> CONCISE   He believed that the Red Sox would win.

Wordy	Concise
at the present time	now
basic essentials	essentials

blend together	blend
it is clear that	(delete)
due to the fact that	because
for the reason that	because
I felt inside	I felt
in most cases	usually
as a matter of fact	in fact
in the event that	if
until such time as	until
I personally feel	I feel
in this modern world	today
in order to	to
most of the people	most people
along the lines of	like
past experience	experience
at that point in time	then
in the final analysis	finally
in the near future	soon
have a need for	need
in this day and age	now

∿ Punctuation

1. The three marks of end punctuation are periods, question marks, and exclamation points.

   a. Periods

   Place a period after a statement.

   Place a period after common abbreviations.

   Use an ellipsis—three periods within a sentence and four periods at the end of a sentence—to indicate that words have been omitted from quoted material.

   > He stopped walking and the buildings . . . rose up out of the misty courtroom. . . . (James Thurber, "The Secret Life of Walter Mitty")

   b. Question marks

   Place a question mark at the end of a direct question.

   Use a single question mark in sentence constructions that contain a double question—that is, a quoted question within a question.

Mr. Petrilla said, "Did he say, 'Are we going?'"

Do *not* use a question mark after an indirect (reported) question.

She asked me what caused the slide.

c. Exclamation points
Place an exclamation point after a word or group of words that expresses strong feeling.
Do not overwork the exclamation point. Do not use double exclamation points.

2. The comma is used essentially to separate and to set off sentence elements.

a. Use a comma to separate main clauses joined by one of the coordinating conjunctions—*for, and, nor, but, or, yet, so.*

We went to the game, *but* it was canceled.

b. Use a comma after introductory dependent clauses and long introductory phrases (generally, four or more words is considered long).

Before she and I arrived, the meeting was called to order.

c. Use a comma to separate words, phrases, and clauses in a series.

He ran *down the street, across the park,* and *into the arms* of his father.

d. Use a comma to separate coordinate adjectives not joined by *and* that modify the same noun.

I need a *sturdy, reliable* truck.

e. Use a comma to separate sentence elements that might be misread.

Inside, the dog scratched his fleas.

f. Use commas to set off (enclose) nonessential (unnecessary for meaning of the sentence) words, phrases, and clauses.

Natasha, *who studied hard,* will pass.

g. Use commas to set off parenthetical elements such as mild interjections (*oh, well, yes, no,* and others), most conjunctive adverbs (*however, otherwise, therefore, similarly, hence, on the other hand*, and *consequently*, but not *then*, *thus*, *soon*, *now*, and *also*), quotation indicators, and special abbreviations (*etc.*, *i.e.*, *e.g.*, and others).

> *Oh*, what a silly question! (mild interjection)
>
> It is necessary, *of course*, to leave now. (sentence modifier)
>
> We left early; *however*, we missed the train anyway. (conjunctive adverb)
>
> "When I was in school," *he said*, "I read widely." (quotation indicators)
>
> Books, papers, pens, *etc.*, were scattered on the floor. (The abbreviation *etc.*, however, should be used sparingly.)

h. Use commas to set off nouns used as direct address.

> Play it again, *Sam*.

i. Use commas to separate the numbers in a date.

> June *4, 1965*, is a day I will remember.

j. Use commas to separate the city from the state. No comma is used between the state and the zip code.

> Walnut, CA 91789

k. Use a comma following the salutation and the complementary closing in a letter (but in a business letter, use a colon after the salutation).

> Dear Jake,
>
> Sincerely,

l. Use a comma in numbers to set off groups of three digits. However, omit the comma in dates and in long serial numbers, page numbers, and street numbers.

> The total assets were *$2,000,000*.
>
> I was born in 1989.

3. The semicolon indicates a stronger division than the comma. It is used principally to separate independent clauses within a sentence.

   a. Use a semicolon to separate independent clauses not joined by a coordinating conjunction.

> You must buy that car today; tomorrow will be too late.

   b. Use a semicolon between two independent clauses joined by a conjunctive adverb (such as *however, otherwise, therefore, similarly, hence, on the other hand, then, consequently, accordingly, thus*).

> It was very late; *therefore,* I remained at the hotel.

4. Quotation marks bring special attention to words.
   a. Quotation marks are used principally to set off direct quotations. A direct quotation consists of material taken from the written work or the direct speech of others; it is set off by double quotation marks. Single quotation marks are used to set off a quotation within a quotation.

> He said, "I don't remember if she said, 'Wait for me.'"

   b. Use double quotation marks to set off titles of shorter pieces of writing such as magazine articles, essays, short stories, short poems, one-act plays, chapters in books, songs, and separate pieces of writing published as part of a larger work.

> The book *Literature: Structure, Sound, and Sense* contains a deeply moving poem titled "On Wenlock Edge."
>
> Have you read "The Use of Force," a short story by William Carlos Williams?
>
> My favorite Elvis song is "Don't Be Cruel."

   c. Punctuation with quotation marks follows definite rules.

     ▪ A period or a comma is always placed *inside* the quotation marks.

> Our assignment for Monday was to read Poe's "The Raven."
>
> "I will read you the story," he said. "It is a good one."

     ▪ A semicolon or a colon is always placed *outside* the quotation marks.

> He read Robert Frost's poem "Design"; then he gave the examination.

     ▪ A question mark, an exclamation point, or a dash is placed *outside* the quotation marks when it applies to the entire sentence and *inside* the quotation marks when it applies to the material in quotation marks.

He asked, "Am I responsible for everything?" (quoted question within a statement)

Did you hear him say, "I have the answer"? (statement within a question)

Did she say, "Are we ready?" (question within a question)

She shouted, "Impossible!" (exclamation)

"I hope—that is, I—" he began. (dash)

5. Italics (slanting type) is used to call special attention to certain words or groups of words. In handwriting, such words are underlined.
   a. Italicize (underline) foreign words and phrases that are still listed in the dictionary as foreign.

   c'est la vie   Weltschmerz

   b. Italicize (underline) titles of books (except the Bible); long poems; plays; magazines; motion pictures; musical composi-tions; newspapers; works of art; names of aircraft; ships; and letters, figures, and words referred to by their own name.

   War and Peace   Apollo 12   leaving *o* out of *sophomore*

6. The dash is used when a stronger break than the comma is needed. It can also be used to indicate a break in the flow of thought and to emphasize words (less formal than the colon in this situation).

   Here is the true reason—but maybe you don't care.

   English, French, history—these are the subjects I like.

7. The colon is a formal mark of punctuation used chiefly to in-troduce something that is to follow, such as a list, a quotation, or an explanation.

   These cars are my favorites: Cadillac, Chevrolet, Buick, Oldsmobile, and Pontiac.

8. Parentheses are used to set off material that is of relatively little importance to the main thought of the sentence. Such material—numbers that designate items in a series, figures, supplementary material, and sometimes explanatory details—merely amplifies the main thought.

   The years of the era (1961–1973) were full of action.

Her husband (she had been married only a year) died last week.

9. Brackets are used within a quotation to set off editorial additions or corrections made by the person who is quoting.

> Churchill said: "It [the Yalta Agreement] contained many mistakes."

10. The apostrophe is used with nouns and indefinite pronouns to show possession; to show the omission of letters and figures in contractions; and to form the plurals of letters, figures, and words referred to as words.

> man's coat   girls' clothes
>
> *you're* (contraction of *you are*)   five *and*'s

11. The hyphen brings two or more words together into a single compound word. Correct hyphenation, therefore, is essentially a spelling problem rather than one of punctuation. Because the hyphen is not used with any degree of consistency, consult your dictionary for current usage. Study the following as a beginning guide.
   a. Use a hyphen to separate the parts of many compound words.

   > about-face   go-between

   b. Use a hyphen between prefixes and proper names.

   > all-American   mid-November

   c. Use a hyphen to join two or more words used as a single adjective modifier before a noun.

   > first-class service   hard-fought game
   > sad-looking mother

   d. Use a hyphen with spelled-out compound numbers up to ninety-nine and with fractions.

   > twenty-six   two-thirds

Note: Dates, street addresses, numbers requiring more than two words, chapter and page numbers, time followed directly by *a.m.* or *p.m.*, and figures after a dollar sign or before measurement abbreviations are usually written as figures, not words.

⌒ Capitalization

English has many conventions concerning the use of capital letters. Here are some of them.

1. Capitalize the first word of a sentence.
2. Capitalize proper nouns and adjectives derived from proper nouns.

   - Names of persons
     Natasha Tolstoy

   - Adjectives derived from proper nouns
     a Shakespearean sonnet   an English class

   - Countries, nationalities, races, and languages
     Germany   English   Spanish   Chinese

   - States, regions, localities, and other geographical divisions
     California   the Far East   the South

   - Oceans, lakes, mountains, deserts, streets, and parks
     Lake Superior   Sahara Desert   Fifth Avenue

   - Educational institutions, schools, and courses
     Santa Ana College   Joe Hill School
     Rowland High School   Math 3

   - Organizations and their members
     Boston Red Sox   Audubon Society   Boy Scouts

   - Corporations, governmental agencies or departments, and trade names
     U.S. Steel Corporation   Treasury Department
     White Memorial Library   Coke

   - Calendar references such as holidays, days of the week, and months
     Easter   Tuesday   January

   - Historic eras, periods, documents, and laws
     First Crusade   Romantic Age
     Declaration of Independence   Geneva Convention

3. Capitalize words denoting family relationships when they are used before a name or substituted for a name.

He walked with his nephew and Aunt Rhody.

but

He walked with his nephew and his aunt.

Grandmother and Mother are away on vacation.

but

My grandmother and my mother are away on vacation.

4. Capitalize abbreviations after names.

    Henry White Jr.   William Green, M.D.

5. Capitalize titles of essays, books, plays, movies, poems, magazines, newspapers, musical compositions, songs, and works of art. Do not capitalize short conjunctions and prepositions unless they come at the beginning or the end of the title.

    Desire Under the Elms   *Terminator*
    Last of the Mohicans   *Of Mice and Men*
    "Blueberry Hill"

6. Capitalize any title preceding a name or used as a substitute for a name. Do not capitalize a title following a name.

    Judge Sterzay   Alfred Wong, a judge
    General Clarkus   Raymond Clarkus, a general
    Professor Fuentes   William Brock, the former president

～ Text Credits

"A Mixed Tex-Cal Marriage" from *Drink Cultura* by José Antonio Burciaga. Reprinted by permission of the Estate of José Antonio Burciaga.

"Shouldn't Men Have 'Choice' Too?" by Meghan Daum. Copyright © 2005 by Meghan Daum. Originally published in *Los Angeles Times*. Reprinted by permission of the author.

Francis Flaherty, "The Ghetto Made Me Do It," *In These Times*, Chicago, April 5, 1993, Viewpoints section. Reprinted by permission of *In These Times*.

From *Memories* by Joan Gould. Copyright © 1989. Reprinted by permission of the author.

"No Tears for Frankie" by Gina Greenlee from *The New York Times Magazine*, June 10, 2001. Reprinted by permission of the author.

Adair Lara, "Who's Cheap?" from *San Francisco Chronicle*. Reprinted by permission of the author.

From Scot Ober. *Contemporary Business Communication*, 6th ed. © 2006 South-Western, a part of Cengage Learning, Inc. Reproduced by permission. www.cengage.com/permissions.

Ryan J. Smith, "From B'wood to the 'hood'" from *Los Angeles Times*. February 19, 2006. Reprinted by permission of the author.

"The Jacket" from The *Effects of Knut Hamsun on a Fresno Boy: Recollections and Short Essays*, by Gary Soto. Copyright © 1983, 2000 by Gary Soto. Reprinted by permission of Persea Books, Inc., New York, and the author.